THE MODERNIST NOVEL

Leading scholar Stephen Kern offers a probing analysis of the modernist novel, encompassing American, British, and European works. Organized thematically, the book offers a comprehensive survey of the stunningly original formal innovations in novels by Conrad, Joyce, Woolf, Proust, Gide, Faulkner, Dos Passos, Kafka, Musil, and others. Kern contextualizes and explains how formal innovations captured the dynamic history of the period, reconstructed as ten master narratives. He also draws briefly on poetry and painting of the first half of the twentieth century. *The Modernist Novel* is set to become a fundamental source for discussions of the genre for students and scholars of modernism and twentieth-century literature.

STEPHEN KERN is a Humanities Distinguished Professor in the Department of History at Ohio State University. His publications include *The Culture of Time and Space 1880–1918* (1983); *The Culture of Love: Victorians to Moderns* (1992); and *A Cultural History of Causality: Science, Murder Novels, and Systems of Thought* (2004).

THE MODERNIST NOVEL:
A CRITICAL INTRODUCTION

STEPHEN KERN

CAMBRIDGE
UNIVERSITY PRESS

CAMBRIDGE UNIVERSITY PRESS
Cambridge, New York, Melbourne, Madrid, Cape Town,
Singapore, São Paulo, Delhi, Tokyo, Mexico City

Cambridge University Press
The Edinburgh Building, Cambridge CB2 8RU, UK

Published in the United States of America by Cambridge University Press, New York

www.cambridge.org
Information on this title: www.cambridge.org/9781107400429

First published 2011

Printed in the United Kingdom at the University Press, Cambridge

A catalogue record for this publication is available from the British Library

Library of Congress Cataloging in Publication data
Kern, Stephen.
The modernist novel : a critical introduction / Stephen Kern.
p.   cm.
Includes index.
ISBN 978-1-107-00811-3 – ISBN 978-1-107-40042-9 (pbk.)
1. Modernism (Literature)   I. Title.
PN56.M54K47   2011
809.3′9112–dc22
2010050048

ISBN 978-1-107-00811-3 Hardback
ISBN 978-1-107-40042-9 Paperback

Contents

Illustrations

Table

Acknowledgments

Thanks to the members of the modernist study group at Ohio State University, who provided a wealth of knowledge and advice, astute readings of chapters, and a supportive community of interest: Morris Beja, Sarah Copland, Katherine Elkins, Lois Florman, David Herman, Martin Hipsky, Sebastian Knowles, Ellen Carol Jones, Karen Leick, Jesse Matz, Brian McHale, William Palmer, James Phelan, Jessica Prinz, and Paul Reitter. Other colleagues read chapters and shared their expertise: Arved Ashby, Alan Beyerchen, Kevin Boyle, John Burnham, Alice Conklin, Thomas Davis, Carole Fink, Steven Fink, David Frantz, Myroslava Mudrak, and Christopher Otter. From outside my university Robert Brenner, Suzette Henke, Brian Richardson, Alpana Sharma, Jeff Wallace, and Philip Weinstein also read individual chapters. Amanpal Garcha read the entire manuscript with special attention to realist novels. Porter Abbott, Jay Clayton, Gerald Prince, and Vincent Sherry responded to specific questions about narrative theory. My students Mark De Groh, Steven Gallick, Ryan McMillin, and Anne Sealey discussed pages in progress, while Nicholas Steneck asked one probing question to which this book is an extended reply. My children Justin and Simone helped sort out what made sense and what did not.

Four long-time friends took on the challenge of this book personally from my initial inquiries to its completion. Rudolph Binion read the book with scrupulous care and rigorous attention to historical accuracy. Brian McHale sharpened my use of narrative theory and addressed countless interpretive problems. Bill Palmer read every chapter along the way and helped me navigate the rocks of dubious science, faulty logic, and unnecessary jargon. Sean Shesgreen commented on each of my chapters as he has on all the others going back three decades, when he has generously shared his subtle aesthetic sensibility and insistence on clarity and simplicity.

Abbreviations

A	James, Henry. *The Ambassadors*. 1903. Harmondsworth: Penguin, 2003
AA	Faulkner, William. *Absalom, Absalom!* 1936. New York: Vintage, 1990.
AD	Faulkner, William. *As I Lay Dying*. 1930. New York: Vintage, 1990.
C	Gide, André. *The Counterfeiters with Journal of "The Counterfeiters."* 1925, 1927. Translated by Dorothy Bussy. New York: Vintage, 1973.
HD	Conrad, Joseph. *Heart of Darkness*. 1902. 4th edn, Harmondsworth: Norton, 2006.
JR	Woolf, Virginia. *Jacob's Room*. 1922. In *Jacob's Room & The Waves*. New York: Harcourt, 1959.
LJ	Conrad, Joseph. *Lord Jim*. 1899–1900. Oxford: Oxford University Press, 1983.
MA	Stein, Gertrude. *The Making of Americans*. 1925. Normal, Ill.: Dalkey, 1999.
MD	Woolf, Virginia. *Mrs. Dalloway*. 1925. New York: Harcourt, 1981.
MM	Mann, Thomas. *The Magic Mountain*. 1924. Translated by John E. Woods. New York: Knopf, 2005.
MQ	Musil, Robert. *The Man Without Qualities*. 2 vols. 1952, 1978. Translated by Sophie Wilkins. New York: Knopf, 1995.
P	Richardson, Dorothy. *Pilgrimage*. 1915–38. 4 vols. London: Virago, 1982.
PA	Joyce, James. *A Portrait of the Artist as a Young Man*. 1916. New York: Viking, 1956.
RP	Proust, Marcel. *Remembrance of Things Past*. 1913–27. 3 vols. Translated by C. K. Scott Moncrieff and Terence Kilmartin. New York: Random House, 1981.
SF	Faulkner, William. *The Sound and the Fury*. 1929. New York: Vintage, 1990.

TL   Woolf, Virginia. *To The Lighthouse*. 1927. New York: Harcourt, 1981.

U   Joyce, James. *Ulysses*. 1922. New York: Vintage, 1986.

WL   Lawrence, D. H. *Women in Love*. 1920. Harmondsworth: Penguin, 1995.

Introduction

The period 1900–40 produced revolutionary developments in science and the arts. The rediscovery of the work of Gregor Mendel in 1900 revolutionized knowledge of hereditary transmission in showing that characteristics of organisms do not blend in offspring but are transmitted in discrete units according to specific laws, which ultimately became the foundation for modern scientific genetics. In *The Interpretation of Dreams* of 1900 Sigmund Freud laid the foundation for his theory of the mind as a network of unconscious processes and the residue of childhood psychosexual experience. Also in 1900, the introduction of Planck's constant to explain the spectra of thermal bodies was the first blow in a series of advances that led to a fully elaborated quantum theory by 1927. Most unsettling was the theory's indeterminacy principle, which put knowledge of subatomic events on a probabilistic basis, thereby limiting the strictly deterministic causality that classical physicists had posited throughout the universe. Albert Einstein's special relativity theory of 1905 maintained that space and time are not absolute and distinct but relative to motion and transform into one another. In 1908 Arnold Schoenberg composed music with no tonal center, while in 1911 Wassily Kandinsky painted no recognizable objects. No single literary change was as revolutionary as these others. However, the sum of formal innovations in the novel was revolutionary in providing new ways of rendering how people experience personal development, courtship conventions, family relations, urban life, national identification, imperial conquest, capitalist enterprise, liberal institutions, religious faith, and artistic creativity.

The Modernist Novel: A Critical Introduction is a study of how these developments were captured in the novels of the period. To achieve that end it offers (1) a precise analysis of modernists' formal innovations defined in the light of contemporary narrative theory; (2) a comparison of modernists' formal innovations with the preceding realists' rendering of the same formal elements; (3) interpretations of how modernists used those innovations to capture the political, social, and economic history of the period; (4) a unifying argument about that history as a subversion and reworking of ten master narratives (personal, courtship, family, urban, national, imperial, capitalist, liberal, religious, and artistic); and (5) a corollary argument about the role that the artistic narrative played as a relatively unchallenged source of meaning in life as the values embedded in the other master narratives came under assault. Together these offerings define literary modernism as a new way of construing the world and interpreting its history.

My focal topics are derived from a definition of a literary narrative as the presentation of a *character* or characters in a sequence of *events* in *space* and *time*, *framed* with a beginning and ending in a *text* that is related by a *narrator*. The words in italics are the major formal elements that make up my table of contents. The term "formal" refers to essential structural features of all narratives. For example, all narratives have characters and plots, and so these are formal elements. All narratives do not have stable or unstable characters, strong or weak plots, so those variants are non-essential modes of the formal elements of character and plot that change historically. I identify subelements for chapter subdivisions such as the stature of characters, the scale of events, the texture of space, and the pace of time. Among these and other subelements I identify the following specific variants in the modernist period: absent protagonists, fragmented characters, "trivial" events, probabilistic causality, weak plots, literary impressionism, stream of consciousness, repetition of traumas and epiphanies, *in medias res* beginnings, unresolved endings, abstract and surreal styles, singular focalization, embedded focalization, and unreliable narrators.

I focus on formal innovations because modernism is primarily a set of new ways of seeing and interpreting the world, and narrative forms are the literary manifestation of those ways. This focus requires an analysis of literary form in contrast to literary content. The form-content distinction is like a third rail of literary analysis: it drives the entire system, but to touch it directly is deadly. The more one attempts to clarify that distinction, the murkier it becomes. Applied to a bottle of wine, the form-content distinction is precise and concrete in that the wine can be physically separated from the bottle. Applied to objects in art, the distinction can still be clearly conceptualized, as one can think of a violin in a cubist painting separate from the formal techniques used to depict it. But applied to human experience in novels, the forms of experience cannot be clearly separated from their substance even conceptually. Nevertheless, I do address the problem by analyzing how specific formal techniques at key moments in the story were used to capture specific contents. In spite of the formidable theoretical challenges of the form-content distinction, my study is grounded in it.

Such systematic pairing of form and content distinguishes my approach as compared with other studies that include substantive history along with formal innovation but treat the two elements separately.[1] I treat them together. Pericles Lewis's study emphasizes a "crisis of representation" in modernist formal innovation but surveys the substance of that crisis in separate sections on political and economic liberalism, imperialism and racism, working classes and gender roles, urbanism and World War I.[2] David Lodge offers an excellent list of formal innovations but without referring to historical content.

Modernist fiction is concerned with consciousness, and also with the subconscious and unconscious workings of the human mind. Hence the structure of external "objective" events . . . is almost completely dissolved, in order to make room for introspection, analysis, reflection and reverie. A modernist novel has no real "beginning," since it plunges us into a flowing stream of experience with which we gradually familiarize ourselves by a process of inference and association; and its ending is usually "open" or ambiguous, leaving the reader in doubt as to the final destiny of the characters. To compensate for the diminution of narrative structure and unity, alternative methods of aesthetic ordering become more prominent, such as allusion to or imitation of literary models or mythical archetypes, and the repetition-with-variation of motifs, images, symbols – a technique variously described as "rhythm," "Leitmotif," and "spatial form." Modernist fiction eschews the straight chronological ordering of its material and the use of a reliable omniscient and intrusive narrator. It employs, instead, either a single, limited point of view, or a method of multiple points of view, all more or less limited and fallible: and it tends towards a fluid or complex handling of time, involving much cross-reference backwards and forwards across the chronological span of the action.[3]

I shall show how these and other formal techniques capture specific historical developments in the modernists' world.

I highlight innovative formal techniques because they are the most significant aspects of the modernist novel. Charles Dickens wrote about life in the big city, but he did not do it the way Joyce did. Joyce's *Ulysses* (1922) is historical in an obvious way in that it shows a distinctive historical moment, Dublin in 1904, but its more important historical aspects are its formal innovations. Navigating through Dublin in 1904, Dickens would have lost his way, but trying to read *Ulysses*, he would have thought he had lost his mind. Modern*ism* is about a new way of interpreting the world more than the substance of that world, just as Pablo Picasso's *Les demoiselles d'Avignon* is more significant historically for its cubist techniques than for its interpretation of five prostitutes. I do not neglect history but reconstruct its contours as they were engaged by modernist formal innovations.

Collectively those innovations constitute a revolutionary set of ways of interpreting the world as in the following examples. Proust's focus on the seemingly *trivial events* of involuntary memory in *Remembrance of Things Past* (1913–27) recalibrates the significance of subject matter, as it gives far more attention to the taste of tea and madeleines than to World War I. *Weaker plots* mirror the increasingly weaker organizing authority of especially the courtship, family, national, and religious master narratives. The relocation of action from out in the world to the interior of mental life by *stream-of-consciousness technique* and *literary impressionism* captures how the chaotic outer world of especially urban life and courtship scenarios was experienced from within. *Multiple narrators* in Faulkner dramatize the murkiness of any single family narrative as well as the Southern national narrative. In James's *The Ambassadors* (1903), *singular focalization* through the experience of the protagonist Lambert Strether mirrors his initial limited vision about life and the narrow-mindedness of the capitalist world that he was engaged to serve. The dozen techniques that Joyce employed in *Ulysses* to capture simultaneous events in Dublin rework the urban narrative by creating the new sense of *simultaneity* made possible by new transportation and communication technologies.

Most attempts to interpret this time of social, political, and ideological turmoil center on its negative aspects: chaos (Erich Auerbach), anarchy (David Kadlec), crisis (David Trotter, Pericles Lewis), disintegration (Georg Lukács), dehumanization (José Ortega y Gasset), decadence (David Weir), disorientation (Michael Valdez Moses), disenchantment (Max Weber), unknowing (Philip Weinstein), irrationality and absurdity (Lionel Trilling), despair (John A. Lester), bewilderment (Paul B. Armstrong), fragmentation (Marjorie Perloff, Sara Haslam), breakdown of form (James M. Mellard), and a meltdown of "all that is solid" (Marshall Berman).[4] While each of these characterizations, aside from that of Lukács, implies positive aspects from deeper understanding, the focal concepts are still negative.

The negative component of my argument about subversion of the master narratives took shape as a modification of Jean-François Lyotard's famous definition of postmodernism as "incredulity toward metanarratives." As a consequence, he argued, "the narrative function [was] losing ... its great hero ... its great voyages, its great goal."[5] Like Lyotard, I focus on the fate of narratives, but in contrast to him, I substitute *master narrative* for his *metanarrative* that suggests narratives about narrative, which is not my subject. I apply his argument to the earlier period of modernism and switch the decisive change from incredulity to subversion, because artists do not merely disbelieve; they also, and more importantly, believe and affirm. I make explicit the interaction of negative and positive elements by adding *reworking* to my definition of the fate of the master narratives. So the thesis of this book about the substantive history of this period is that it involved a subversion and reworking of the master narratives.

The unifying positive attitude among modernists took shape around a celebration of art. This shared value is not surprising in that leading literary modernists were artists, and many of their works focused on creativity as the most prized source of meaning in life. By his famous exhortation to "make it new" Ezra Pound implied that it did not matter what *it* was as long as it was new, but it did matter to modernists interested in depicting their world. Modernists looked to art for reassurance that life had meaning beyond their everyday concerns, especially as the values and institutions that supported those concerns came under attack.

If I could conjure up a source for this study it would be a journal that Joyce kept while writing *Ulysses* in which he recorded when and how he sought to capture the circumstances of Dublin in 1904 and found inadequate the narrative techniques of his realist predecessors such as Balzac and Dickens. It would also explain which techniques he developed to capture those circumstances and why. While modernists did not provide such a dream document, they did note an assortment of innovative intentions, especially James, Proust, Stein, Woolf, Lewis, Gide, Breton, Broch, and Musil. Absent such a document for Joyce or any modernist, I contrast the modernists' techniques with those of their predecessors, the realists.

Woolf's impassioned questions about popular realist novels of her time – "Is life like this? Must novels be like this?" – I hear behind all modernists' efforts to capture what life is like and how novels ought to be written.[6] Modernists indeed sought to render the world as it really is, while realists saw themselves as modern in their time. So I use *realism* and *modernism* not to categorize what is real or modern, because those features can be attributed to both styles, but to refer to techniques distinctive to the periods that are known by those terms. The remainder of this study offers extended definitions of those terms, but a brief introductory definition is in order here. Realist literary techniques, from roughly 1840 to 1900, typically include (1) narration by an "omniscient" third-person narrator or a first-person narrator who knows everything he or she needs to know about the story, (2) a presumption of the adequacy of language to convey that knowledge, (3) characters with integrated personalities who act in coherent if not predictable ways in accord with those personalities, (4) events that take place in a uniform space in clearly identified chronology, (5) a strong plot of important events that are causally linked, begin at an originary moment in time, and move toward closure to produce an intelligible overall meaning. Modernists alter these techniques, as Woolf put it, to capture what life is like.

The differences between realism and naturalism, roughly 1870 to 1890, are important, but I treat both under the rubric of realism because my purpose is to track a broad historical change from the mid nineteenth to the early twentieth century. The difference between the realist Flaubert and the naturalist Émile Zola, especially in their use of plots, pales in a comparison of both with the modernist Proust, whose weak plot centers on discovering why the taste of tea and madeleines filled him with such intense momentary joy and how to make it endure. My argument about distinctive features of the modernist novel is based on a comparison of modernist literary techniques with literary techniques of the immediately preceding period of the realist novel, not with anticipations of modernism in earlier times such as the mock hero and multiple styles in Miguel de Cervantes's *Don Quixote* (1605–15), the achronology and unresolved ending in Laurence Sterne's *Tristram Shandy* (1759–69), the endless deferrals of action and intense self-consciousness about narration in Denis Diderot's *Jacques the Fatalist* (1796), or the physically horrific protagonist and embedded narratives in Mary Shelley's *Frankenstein* (1818). My focus mirrors that of the modernists themselves who were schooled on realism and reacted to it more energetically than to the entire preceding span of literary history.

For thirty years critics have worked to expand the modernist literary canon for theoretical, disciplinary, and political reasons. I believe that it is time to reaffirm the valued status and galvanizing function of the canon's special evidentiary role. As a historian whose field is balkanized by the vastly different sources that historians use from all over the globe and across long stretches of time, often from obscure archives of unpublished manuscripts, I am particularly appreciative of the field of literary criticism that does have a canon that enables critics to respond to analyses of the sources of one another's studies with exceptional focus and passion precisely because they have read them, taught them, and written about them over many years. And so my focus on enduringly valued novels counters the trend in modernist studies to expand the source base of modernism temporally, vertically, and spatially, as one recent survey notes.[7] While these expansions introduced important new titles, repositioned the status of renowned works, and inspired illuminating analytical techniques, they also disjoined and dispersed interpretations of modernism, including the modernist novel.

Expanding the time frame of modernism back to the mid nineteenth century or before compromises its status as a historically distinct period. Expanding sources downward from high culture toward more popular and formally less challenging novels entails slighting works of exceptional quality and diffuses the common source base that gives the study of modernism focus and creates a vibrant community of interest. Expanding the spatial range of sources globally makes it difficult to identify a common culture based on shared experiences. Europeans and Americans at around the same time experienced urbanism, feminism, monopoly capitalism, a surge of secularism, and the two major diplomatic alliance systems that drew the nations of Western Europe and America into World War I. Before the war Westerners communicated with increasing speed by telegraph and telephone and traveled freely without passports to different countries by new automobiles and faster trains and later by airplanes. In the interwar years they dealt with fascism, Nazism, and communism. The major historical developments that link Westerners and the rest of the world – imperialism and decolonization – divide between the strikingly different experiences of colonizers and colonized. Western writers rapidly exchanged work published in new journals and translated into their respective languages so that they made up a mutual readership and addressed a common public. In Bloomsbury, Schwabing, Montmartre, and Greenwich Village they gathered to discuss their craft. Even in exile they remained in European and American cities – Joyce wrote *Ulysses* in Trieste, Zurich, and Paris and not in Tokyo, Cairo, and Bombay. The American exiles James, Stein, Hemingway, Fitzgerald, Dos Passos, and Barnes were drawn to Europe and not to Asia or South America. Early on most devotees of serious literature read Flaubert, and then James and Conrad, and by the mid 1920s many had read Joyce. Proust won the Goncourt Prize in 1919, and Mann won the Nobel Prize in 1929. Modernists' novels are set primarily in Europe and America and concern people from those areas, and while they had unique styles, they shared concerns about the Western world.[8]

I rely on canonical novels not to enshrine a pantheon of classics but because they generally made the most historically distinctive formal innovations, which is what made them classics in their time. The modernist canon is also more familiar to readers, which makes it possible to refer to well-known novels succinctly without the extensive introduction of character and plot necessary with less familiar novels. Thus I can assume that my readers may know something about the character of Leopold Bloom and the plot of *Heart of Darkness*. I draw on Joyce's *Ulysses* more than any other novel because it is a particularly rich source of modernist literary creativity.

My sources are primarily modernist novels. By way of introduction to most sections, I draw on a few realist novels with extreme brevity to sharpen my arguments about historical change. Such an evidentiary imbalance invites a reading of the earlier period as a mere prelude to the modernist period and may imply progress. I work to avoid such a Whiggish interpretation even if some modernists did indulge in one. In 1921 Gide noted in his journal, "I shall not be satisfied unless I succeed in getting still farther from realism."[9] Proust recoiled from the deficiencies of the Goncourt brothers' realism and in *Remembrance of Things Past* rejected "the falseness of so-called realist art" (*RP*, III, 915). In 1919 Woolf targeted classical realism in the work of her contemporaries in proposing that "the sooner English fiction turns its back upon" the "materialist" novelists H. G. Wells, Arnold Bennett, and John Galsworthy, "the better for its soul."[10] Five years later she added more strongly that those writers "have made tools and established conventions which do their business. But those tools are not our tools, and that business is not our business. For us those conventions are ruin, those tools are death."[11] In contrast to such views, I trace not a story of progress in literary excellence but the logic of change between two periods as avant-garde novelists developed narrative tools to capture their age in ways that they believed earlier techniques were not as well suited to accomplish.

This study offers literary critics, historians, and narrative theorists a new look at modernism. To literary critics it offers a systematic survey of the formal innovations of the modernist novel element by element and historicizes those formal innovations in two ways: by comparing them with what their realist predecessors did and by showing substantively how those innovations were used to capture changing historical circumstances. It offers historians a definition of the master narratives, an interpretation of the history of the modern period as a subversion and reworking of those narratives, and a suggestion that the new ways of writing novels may also have spilled over into the writing of history. I accent form over content not because I believe that new ways of writing about World War I were more important than new facts about the war but because from a historiographical perspective, the distinctive feature of the history written at that time was its form more than its content. Finally, this study offers narrative theorists, whose scholarship is largely ahistorical, some explanation as to why formal elements may have changed as they did in this period in response to literary as well as historical developments. A few narrative theorists note how specific narrative techniques emerge at certain historical moments but rarely address why such techniques came into use at those times.[12] Modernists innovated formally for compelling reasons, namely to be original and creative and to capture the substantive circumstances of their age.

Master narratives make sense of experience for large numbers of people. My definition of them follows that of Allan Megill, who defined them as an "authoritative account of some particular segment of history."[13] They pull together major developments that were the foundation for historical understanding and a source of meaning leading up to and including the modernist period. I cast the substantive history of this period into master narratives because it was conceptualized as narratives, and such formulations facilitate showing how formal narrative techniques were used to capture its substance. In this half of the introduction I organize the ten master narratives according to two principles: for the first six, according to the increasing number of people involved (from individuals and couples to nations and empires), and for the final four, according to the increasingly spiritual nature of the activities involved (from making money and seeking justice to believing in God and creating art).

The personal narrative is the story of an individual life from birth to death. In the realist period that narrative was of someone who moves in uniform space and time acquiring knowledge and governed by an ethical imperative that individuals should treat others as ends, not as means.[14] That person's separate mental faculties are components of an essentially unified subject.

The major legal achievements with respect to personal autonomy were the abolition of the slave trade from Africa in the early nineteenth century, the emancipation of the Russian serfs in 1861, the Fourteenth Amendment to the Constitution in the United States in 1868 that guaranteed equal protection to all people under the law, and electoral reforms throughout the nineteenth century all across Europe that allowed more people to participate as citizens in the affairs of state by voting in increasingly democratic elections. The legal system was strongly voluntarist as jurists located criminal responsibility squarely in the individual self. Realists celebrated individuals with resolute wills and strong character, and while they acknowledged that some people lacked these qualities, they did not question whether a self underlay them. Later in the century observers tended more and more to explain aspects of the personality from social causes, but still retained a notion of a unified and responsible self.

The courtship narrative is the story of gender roles, sex, and love relations. In the nineteenth century, middle-class men and women developed sharply contrasting gender roles. Men learned to work in the world, earn money to support a wife and children, and assume leading roles in the community, church, business, army, or state. Women learned to attract a man and wait for him to court while learning to sew, cook, play piano, dance, read, and teach children – skills for marriage and motherhood. Commentators viewed male and female as opposites, physically and mentally. Men were physically strong, rational, active, cool-headed, and adventurous, while women were physically weak, intuitive, passive, impulsive, and flirtatious. Sexual activity was oppressed from the outside by public censorship and suppressed from the inside by prudery. Still, men were somehow to acquire sexual experience to guide wives. The man decided when, where, and whom to court, while chaste and chaperoned women awaited his attention and marriage proposal. Then for a brief moment power shifted and women could play the active role in deciding yes or no. Women were more committed to the morality of love based on honesty, fidelity, and commitment, while men made moral choices in the public sphere.

After around 1890 this narrative was subverted by movement toward gender depolarization from findings in genetics (sex is determined by only one out of twenty-three pairs of chromosomes, the rest being bisexual), endocrinology (both males and females produce all three sex hormones – androgen, estrogen, and progesterone), embryology (fetuses are bisexual in early stages, and maleness emerges out of femaleness in later stages), gynecology (hermaphroditism is evidence of latent bisexual tendencies in both sexes), sexology (intermediate sex types exist and are called "inverts" and "bisexuals"), evolutionary biology (a latent human bisexual disposition derives from bisexual animal progenitors), feminist theory (Victorian ideas about an absolute sexual dichotomy are wrong), and psychoanalysis (psychosexual development is bisexual in oral and anal stages). Gender depolarization is further reflected in the growing concern among social commentators and moralists about "masculinization" of women and "feminization" of men. This subversive realignment centered on more aggressive gender roles for women, who began to engage in sports, ride bicycles, raise hem lines, stop wearing corsets, start wearing make-up, cut their long hair, travel without chaperons, discuss sex, use contraception, choose to have premarital sex, explore lesbian love, wait longer to marry, attend universities, enter "men's" professions (especially during World War I), join women's movements, access artistic academies, do nude self-portraits, develop a self-consciously female writing style, and vote.[15]

Courtship was reworked by men and women who took into account new gender roles pioneered by more active women in sex, marriage, motherhood, professions, society, politics, economics, and art. Women became more aggressive in pursuing, touching, and kissing men as well as in discussing sex, initiating sex, and proposing marriage. In *The Family* (1906) the American anthropologist Elsie Clews Parsons recommended trial marriages in which men and women could discover if they were sexually compatible before marrying. Couples rejected the romantic ideal of fusion in love so popular in the realist period and affirmed the desirability of maintaining autonomy in loving as they pursued less scripted courtship scenarios.

Marital relations in England, for example, were transformed by a series of Parliamentary acts that gradually accorded legal selfhood to women and equalized the grounds for divorce. In 1850 the English wife's legal existence had been absorbed into that of her husband in a condition known as coverture: "the husband and wife are one person; that is, the very being, or legal existence, of a woman is suspended during marriage, or at least incorporated and consolidated into that of the husband, under whose wing, protection and cover she performs everything."[16] An act of 1884 abrogated the husband's legal right to imprison his wife. An act of 1923 gave a wife the power to obtain a divorce on the basis of adultery alone without additional aggravating grounds. In 1937 wives were given the right to sue for divorce on the ground of desertion, cruelty, or insanity alone, without also proving adultery.

The family narrative offered a source of meaning for individuals in a single family and for families across generations. Both narratives were subverted by a number of developments. In the 1870s marital birth control became more widespread in the middle and lower classes, and the number of children per family dropped, eroding the size of families and increasing tension within them.[17] A decade later, as feminist movements gained traction, women resisted conventional familial roles as subservient wives and child-bearing machines and sought new sources of fulfillment outside the family. By the end of the century, as the "New Woman" cultivated new amorous and professional opportunities, and as new divorce laws allowed married women to break free, the family became an increasingly explosive unit. Late Victorian anthropologists and sociologists questioned the universality of the family and came to view it as a social and historical construct rather than a divinely ordained institution, further undermining its authority. The rediscovery of Mendel's theory of hereditary transmission in 1900 initiated the emergence of modern genetics, although popular thinking continued to be mired in erroneous understandings of the mechanism of heredity that predominated in the nineteenth century. Even experts in psychology, sociology, and eugenics continued to view the family as a conduit for an increasing pool of diseases such as tuberculosis and syphilis as well as vices, such as alcoholism, that collect in the blood, which they wrongly believed to be the carrier of hereditary degeneration. In 1896 Freud identified strong conflicting feelings for both of his parents and in 1910 first used the term "Oedipus complex" to name them. He introduced this aspect of psychoanalytic theory to codify psychodynamics that he believed to be universal but especially acute at that time when fathers dominated families and some aggressive physicians even threatened masturbating boys with castration. The increasing diversity and intensity of urban life pulled people in diverse directions that further destabilized families, while World War I ripped them apart by brutalizing, wounding, and slaughtering millions of husbands and fathers.

After the war Europeans scrambled to restore pre-war courtship scenarios as well as familial values. That reworking was especially urgent in France, which had suffered a worrisome depopulation in the pre-war years that commentators explained from infertility, secularization, moral decay, sexual promiscuity, widespread contraception, physical and moral degeneration, breastless and hipless "*garçonnes*," and emasculating feminists who rejected having children. The reconstructing of gender in postwar France, like the reconstructing of the family, was only partly successful, as women in France as well as across Europe and America were unwilling and unable to renounce entirely the new professions, life styles, and aspirations made possible by early feminism and further realized during the war.[18]

The urban narrative covers the massive movement of people from the country to the city. While the realist city was big, the modernist city, except for Dublin, was generally much bigger, as Table 1 shows.[19] Urban experience

Table 1 *Population change in major cities 1850–1910*

	1850	1910
Berlin	419,000	2,071,000
Dublin	272,000	305,000
London	2,685,000	7,256,000
New York	515,547	4,776,883
Paris	1,053,000	2,888,000
Petersburg	485,000	1,962,000
Prague	118,000	224,000
Vienna	440,000	2,031,000

was also transformed by new communication technologies (telephone, wireless, cinema, electric signs, cheap daily newspapers) and new transportation technologies (automobiles, busses, electric trams, airplanes) that increased the pace and scale of human interactions. Electric motors and assembly lines revolutionized production. Big cities were torn up by the construction of grand boulevards, sewers, subways, and skyscrapers, while steamships exchanged people from around the world, which increased social mobility and cultural diversity.

The movement of populations to cities transformed simpler rural societies into more complex urban centers. The story of the "Young Man from the Provinces," as Lionel Trilling put it, who is poor but intelligent and full of hope and travels to the city to seek his fortune is one of realism's dominant narratives.[20] In the modernist novel young men are already residents of large cities, and the country is generally a background region from which their ancestors emigrated.

Some observers focused on negative aspects of urban life with slums, pollution, crime, and alienation. In "The Metropolis and Mental Life" of 1902, the German sociologist Georg Simmel observed how cities generate a disorienting intensification of nervous stimulation that leads to either anxiety or a "blasé attitude" and transforms personal into impersonal values based on monetary exchange. Others celebrated how cities promote cosmopolitanism, artistic innovation, and professional specialization. In 1909, the founder of Italian futurism, Filippo Marinetti, rhapsodized: "We will sing of the multi-colored polyphonic tides of revolution in modern capitals . . . of the vibrant nightly fervor of arsenals and shipyards blazing with violent electric moons."[21] The urban narrative traced how millions left the countryside and streamed into increasingly large urban centers that transformed traditional social life.

The national narrative is about the integration of people into ethnic, cultural, and ultimately political units with a sacred originary moment mired in legend and continuing progress toward a future of increasing territorial control, financial prosperity, social stability, political authority, and cultural supremacy. While England and France were unified throughout the realist and modernist periods, the United States and European countries east of France fought a number of wars between 1859 and 1871 to become unified nation states. Across these years religious and dynastic grounds for national unity were replaced by music and national anthems, symbols and national flags, festivals and national holidays, print journalism and nationalist propaganda, and, most forcefully, by xenophobia from imperial conquests and foreign wars. World War I was caused in large part by the intensification of aggressive nationalism. The war amplified nationalism with the patriotism that fired civilians and soldiers in the early days, as when two million Englishmen volunteered to fight between August 1914 and June 1915; but it also shattered nationalism after four years of slaughter over a pack of "old men's lies," as Pound put it in *Hugh Selwyn Mauberley* (1920): "There died a myriad, / And of the best, among them, / For an old bitch gone in the teeth, / For a botched civilization."

The material ground for nationalism in sovereign countries was restructured after the war with the Peace of Paris, which largely ignored Woodrow Wilson's principle of the self-determination of nationalities that was supposed to regulate the creation of nations in accordance with the will of the people. Wartime grievances and postwar insecurities undermined the implementation of that principle, and Europe was recreated with millions of politically oppressed nationals, a breeding ground for future conflict. One nationalities problem was addressed, if not resolved, with the creation of the Irish Free State in 1922, the same year Joyce published *Ulysses*. But the novel was written during years when the cause of Irish nationalism was a source of intense conflict that reverberates throughout the text.

Popular response to nationalism after 1914 centered on the war that transformed gender roles, love relationships, social organization, economic institutions, and the political stability of Europe. The war's role in modernist literary innovation, however, was more of an interruption than a defining moment. Jean-Michel Rabaté implies as much in his full-length study of everything new that occurred in 1913, a year he tags as "the cradle of modernism."[22] Most of the formally innovative modernists did not fight and rarely depicted the horrors of the trenches, but their oblique approach to the war cannot be explained simply by the fact that they were not there. Their formal concerns led away from spectacular events such as bodies blown to bits. They sought to rethink the sort of experiences that are suitable subjects for art generally and were inclined to focus on seemingly trivial experiences in which they found a wealth of riches that they worked to capture with new formal techniques. Therefore, the war was a huge distraction for most modernist writers, as most of the formal innovation in their novels was manifest in nascent form in the pre-war years. They did not ignore the war. Indeed, many powerful moments in their novels treat the war but do so indirectly as it was registered by those who did not fight or by those who did fight but experienced it most forcefully afterwards as emotional exhaustion or shell shock.

The imperial narrative is the story of the increasing territorial, financial, political, and cultural dominion by the nations of Europe and America over other areas, mainly of Africa and Asia. Between 1876 and 1915 Britain acquired 4 million square miles, France 3.5 million, and Germany and Italy around 1 million each. This enormous expansion was made possible by superior science, technology, politics, and weaponry. New steel hull boats and railroads enabled Europeans to conquer the interior of Africa. A Congress of European States in Berlin in 1884–85 devised rules to "legitimate" such domination, empowering nations to establish a mandate over territories if they promoted "welfare" for the "backward people" there with military presence and civil administration. New machine guns and artillery enabled small numbers to conquer huge populations: in 1898 at Omdurman the British killed 11,000 Sudanese with machine guns while suffering only 28 deaths themselves. In the Belgian Congo between 1885 and 1895, up to 10,000,000 people were starved to death, killed off by exposure and disease, or brutally murdered, all to get natives to collect ivory and rubber.[23] By 1900 in Africa only Abyssinia and Liberia remained independent.

Europeans had various reasons to take colonies in addition to natural resources, markets, cheap labor, and investment. France sought to undo the humiliating defeat by Germany in 1870 and win political prestige, Britain wanted to run a railroad from the Cape to Cairo and protect the Suez Canal out of economic interest, and Germany grabbed colonies as a latecomer to imperialism. All nations were driven by the axiom that great nations must be big and therefore must expand or die, and repeatedly invoked the analogy of countries as like trees that must expand their branches over as high and wide an area as possible to capture a fair share of sunlight and not wither in the shade of another country. They each gilded the imperial narrative with myths: the British bore a "white man's burden" to civilize primitives; the French pursued a righteous "civilizing mission" to bring the French language and culture to inferior peoples; the Germans conquered savages on behalf of "German culture." This spectacular land grab itself bolstered myths about the superiority of the white race, Christian religion, and Western society. Those imperial values were promoted by the German Colonial Society, the Committee for French Africa, and the British Royal Colonial Institute, whose members wrote books, built museums, and lobbied for aggressive foreign policy. Herbert Spencer philosophized about imperialism with Social Darwinism, Rudyard Kipling poetized imperialism's self-sacrificing virtue, while Josiah Strong celebrated its destiny to bring Christianity to heathens. Leading intellectuals including G. W. F. Hegel, Alfred Russell Wallace, Francis Galton, and Benjamin Kidd characterized Africans as moral primitives or "half-witted" savages being uplifted by European culture.

In the 1880s the British Labour Party urged the government to end the transport of Chinese laborers as indentured workers in South Africa, and in

1893 Ghandi protested the treatment of Indians in Natal. The anti-imperialist Ethical Union formed in 1896 saw imperialism as ethically objectionable and inimical to progress. British Liberal and Labour Party leaders protested, especially during the Boer War of 1899–1902, as Britain found it unexpectedly difficult to put down a colonial uprising. In 1897 the imperial apologist Kipling wrote in "Recessional": "Far-called, our navies melt away ... Lo, all our pomp of yesterday / Is one with Nineveh and Tyre!" The British reformer E. D. Morel organized the Congo Reform Association in 1904 to expose atrocities in the Congo, encouraged by Roger Casement, author of a Congo Report submitted to the British Parliament in 1904. French anti-imperialists emphasized the financial drain of imperialism and the contradiction between it and the values of their republican government based on French Revolutionary ideals of liberty, equality, and fraternity. French religious leaders protested the Arab slave trade in Africa. The myth of white racial superiority suffered a stunning setback in 1896 when 70,000 Abyssinians crushed the Italian army and killed 6,000 of its soldiers at Adowa. In 1905 the Japanese defeated the Russians at Port Arthur. The imperial narrative was subverted because it failed to produce wealth, power, or prestige more than because activists protested its immorality.

The imperial narrative was also challenged by intellectuals and artists who pursued the study of anthropology and celebrated cultural pluralism. In 1911 Franz Boas argued that *The Mind of Primitive Man* (his title) was as complex as the mind of the civilized man, equally capable of linguistic, social, and artistic achievement. The immorality of imperialism was highlighted by artists and intellectuals increasingly inspired by new values and possibilities from "primitive" cultures, as evident in Picasso's *Les demoiselles d'Avignon* (1907) and Stravinsky's *Sacré du printemps* (1913). The official public reworking of the imperial narrative was decolonization among scores of colonial states that achieved their first tangible political victory after World War II with the independence of India and Pakistan in 1947.

The capitalist narrative covers the economic system and its related social, political, and scientific developments in a story of material progress. Capital accumulation made possible an increasing availability of credit and expansion of industry and trade. Money based on the gold standard was established in England in 1821 and in Western Europe and the United States in the 1870s, where it lasted until 1914, which closed a period of exceptional monetary stability. New technologies for the manufacture of steel, machines, and fertilizers led to even more production as did improvements in technique such as time management and assembly lines. The increasing division of labor meant more efficient and specialized production and cheaper products. The rationalization of production by a professional managerial class and expanded vertical and horizontal integration of large trusts increased the scale and scope of production. Increasingly sophisticated advertisements informed more customers of the qualities and availability of an ever-expanding range of products. The growth of the railroad network and the emergence of steamships, automobiles, and trucks accelerated and expanded production and distribution. While these improvements were undertaken to enrich investors, they also contributed to the wealth and stability of nations and ultimately to the prosperity of the middle and lower classes by providing them with employment, goods, and services.

The liberal narrative is the progressive realization of the ideals of the Enlightenment. The philosophy at the heart of that narrative is that man is born a blank slate with natural rights. He can be educated and use reason to determine his best interest and participate in politics responsibly as a citizen by voting for representatives in a government based on the rule of law. While serving public utility, such governments must not impinge on individual rights to free speech, press, assembly, religion, and so forth.

One focus of this narrative in the nineteenth century was an extension of the right to vote. European liberals promoted a limited suffrage based on property holdings and education but also worked to promote public education and thereby lay the foundation for electoral reform, which accelerated after 1870.[24] The social basis for these changes was a restructuring of the social hierarchy as the poor became more prosperous and the middle class grew. These political and social changes continued throughout the nineteenth century as liberals struggled to achieve electoral reform, avoid full democracy, and institute laws to protect civil rights from governmental interference.

The liberal project ran into a number of challenges that gradually undermined its effectiveness. Liberalism's essence subverted the French Revolution's commitment to liberty, equality, and fraternity by limiting citizenship and voting rights to the wealthy and educated with the *capacity to vote*, thereby avoiding the more radical notion of all citizens having a natural *right to vote*. Conversely, liberal success in increasing the number of people with the capacity to vote expanded the political clout of the lower classes. The *embourgeoisement* of the lower classes and democratization of society undermined the appeal of the exclusionary liberal discourse. The appeal of liberalism with its tortuous equivocation between equality and privilege became increasingly less urgent as, after 1880, the legal privileges, social prominence, and political clout of the European aristocracy declined.[25] Social restructuring necessitated a politics that addressed a mass society to which socialists more than liberals appealed with goals of social ownership and a proletarian revolution on behalf of everyone. Liberalism also declined after 1885 because of its inability to address the emerging mass politics and consumer culture. The old liberals focused on constitutional and electoral matters, while the new parties were fired up by single issue lobbies such as the Navy League in Germany and Irish Home Rule in England. The nuances and complexities of liberalism could not compete with the rousing rhetoric of nationalism fueled by war cries or imperial conquests.

In the early twentieth century, the partial success of liberals' democratization and egalitarianism triggered counter-movements and ideologies such as Social Darwinism, anarcho-syndicalism, chauvinistic nationalism, racism, and antisemitism. Liberalism was further subverted by Fascists in Italy and then by Nazis in Germany, who tagged the philosophy as weak and associated with the failures of the Weimar Republic. Marxists also challenged it from the left as an ideological cover for a self-interested bourgeoisie that had betrayed workers since the French Revolution. Liberalism also changed into a call for technocracy, bureaucracy, and scientific rationalism. In place of voting capacity based on property and wealth, liberals focused on overall capacity based on education and professional expertise.[26] Liberalism was reworked by reaction against exclusionary ideologies in the form of anti-fascism and anti-communism, as it also became a "New Liberalism" sustained by economic interests such as free trade and urban consumers and committed to the expansion of the regulatory and welfare state.[27]

The religious narrative encompasses the creation, incarnation, crucifixion, resurrection, second coming, Last Judgment, and Kingdom of God of Christian history. For centuries that narrative also sanctified birth, marriage, and death; grounded morality and political sovereignty; offered hope for miracles through divine intervention; framed history governed by divine providence; promised salvation in an eternal afterlife with Jesus Christ and God; and inspired art, music, and literature. It set the calendar with religious holidays and sabbaths to worship God, pray for God's help, and meditate on how to live a Christian life. Finally, it offered believers a reassuring account of what happened "in the beginning" and a vision of what was to be hoped for in the end.

The hold of that powerful narrative was subverted in the modernist period by the growth of more secular and culturally pluralistic large cities, the rising authority of science, and the formal separation of church and state, instituted legally in France in 1905. Evidence of the modernist threat to Roman Catholicism is the 1907 encyclical of Pope Pius X, *Lamentabili Sane Exitu* (a lamentable departure indeed), which condemned modernism, by which he meant rationalism, materialism, liberalism, and anti-clericalism. The collapse of religiously anointed monarchies and their hereditary aristocracies in Russia, Germany, and Austria-Hungary during and after World War I further secularized life at the highest levels of power. Throughout the modernist period attendance in church and religious schools in Europe declined significantly. Fascist Italy, Nazi Germany, and Soviet Russia moved against conventional religious institutions but at the same time reworked conventional orthodoxies into new political religions, enshrining their respective leaders as messiah-like rulers and adopting myths, symbols, and ceremonies from the religions they opposed.[28]

The artistic narrative like the personal narrative refers to a single life story. Modernists conceptualized creativity as a narrative which personally gave them fits of suffering and self-doubt but emerged as the most venerated source of meaning in life. Early on Nietzsche urged followers to learn from artistic accomplishment and then adapt that process to life itself. Only after such a struggle does life become authentic and meaningful, no longer a regret from which one hopes to be saved but an achievement that is its own deliverance. He concluded *Thus Spoke Zarathustra* with the philosopher joyously affirming his existence that has been crafted artistically. Writers celebrated a life devoted to art in their most personal works. Rainer Maria Rilke's fictional journal *The Notebooks of Malte Laurids Brigge* (1910) is about a poet learning to write. Joyce's fictional autobiography, aptly titled *A Portrait of the Artist as a Young Man*, is about Stephen Dedalus, whose name in Greek means "fabulous artificer" and who struggles to define his creative vocation as he detaches from the Catholic Church. In *The Counterfeiters* Gide projects his authorial role in a narrative about Edouard, who is trying to write a novel also titled *The Counterfeiters* and assess its worth in the novel as well as in a fictional journal appended at the end, a path-breaking autopsy of literary creation.[29] Dos Passos dramatizes the progress of a narrator's self-reflexive voice through fifty-one autobiographical "Camera Eye" sections dispersed throughout his epic trilogy *U. S. A.* (1930, 1932, 1936). The climax of Proust's *Remembrance* comes in waves of illumination about the importance of art. The novel is about the narrator's search for a way not only to recapture in memory a past that is lost but to prolong the fleeting joy of its retrieval and find a way to preserve it in full consciousness. In the end he discovers that "the work of art was the sole means of rediscovering Lost Time" and concludes that "the supreme truth of life resides in art" (III, 935–39). Sartre ends *Nausea* (1938) with its protagonist envisioning liberation from an absurd existence by resolving to become a writer.

The master narratives are archetypical constructs I use to conceptualize and order historical developments. The overall tag suggests that they are of the same order of generalization, but they are not. The personal and artistic narratives reconstruct the story of an individual life, while the courtship narrative is that of a single couple. The other master narratives (family, urban, national, and so forth) cover large numbers of people over the entire time span of my study. People in the modernist period did not experience the master narratives as such, and novelists did not use those terms. Thus, "the urban narrative" does not appear in *Ulysses*, "the liberal narrative" is not in Kafka's *The Trial* (1925), and "the imperial narrative" is not in *Heart of Darkness*. But Joyce did live in and have strong feelings about Dublin, Kafka did work in the dehumanizing labyrinths of Prague's legal bureaucracies, and Conrad did skipper a ship into the Congo and observe imperialist abuse. In recasting their personal experience into novels, these writers devised new formal techniques to address historical realities of their time and produce monuments of literature that in turn impacted on how their readers viewed contemporary developments such as urban life, liberal justice, and imperialism. I generalize these specific experiences into master narratives to identify the larger historical significance of these episodes in the authors' personal lives and the lives of the characters on whom they projected those experiences. Those generalizations put together make it possible to interpret the larger historical significance of modernist novels into a single reading of the fate of narrative in literary culture, which I take to be the heart of modernism.

CHAPTER I

Character

Characters are persons who perform actions in stories. In realist novels they are generally present in the action, substantively complete in their composition and therefore fully "in character," structurally solid as a coherent unit, stable in basic identity over time even as they respond to changing circumstances, admirable (as protagonists) if not classically heroic, and oriented to life in a purposive way. In modernist novels the formal features of presence, substance, structure, stability, stature, and purpose change in subverting and reworking the historical content of the master narratives.

PRESENCE: CONSPICUOUS ABSENCE

That main characters are present and center in the action that moves stories would seem to be a truism. Throughout the realist period such was the case, but in the modernist period some characters began to disappear significantly. Realist presence gave way to modernist absence in stories about a black, a lesbian, and a young man, who subvert conventionally biased distinctions that ground the imperial, courtship, and national narratives.

In Conrad's *The Nigger of the "Narcissus"* (1897), the black seaman James Wait is from the British West Indies and as a colonial subject is the victim of racial prejudice. His presence is announced prominently in the title, but he is conspicuously absent in the story even as he dominates the action. He is late to board the *Narcissus*, his name on the ship's list is a smudge, and he spends most of the time below deck. He is isolated from the crew because of illness as well as race and is absent from the main action of a storm and a near mutiny, which his laziness and apparent malingering trigger. He is repeatedly identified with mist, fog, and darkness, and he leaves the ship early, because he dies and is buried at sea. Still, his absence dominates the novel. As the narrator explains, "he made himself master of every moment of our existence," adding that "through him we were becoming highly humanized, tender, complex, excessively decadent: we understood the

subtlety of his fear, sympathized with all his repulsions, shrinkings, eva-
sions, delusions – as though we had been over-civilized, and rotten, and
without any knowledge of the meaning of life."[1] One sailor blames the
storm on his presence, and his death seems to restore calm. In a preface to
the 1914 American edition, Conrad explained that "in the book [Wait] is
nothing; he is merely the center of the ship's collective psychology and the
pivot of action." While Conrad intended to celebrate human solidarity
during a storm at sea, he forged it amid divisive racial prejudice among his
sailors through a character who controls the story by his absence.

Djuna Barnes's *Nightwood* (1936) subverts the courtship narrative through
the perspective of a bisexual outsider, Robin Vote, who is chronically absent
from the lives of her male and female lovers. Introduced as one who has fainted
and is therefore unconscious, she marries Felix Volkbein but remains uncom-
municative. Her clothes are of another period, and she is unable to grasp what
Felix says or respond to his love. She leaves him, wanders to other cities, and
meets Nora Flood whom she also repeatedly abandons. Robin's absence
drives Nora to grasp the constraints of heterosexual courtship conventions.
Dr. O'Connor explains to Nora how those conventions keep some people
from gratifying unconventional urges: "what is this love we have for the invert,
boy or girl?"[2] Robin's physical absence dramatizes what is emotionally absent
from dehumanizing gender and courtship conventions, especially for lesbians.
In realist novels, a character's lover might be absent, but the character always
has an identifiable beloved, whereas Barnes's absentee is fundamentally
estranged from love itself, which is impossible for her in her time.

The most significantly missing character is in Woolf's *Jacob's Room*
(1922), which tells the story of Jacob Flanders, whose conspicuous absenteeism symbolizes the approximately 885,000 Englishmen who were killed in
World War I, half of them blown to bits and unrecovered, with only around
10 percent returned to England for burial. While the conditions of trench
warfare forced soldiers to live with dead bodies, civilians did not see them.
They were buried where they fell, if they were recovered at all, and beginning in 1916 the Defence of the Realm Act banned publishing photographs
of dead soldiers.[3] Amid the chaos, countless caskets were empty, while many
contained parts of two or more bodies. From Jacob's titular empty room
and his brother's opening unanswered call, "Ja-cob! Ja-cob!" to the concluding gesture of his mother holding up his old shoes, Woolf's novel offers
a historically unprecedented rendering of the number of ways a character
can be absent or deficient and still profoundly impact others as he himself is
groomed to become cannon fodder. I count sixty-four instances of Jacob's
absenteeism in five modes, including the following:

1. *Physically*: late, never came, already gone, out in front, lags behind, not in his room, left the house, turned to go, lost during a hunt, gone to Paris.
2. *Intentionally*: does not want to play, hides from his mother, disobeys his mother, covers his face with a handkerchief, ignores a woman in a railway car, fails to read Shakespeare, remains silent.
3. *Cognitively*: asleep, does not hear, bored, absent-minded, looks vacant, opens hymn book at wrong place, does not know history, knows nothing about music, cannot dance.
4. *Objectively*: cannot be found, Mr. Floyd walks by him at Piccadilly, Professor Huxtable walks past him at Cambridge, his article is rejected for publication, a maid misunderstands his name, Evan Williams cannot find him, calls to him go unanswered.
5. *Symbolically*: a creaking wicker chair, a galloping riderless horse, Jacob's empty room, his empty shoes.

These conspicuous absences magnify formally the absurdity of the mass death from war that Woolf evokes as an ominous background beginning with Jacob's surname *Flanders* that conjures up the killing fields of Belgium and Northern France. The soldiers sliding back in the muddy maze of trenches are suggested symbolically by the crab that young Jacob captures in a bucket, futilely circling the sandy bottom, "trying with its weakly legs to climb the steep side; trying again and falling back, and trying again and again" (*JR*, 14). Woolf cuts from explaining how "character-drawing" can produce only "exquisite outlines enclosing vacancy" to evoking powerfully how guns fire and "a dozen young men in the prime of life descend with composed faces into the depths of the sea," while on land an entire army "falls flat, save that . . . one or two pieces still agitate up and down like fragments of broken match-stick" (155–56). The novel ends in Jacob's empty room with his friend Richard futilely calling out "Jacob! Jacob!" and his despairing mother holding up his empty shoes, a moment that poignantly recalls her question that opens the novel: "Where *is* that tiresome little boy?" Woolf exploits the innovative formal strategy of conspicuous absence to assail the war and the men who caused it, rewriting the national master narrative from a story of patriarchal pomposity and progress to one of deadly hubris and decline.

The innovative narrative technique of a conspicuously absent main character enabled Conrad, Barnes, and Woolf to subvert respectively the imperial, courtship, and national narratives with novels that do not merely moralize about victimizing specific populations but dramatize the annihilating experience of being excluded from privileged sanctuaries by racial intolerance, homophobic intolerance, and nationalist chauvinism.

SUBSTANCE: CONCRETE NOTHINGNESS

Realist characters, whether miserly like Monsieur Grandet in Balzac's *Eugénie Grandet* (1833), loyal like Abel Magwitch in Dickens's *Great Expectations* (1860–61), or passionate like Anna in Tolstoy's *Anna Karenina* (1851), are what they are inside to outside and remain so throughout the story. In response to challenging circumstances, they become more fully realized as characters. Such existential plenitude was resisted by some modernists who increasingly questioned whether a person can actually *be* anyone thoroughly. A modernist theory of the positive function of negation as the essence of character is Sartre's *Being and Nothingness* (1943), which views human existence as devoid of any inherent meaning, with, rather, nothingness at its core. People experience "concrete nothingness" in many ways: as in questioning, absence, regret, and the ever-present possibility of death. Unlike the being of nonhuman things that are always totally what they are, wall-to-wall being, human existence is never completely anything; it is rather a constant slippage from being one with itself as it struggles with the fundamental "elsewhere of consciousness" in any given moment and endlessly moves away from its lost past and toward its uncertain future, always tempted to flee from the responsibility of endlessly defining itself that is required by its freedom.

Sartre forecast this philosophy in his earlier novel *Nausea*, about Antoine Roquentin, the main character who, as a first person narrator, is always present and in the reader's mind but nevertheless embodies concrete nothingness, which he occasionally contemplates explicitly: "I am the one who pulls myself from the nothingness to which I aspire."[4] Plagued by chronic nausea when contemplating his life, he grasps its nature when looking at the meandering root of a chestnut tree, which is simply there – excessive and superfluous (*de trop*), without any reason for or justification of its existence. But human existence is even more formless than the root, because it is essentially a gaping nothingness that is the key to its essence as conscious, free, and responsible for itself. Roquentin's experience is ultimately liberating, however, because if one is essentially nothing, one can become anything. Sartre's novel challenges the personal narrative of realist fiction as well as the liberal narrative as Roquentin rejects the bourgeois world of Bouville (Mudtown) where he lives. In the end he affirms art as a purpose by drawing inspiration from a jazz singer and by resolving to become a writer.

Sartre defines man as "a being which *is* what-it-is-not [because consciousness is always beyond itself] and which *is not* what-it-is [because it must change]." Those paired paradoxes echo Martin Heidegger's earlier quip in *Being and Time* (1927) that "Everyone is the other, and no one is himself." Such existential paradoxes permeate modernist fiction. The narrator in Ford's *The Good Soldier* (1915) wonders "who in this world can give anyone a character?" His skepticism centers on the inability to assign clear motivation.[5] Woolf offers a motto for modernism with the reflections of her protagonist in *Mrs. Dalloway* (1925): "She would not say of any one in the world now that they were this or were that" and, at the end of that paragraph, more specifically, "she would not say of Peter, she would not say of herself, I am this, I am that" (*MD*, 8–9). The wise but unstable Darl Bundren in Faulkner's *As I Lay Dying* (1930) concludes: "I don't know if I am or not. Jewel [Darl's brother] knows he is, because he does not know that he does not know whether he is or not" (*AD*, 80). Joyce dramatizes the impossibility of self-definition when Leopold Bloom, after a seaside encounter with Gerty MacDowell, attempts to write a message about himself for her in the sand but can only come up with "I," and then a moment later, "AM. A." and finally rubs out the incomplete sentence. The conclusion of Descartes's *cogito ergo sum* – *I think, therefore I exist* – the proof of his existence that he held to be indubitable and that grounded philosophical inquiry into existence for three centuries, eludes Bloom who sweeps it away with his boot. In the "Lestrygonians" episode Bloom records the blunt existential conclusion, "No-one is anything" (*U*, 135).

Concern about how public roles drain inner substance energizes Musil's *The Man Without Qualities* (1930–43), the most sustained challenge to the substantiality of a character in modernist fiction. In contemporary Austria, the narrator explains, one's qualities or characteristics are diffused by multiple roles, as an individual has a professional, national, civic, class, geographic, sexual, conscious, unconscious, and private character. The protagonist Ulrich attempts to unite them, "but they dissolve him, so that he is really nothing more than a small basin hollowed out by these many streamlets." This "empty, invisible space" offers the possibility to create his own characteristics, an undertaking that most people fail to engage in (*MQ*, 30). After a losing battle in youth, people accept the public persona that enfolds their lives. Some may come up with "a slogan in which they think they can recognize themselves ... a new mustache or a new idea," but such gestures fail to counteract the "heavy world, weighing on tongue, hands, and eyes ... and inside nothing but an unstable, shifting mist" (137). Ulrich is the man without everyday qualities who attempts to shape his interior space as his own (7). To do so he must divest himself of "all those prefabricated compartments and forms of life, semblances of reality, the molds set by earlier generations" (135). He is without public characteristics because he resists those pressures.

This existential insubstantiality highlights by contrast the stifling, all-too-substantial values of an Austro-Hungarian Empire that was dominated by aristocratic standing larded up with family pedigree. Ulrich's critique of "pseudoselves" exposes the pseudoreality of the Empire as self-deceived about its imperial strength and propped up by imperial propaganda and bourgeois liberalism. In elaborating on the gaping emptiness at the core of his protagonist, Musil suggests an analogous emptiness behind the over-inflated patriotic, imperial, and liberal narratives that held together the Empire in its final year of peace; but while Ulrich's emptiness was a realm of potential free action, the Empire's emptiness was a hollow shell that crumbled in military defeat at the end of the war.

STRUCTURE: BLURRING AND FRAGMENTATION

As Leo Bersani argues, "The richly detailed textures of characterization in realist fiction seldom subvert the coherent wholeness of personality ... Psychological complexity is tolerated as long as it doesn't threaten an ideology of the self as a fundamentally intelligible structure unaffected by a history of fragmented, discontinuous desires."[6] The minds of such characters are made up of separate faculties that cohere in a unified subject. Major challenges to that view were made by Ernst Mach and William James, who held that the self was nothing but consciousness itself. For Mach, "the ego is not a definite, unalterable, sharply-grounded entity" but rather "a mass of sensation, loosely bundled together."[7] For James the self is a "stream of thought, of consciousness."[8] Freud saw the self as a fragmentary mental agency that lacks autonomy. "The ego," he announced, "is not even master of its own house," as the mind is undergirded by myriad intersections of unconscious processes.[9] In accord with such challenges, several modernists created characters whose basic structure is blurred or fragmentary.

Modernists created characters as a mass of sensations whose ego boundaries are blurred with identities distributed between themselves and others or outside objects. In Rainer Maria Rilke's *The Notebooks of Malte Laurids Brigge* a tram rides over and into the narrator as he sleeps.[10] Not content to relate merely how a person moves about a city, modernists make city experience constitute the person. The two subjects in the title of Alfred Döblin's *Berlin Alexanderplatz: The Story of Franz Biberkopf* (1929), the city and the man, interpenetrate as when Biberkopf, just out of prison, is assaulted by the fear that sliding rooftops will crash into his head, and inanimate objects like cars and houses come alive. In a review of *Ulysses* in 1928, Döblin noted the destabilizing impact on personal identity of cinema and newspapers along with "the streets, the scenes changing by the second, the signboards, automobile traffic."[11] The titular hero of Wyndham Lewis's *Tarr* (1918) believes that "all personality [is] catching: we are all sicknesses for each other."[12] His nemesis, the artist Otto Kreisler, boasts, "I am as many people as the different types of people I have lived amongst" (258). This *boulevardier* is swept up in the vortex of city life, existentially usurped by people he meets on the street and by advertisements and newspaper headlines he sees. Writing at the end of World War I, Lewis parlays his characters' blurring into a critique of chauvinistic nationalism, which is undercut by the contagious internationalism of his main characters.

Clarissa Dalloway merges with London as she wonders during a walk, "did it not become consoling to believe that . . . somehow in the streets of London, on the ebb and flow of things, here, there, she survived, Peter survived, lived in each other, she being part, she was positive, of the trees at home; part of the people she had never met" (*MD*, 9). In Woolf's *The Waves* (1931) six characters merge repeatedly in waves of experiences that flow through one another. Bernard notes that when he and the five others sit close, "we melt into each other with phrases."[13] While this novel concerns mainly the personal and courtship narratives, it also subverts the imperial narrative with a seventh character, Percival, a conspicuously absent mock-hero who is degraded as he falls off a horse during his imperial escapades in India.

Joyce's Bloom wonders what it would be like to be a cat, a blind man, or a seagull. To underscore his and Stephen's fusion with each other the narrator refers to the two of them as "Stoom" and "Blephen." At the cemetery Bloom thinks about Hindu widow suicide and then other burial customs, musing "If we were all suddenly somebody else" (*U*, 91). His empathizing undercuts the chauvinism of Irish nationalism and antisemitism. During lunch he thinks about a slaughterhouse, as though he himself were being butchered, an empathetic moment that Joyce captures with fragments and coinages that render the sights and sounds of the carnage and suggest its acrid smell and slimy surfaces.

Wretched brutes there at the cattlemarket waiting for the poleaxe to split their skulls open. Moo. Poor trembling calves. Meh. Staggering bob. Bubble and squeak. Butchers' buckets wobbly lights. Give us that brisket off the hook. Plup. Rawhead and bloody bones. Flayed glasseyed sheep hung from their haunches, sheepsnouts bloodypapered snivelling nosejam on sawdust. (140)

Realists such as Upton Sinclair in *The Jungle* (1906) criticized the meat-packing industry from the outside with descriptive prose and forceful polemics, whereas Joyce suggests how Bloom experiences the slaughter as if he had fused with the butchers, shoppers, and observers.

Realists celebrated strong characters by making them central to the narrative, and while they acknowledged that some were weak, they did not question whether a singular self undergirded them. Even split person-alities in realist novels are neatly divided as with Dr. Jekyll and Mr. Hyde, whose unified selves in their fully good and evil modes take over sequen-tially. In contrast, modernists splintered personalities that are simultane-ously present as fragmentary aspects of a hybrid entity.

A few modernists captured fragmentation from shell shock.[14] Rebecca West's protagonist Chris Baldry in *The Return of the Soldier* (1918) suffers from shell shock that splits his personality and his life between a pre-war lover he adores and the woman to whom he is married but does not even recall in a home he can no longer recognize. Shell-shocked Ludwig Gödicke in Broch's *The Sleepwalkers* (1931) experiences the "scattered fragments" of a "series of persons living within him" that do not hang together.[15] In ten essays on the "Disintegration of Values" that interrupt the story, Broch theorizes how Gödicke's fragmentation personifies the loss of national cohesion that plagued postwar Germany. In *Mrs. Dalloway* "the throb of the motor engines sounded like a pulse irregularly drumming through [shell-shocked Septimus Smith's] entire body," while the leaves in Regent's Park "connected by millions of fibres with his own body" (*MD*, 15, 22).

Some modernist homosexual characters are fragmented by conflict over their sexuality. In Gide's *The Immoralist* (1902) Michel is split between his tepid feelings as a husband and his passion for Arab boys. In *Remembrance of Things Past* Proust explains his homosexual characters' dilemma because they are even rejected by other homosexuals "in whom they inspire only disgust at seeing themselves as they are" (II, 637–38). The lesbian novelist Bryher (Winifred Ellerman) opens her autobiographical *Two Selves* (1923) with a syntactically fragmented statement of her fragmentation: "Two selves. Jammed against each other, disjointed and ill-fitting. An obedient Nancy with heavy plaits tied over two ears that answered 'yes, no, yes, no,' according as the wind blew. A boy, a brain, that planned adventures and sought wisdom. Two personalities uneasy by their juxtaposition."

A few modernists saw fragmentation as a source of life-affirming com-plexity, as Strindberg explained in the foreword to *Miss Julie* (1888): "My souls (characters) are conglomerations of past and present stages of civilization, bits from books and newspapers, scraps of humanity, rags and tatters of fine clothing, patched together as is the human soul." In the preface to *A Dream Play* (first performed in 1907), he adds how in that play "the characters are split, double and multiply; they evaporate, crystallize, scatter and converge." In Hermann Hesse's *Steppenwolf* (1927), Harry Haller discovers his "schizomania" as a key to existence and aspires to cultivate his "hundred or a thousand selves."[16]

A formally innovative rendering of character "in pieces" is in Gertrude Stein's *The Making of Americans* (1925), most of which she wrote from 1906 to 1911 when Picasso did a portrait of her (1906) and went on in 1910 to create his most fractured cubist portraits of Ambroise Vollard and Daniel-Henry Kahnweiler. While Picasso produced single images of fragmented faces simultaneously from different perspectives, Stein offered multiple images of persons sequentially from slightly different perspectives in slightly varied sentences. To capture this fragmentation she devised the techniques of beginning again and repetition to reconfigure characters' subtly different modes like a cubist composition coming into being over time. Early on the narrator is confident she can catch the "bottom nature" of characters with repetitive descriptions of how they repeat themselves. After several hundred pages she explores contradictions in their bottom natures, how they are "dependent-independent" or "independent-dependent," turning on which trait is dominant. Eventually, she concedes that some people do not have a bottom nature: "There are very many of them . . . pieces that never make of them a whole one, not because of complication in them, not because of difficulty envisaging them but because really such of them are in pieces inside them" (*MA*, 311). Later she gives up identifying a bottom nature: "Perhaps not any one really is a whole one inside them to themselves" (519). In contrast to her novel's title, she actually crafts the *un*making of an American family. The Hersland family declines from personal and historical experience including patriarchal domination and bourgeois conventions, but more significantly it expires in the formal invention of narratives repeated so many times that, like a word too often repeated, they lose all meaning. Stein struggles to find a new way to render the numbing sameness of character as well as the myriad varieties of people. Her narrative technique of beginning again with slight variations captures an inescapable truth about characters whose language and lives are tediously repetitive. She so suffocates her fragmented characters with repetition that they all but disappear from the story.

Modernists subverted and reworked the coherent ego of realist characters with blurring and fragmentation that modified a variety of master narratives. Blurring captured urban influences on character: penetration in Rilke, assault in Döblin, contamination in Lewis, exhilaration in Woolf, and empathy in Joyce. Fragmentation was evident in shell shock that subverted the nationalist narrative, homosexuality that subverted the courtship narrative, and anti-patriarchy that subverted the family narrative.

STABILITY: VOLATILE EGOS

In a letter of June 5, 1914, D. H. Lawrence announced, "You mustn't look in my novel for the old stable *ego* of the character." He proposed to craft "another ego" passing through various "allotropic states" to reveal a less stable one than his realist predecessors offered. While allotrope suggests a static state (diamond is an allotrope of carbon), Lawrence meant temporal instability. He overstated his upcoming historical contribution, because realist novels are full of unstable egos; but their instabilities develop from clearly identified causes: greed in Vautrin (*Old Goriot*, 1834), revenge in Captain Ahab (*Moby Dick*, 1851), jealousy in Bradley Headstone (*Our Mutual Friend*, 1864–66). Throughout the story these unstable characters are ready to explode, and the climax comes when they do. In contrast, modernists believe that everyone is unstable even when external pressures are mild. The instabilities of modernist characters are not the result of clearly identified specific circumstances, as is the case with so many of Dickens's characters, but are rather a function of human existence per se. These instabilities are manifest in a character's name, religion, nationality, race, family, profession, gender role, and mental state.

Characters with many names are a simple indication of instability and variability. Miriam Henderson in Richardson's *Pilgrimage* (1915–38) is also Mim, Hendie, Chickie, Mimmy, Mirry, Miriorama, Miriametta, Mira, and Mirissima, nicknames used by different persons addressing her different social personas. In *Ulysses*, Bloom is also Poldy, Papli, Jewman, Leopopold, Leeolee, L. Boom, Ben Bloom, Booloohom, Henry Flower, Ruby Cohen, Sir Leopold, Herr Professor Luitpold Blumenduft, and Jollypoldy the rixdix doldy, among others. These names suggest changing aspects of his fantasy life, conscience, and character, which include his religion. Father Farley refers to him as "an episcopalian, an agnostic, an anythingarian" (*U*, 400). His friend Ned Lambert asks, "Is he a jew or a gentile or a holy Roman or a swaddler or what the hell is he?" (276). Bloom is a part Jew who was baptized into the Irish Protestant Church under the direction of his converted father and was re-baptized as a Catholic for his marriage to Molly. He owns a Catholic cemetery plot, is uncircumcised, and first thing in the morning of the story eats pork kidney. In the hallucinatory "Circe" episode, characters young and old, rich and poor, living and dead appear to define Bloom's multifarious identities symbolized by nineteen costume changes. He is even interpreted surrealistically by a bar of soap, a crab, a fan, a hoof, and a yew tree. Positively these characters and objects view him as intelligent, thoughtful, generous, and capable of performing miracles or building a utopian city. They call him Mayor of Dublin and emperor-president Leopold the First, even the Messiah. Others voice his dark side as a "fiendish libertine" and "vile hypocrite." This multiplicity of perceptions provides a new kind of stability-out-of-instability for Bloom in steering a resolute course in his love for Molly and faith in others amid the rip tides of these diverse influences.

In Faulkner's *Light in August* (1932) uncertain racial identity torments Joe Christmas, who acknowledges, "I got some nigger blood in me."[17] But he does not know how much, or if it is there at all. His dilemma is the pivot of the novel that assails the inhumanity of racism. In an interview Faulkner summed up Joe's character in terms of stability: "I think that was his tragedy – he didn't know what he was, and so he was nothing. He deliberately evicted himself from the human race because he didn't know which he was." "The most tragic condition a man could find himself in," Faulkner added, is "not to know what he is and to know that he will never know."[18] Joe's unstable racial identity subverts the moral stature of the Southern national narrative, which drains away as Joe bleeds to death from castration by racial bigots.

The force of ancestry loomed large among Victorians, who were ignorant about genetics. They believed in telegony, which refers to the direct influence of impregnation on a female's reproductive system and all her subsequent offspring. Thus, if a woman has a child sired by one man and a second child sired by another man, the second child will partly resemble the first father, whose characteristics, they believed, remained in her blood after delivery. Lacking a correct understanding of the function of the placental barrier and believing erroneously that mothers share fetal blood, they concluded that traces of the first father remain forever in her blood and hence in her reproductive system.[19] Victorians' misunderstanding of hereditary transmission fueled wild fears about how children inherit birth defects and vices along with their parents' property and social standing. Family lineage thus played a major role in defining character. Modernists, who had a better grasp of the nature of heredity, did not so readily explain character from a family's blood line, and characters search in vain for stability and meaning deriving from family heritage. In *Nightwood*, Barnes mocked such a search in Felix, a Jew, who adopts the sign of the cross, claims to have descended from an Austrian aristocratic family, and styles himself a Baron. He attempts to ingratiate himself in a world of fake family narratives based on fake titles and origins. While he is destabilized trying to establish a fake family identity, Gide's character Bernard in *The Counterfeiters* is destabilized when he learns that he is illegitimate and not the son of the man he thought was his father.

Realist characters take different jobs but in so doing maintain their personal identity, while in modernist novels such changes can be symptoms of a fundamental instability in character. In Kafka's *The Castle* (1926), the protagonist, who has no first name and only the initial of his last name, K., introduces himself as a land surveyor to a group of villagers who question his professional credentials and eventually erode his personal identity. His two assistants do not bring any surveying instruments, and they know nothing about surveying. In time he wonders whether he ever was a surveyor – if indeed it is possible to be a surveyor – and becomes a school janitor and finally a horse groom. These are not mere job changes but responses to disorientation in a world where no one has a stable identity, and even the castle that hired K. dissolves in fog and darkness. Among the many connotations of *kafkaesque* is instability of character that is reinforced by an intrusive and unfathomable social world.

Victorians typically believed that gender character was determined fully and indelibly by sexual differences: men are polygamous, active, and rational, while women are monogamous, passive, and intuitive. Sexual difference, determined by an initial visual inspection of the genitals, shapes gender roles and the entire personality so completely, Victorian experts held, that male inverts are necessarily also transvestites and effeminate and cannot whistle because whistling is a masculine skill.[20] Thus dichotomous gender roles penetrate the deepest layers and fullest reaches of the entire personality. Thinkers in the modernist period reworked that male-female binary with affirmations of gender depolarization from genetics, endocrinology, embryology, evolutionary theory, feminist theory, psychoanalysis, sociology, and anthropology as well as literature and art.[21] Bloom is one example, as several times during the novel he fantasizes what it would be like to be a woman, and during the "Circe" episode he becomes "the new womanly man" and gives birth to eight children. For Joyce such mental experimentation is a source of richness that strengthens character, although it also destabilizes the dichotomous gender roles that grounded the conventional courtship narrative.

Some characters lose their identity by fusing with others, at least in the imagination. In Woolf's *The Waves* Bernard says: "I changed and changed;

was Hamlet, was Shelley, was the hero, whose name I forget, of a novel by Dostoevsky; was for a whole term, incredibly, Napoleon; but was Byron chiefly" (184). Gide's intention to create unstable characters is presented in *The Counterfeiters* by the fictional novelist Edouard in a notebook entry on "Inconsistency" that rejects "characters in a novel or a play who act all the way through exactly as one expects them to," adding that "this consistency of theirs, which is held up to our admiration, is on the contrary the very thing which makes us recognize that they are artificially composed" (*C*, 336–37). The inconsistency of Gide's characters insures their instability, at least as compared with the predictable types in Zola's naturalistic novels, whose characters are over-determined by psychological typing. Zola's characters are destabilized by hereditary taints or by overwhelming emotions such as jealousy and lust that compel them to rape or kill, while Gide's are destabilized in moments of calm reflection when they ponder the counterfeit nature of human existence generally, including social life and religious faith, even love and art.

Gide's innovation of unstable character enabled him to assail contemporary values embedded in the national, imperial, religious, courtship, family, and liberal narratives that he also subverted and reworked in his own life. Born into a patriotic and pious French Protestant family, he abhorred nationalism and imperialism and became an atheist. He defied gender roles as the first prominent French intellectual to acknowledge his homosexuality in print. He married a cousin but never had sex with her and later intentionally sired a child out of wedlock to challenge the sanctity of marriage. His novels questioned patriarchal authority by mocking cold and menacing fathers, and he subverted family values in maintaining that he preferred his characters to be orphans, unmarried, and childless. His novels about crime challenged the liberal narrative of the French penal system that based punishment on clearly determined motives for crimes, which he believed to be an artificial juridical construct.

The ultimate instability of character is insanity. In *As I Lay Dying*, one of the fifteen narrators, Darl, is part of a dysfunctional family that journeys for nine days to bury their dead mother Addie, rotting and stinking in her coffin. Darl is the most insightful family member but also the most unstable, and in the end he is committed to an asylum after burning a barn, hoping to incinerate his mother's body inside and stop this morbid funereal journey. Along the way he thinks about personal identity in an increasingly deranged family without compass or direction: "How do our lives ravel out into the no-wind, no-sound, the weary gestures wearily recapitulant: echoes of old compulsions with no-hand on no-strings: in sunset we fall into furious attitudes, dead gestures of dolls" (*AD*, 207). Faulkner uses unconventional syntax to capture an unstable mind in a family gone mad. Victorian families in Emily Brontë's *Wuthering Heights* (1847) and Charles Dickens's *Dombey and Son* (1846–48) are full of anxiety and instability, but they are nonetheless central to individuals' and characters' motivations, actions, and identities; and it is unlikely that even under extreme distress they would be described the way Faulkner did as "old compulsions with no-hand on no-strings."

STATURE: A NEW KIND OF HERO

While the first four sections on presence, substance, structure, and stability center on more distinctively formal aspects of characters, the following sections on stature and purpose center more on an overall interpretation of the substance of characters. Stature is based on moral, aesthetic, and existential value judgments, while purpose is based on judgments about the goal orientation of a life.

For realists, stature was largely about moral character. Some realist novels have genuine villains such as Bill Sikes, Uriah Heep, Alec d'Urberville, Vautrin, and Javert. The modernist would-be villain Biberkopf is an alcoholic, burglar, rapist, pimp, murderer, and peddler of Nazi newspapers, but his stature is not defined by moral judgments about these activities. What defines it is rather his "hard, true, and enlightening existence," his hallucinatory insights in a confrontation with death as he goes mad in a prison asylum.[22] Camus's Meursault in *The Stranger* (1942) is also a murderer, but that novel is conceived precisely to challenge moral judgmental categories altogether.

Other realist novels have virtuous heroes: Daniel Deronda is kind and helpful, Sydney Carton is ultimately loyal and self-sacrificing, Jean Valjean is strong and courageous. For modernists, stature is less about moral character and more about creativity and fulfillment. In assessing modernist protagonists, critics use the term *anti-hero* for one who lacks classical virtues of strength, beauty, courage, wisdom, and pride. As Lionel Trilling wrote: "Nothing is more characteristic of the literature of our time than the replacement of the hero by what has come to be called the anti-hero, in whose indifference to or hatred of ethical nobility there is presumed to lie a special authority."[23] But protagonists are never just anti. Modernist protagonists are rather neo-heroic, that is, admirable in new ways even when they are physically unattractive, sexually unconventional, impotent, cowardly, immoral, or even dead. The most famous one is a cuckold.

Clarissa Dalloway describes herself as having a "narrow pea-stick figure; a ridiculous little face, beaked like a bird's," but she also stabilizes the world around her emotionally and is especially sensitive to the feelings of others (*MD*, 10). In *Women in Love* (1920) Rupert Birkin is "very thin and hollow, with a ghastly look in his face," although he is also emotionally inventive and determined to forge a thoughtful love with Ursula Brangwen (*WL*, 124). Franz Biberkopf has "pimply cheeks, red lines on his forehead, a nose like a cucumber, and ghastly old goggle-eyes like a cow's," but he is also tenacious in the face of difficulties and loyal even to a crook who throws him out of a moving car (164).

The most sexually unconventional modernist female character is Molly Bloom in *Ulysses*, whose concluding monologue reveals a historically inno-vative view of the female body, sexual appetite, and gender role. In a letter Joyce explained that the "four cardinal points" of the final episode were "the female breasts, arse, womb and cunt expressed by the words *because, bottom* (in all senses bottom button, bottom of the class, bottom of the sea, bottom of his heart), *woman, yes*."[24] His pairings suggest that sex is the center of her being: her breasts explain sexual attraction, her "arse" is the bottom of all things, her womb is woman's central meaning, and her sex organ generates a continual desire for the orgasmic *yes*.

Molly's breasts are not the perfect orbs idealized by Renaissance sonneteers but earthy organs for nourishing babies and preoccupying men. Earlier, Leopold viewed her "large soft bubs, sloping within her nightdress like a shegoat's udder" (*U*, 51). In the final episode Molly wonders about the veins in them and marvels at how nipples get firmer from touch. When she was pregnant with Milly they were so full that Leopold had to suck her nipples to relieve the pressure. Molly is proud of her bottom but insulted by the way Leopold is attracted to her "wrong end." The insult to her dignity from his fascination with these "2 lumps of lard" where women "havent 1 atom of any kind of expression" reaches a high point near the end of her monologue when she fantasizes about repaying his attraction with a crude gesture: "if he wants to kiss my bottom Ill drag open my drawers and bulge it right out in his face as large as life he can stick his tongue 7 miles up my hole" (639, 642). Molly reflects briefly on her womb with recollections of a previous pregnancy and the immediate onset of menses as she sits on her commode with blood "pouring out of [her] like the sea" (633). She is frequently aroused, capable of intense sexual feelings accompanied by fantasies as erotic as those of the gypsies and murderers that she fantasizes about seducing. She masturbates frequently and fantasizes about seducing young boys and priests and in particular Stephen Dedalus: "I wouldnt mind taking him in my mouth if nobody was looking as if it was asking you to suck it so clean and white . . . even if some of it went down what its only like gruel or the dew" (638). Recalling her sexual pleasure earlier that afternoon with Blazes Boylan, she thinks: "I wished he was here or somebody to let myself go with and come again like that I feel all fire inside me or if I could dream it when he made me spend the 2nd time tickling me behind with his finger I was coming for about 5 minutes with my legs round him I had to hug him after O Lord I wanted to shout out all sorts of things fuck or shit or anything at all" (621). Such fantasies were thoroughly suppressed, if not non-existent, in the heroines of Dickens, Balzac, and Flaubert.

It took ten years for that literary revelation of the female body, sexual desire, and gender roles to germinate in Joyce's writing, as is suggested by the sexually explicit love letters he exchanged with Nora Barnacle in December of 1909. He left her in Trieste in order to help set up the first cinema theater in Dublin where he wrote back of his loneliness and deep love for her. Gradually, with her apparent epistolary cooperation, he began to share wild sexual fantasies. On December 2, he wrote: "Side by side and inside this spiritual love I have for you there is also a wild beast-like craving for every inch of your body, for every secret and shameful part of it, for every odour and act of it." He imagined "feeling your fingers fondling and tickling my ballocks or stuck up in me behind and your hot lips sucking off my cock while my head is wedged between your fat thighs, my hands clutching the round cushions of your bum and my tongue licking ravenously up your rank red cunt." That letter concludes with a reference to her as his "beautiful wild flower of the hedges," a description used several times in these letters and then three times in a slightly varied form as "a flower of the mountain" in the final climactic pages of the novel.[25] The next day he referred to her sexual assertiveness. "It was not I who first touched you long ago . . . It was you who slid your hand down down inside my trousers . . . and frigged me slowly . . . It was your lips too which first uttered an obscene word."[26] By December 9, he acknowledged her letter, "which you say is worse than mine," and went on to urge her to write more explicit things to help him masturbate, which she apparently did.[27] By the end of the month, the letters intensified in sexual explicitness to include fantasies of flagellation, fetishism, sodomy, scatology, voyeurism, and endlessly inventive styles of masturbation for both of them. While her letters from this period have not survived, what one can glean of their content from Joyce's responses suggests their enormous historical significance for Joyce's final depiction of female sexuality in *Ulysses*, because they evidently offered in writing the uninhibited expression of the sexual desires and activities of a woman, which Joyce ten years later transposed into Molly's interior monologue that captures *the* sexually unconventional female character of the modernist canon.

As modernist women campaigned for rights and became sexually empowered, they confounded men's gender roles and patterns of loving. The men responded in inventive ways. That sexual challenge to men was particularly intensified by war. The classic mythology of war was that men do heroic deeds including defending women from sexual assault, but the reality of World War I was that men were degraded by trench life while women were cultivating themselves at home by raising children, going to school, taking "men's" jobs, and learning how to love more assertively and rewardingly. When the men came home reality slammed into myth, and male sexual prowess shrunk. In *The Sun Also Rises* (1926) Hemingway crafted one dramatic casualty of war with Jake Barnes, whose war injury allows him to still feel sexual desire but makes him unable to perform. He is obliged to cultivate a special sort of understanding in his relationship with Brett Ashley that transcends conventional jealousy during her affair with a matador. Jake is no conventional old and silly cuckold, and throughout he seems to be in control of their strained love relationship even though its consummation is impossible. His injury confounds not only the courtship narrative but also the nationalist narrative that came to disaster in the war.

Some characters lack conventional courage but have a new source of stature in compensatory traits. In Conrad's *Lord Jim* (1899–1900) the chief mate of the *Patna*, Jim, grew up with the heroic ideal of nineteenth-century sea romances, as "he saw himself saving people from sinking ships, cutting away masts in a hurricane, swimming through a surf with a line" (*LJ*, 6). But Jim acts cowardly when as an officer he jumps ship, abandoning 800 Muslim pilgrims when he thinks (it turns out incorrectly) that the ship is sinking. Conrad is not interested in passing moral judgments as Jim himself remarks: "There was not the thickness of a sheet of paper between the right and the wrong of this affair" (130). Judgments about courage are irrelevant to assessing Jim's stature, as a French officer on the ship that rescued the *Patna* notes: "one is no cleverer than the next man – and no more brave . . . Man is born a coward" (146). Conrad is interested rather in the workings of a mind processing such a mistake. He probes aesthetic and existential questions more than moral ones, that is, whether one lives an authentic and full life rather than a conventionally courageous or moral one.

Other modernist protagonists are downright immoral. Gide's protagonist Michel in *The Immoralist* (1902), in pursuing Arab boys, drags his tubercular wife to North Africa and ultimately causes her death. In *Heart of Darkness*

Kurtz is the spiritual leader of Congolese who engage in cannibalism and head-hunting, and he himself has no doubt committed numerous "horrors." Mann's Gustav von Aschenbach in *Death in Venice* (1912) fails to warn a family of a cholera epidemic in Venice because he has fallen in love with the family's young son and does not want them to leave, even if staying endangers their lives. Although these protagonists violate moral standards, they have a stature that comes from expanding their horizons existentially as well as geographically by cultivating aspects of existence that were constrained by those standards. Their stature negates conventional heroism as well as morality, but their purpose is to transcend codes rather than negate them.

World War I further eroded the stature of courage, at least military courage, as the new weaponry turned hard-charging soldiers into cannon fodder. In *Under Fire* (1917) Henri Barbusse detailed the degrading impact of artillery on men's bodies: a head flattened like a pancake, femurs and backbones sticking out of clothes, a man split apart from skull to hips. In his epic trilogy, *U. S. A.*, John Dos Passos devoted one section to the character who was celebrated as a symbol of heroism, the Unknown Soldier, with a literary collage of a Congressional document, President Warren Harding's speech, and newspaper reports interlaced with accounts of the soldier's medical exam, war experience, and preparation for burial.

MEDICAL EXAM: "they weighed you, measured you, looked for flat feet, squeezed your penis to see if you had clap, looked up your anus to see if you had piles, . . . charted your urine and your intelligence."

WAR EXPERIENCE: "The shell had his number on it. . . the blood ran into the ground, the brains oozed out of the cracked skull and were licked up by the trenchrats, the belly swelled and raised a generation of bluebottle flies."

PREPARATION FOR BURIAL: "In the reek of chloride of lime and the dead, they picked out the pine box that held all that was left of enie menie minie moe . . . containing what they'd scraped up of Richard Roe . . . how can you tell a guy's a hundredpercent when all you've got's a gunnysack full of bones."[28]

This collage of voices, points of view, and literary styles subverts the national narrative that the Tomb of the Unknown Soldier was intended to memorialize by focusing on the soldier's meaningless death and the boiler-plate sentiments that accompany his burial. Dos Passos establishes the soldier's dignity with other accounts of his places of residence, upbringing, and jobs, interlaced with his plaintive voice repeatedly asking, "*how I can get back to my outfit.*" The Unknown Soldier was always lost.

While Dos Passos's soldier was unknown, the best-known modernist character blatantly challenged conventional ideas about heroism. Joyce crafted Leopold Bloom to be a modern version of the handsome, athletic, virile, cunning, and courageous Odysseus from Homer's *The Odyssey*, who spent twenty years fighting in the Trojan Wars and sailing the Mediterranean, cavorting with nymphs and goddesses and battling mythical monsters before returning to his wife Penelope. In contrast, Joyce's soft, overweight advertising salesman Bloom is a pacifist landlubber who carries a rolled-up newspaper in place of wielding the Odyssean sword, brandishes his cigar in place of the Odyssean spear, and flosses his teeth in place of stringing the Odyssean bow.[29] Odysseus was the loyal son of Laertes, the protective father of Telemachus, and the devoted husband of Penelope; Bloom is in some ways a failure as a son, a father, and a husband, because his father committed suicide, his son is dead, and he has not had sexual intercourse with his wife in over ten years. He is introduced as a man of earthy tastes: "Mr Leopold Bloom ate with relish the inner organs of beasts and fowls ... Most of all he liked grilled mutton kidneys which gave to his palate a fine tang of faintly scented urine" (*U*, 45). During a day of traveling around Dublin, he defecates,[30] worries about his hemorrhoids, runs clumsily on "flurried stork's legs," views his penis in a bath as a "languid floating flower," checks a statue of Venus in a museum to see if it has an anus, exits a pub gassy with the sound of his flatulence ("Pprrpffrrppffff"), masturbates while gazing at a woman on the beach, hallucinates himself transformed into a woman, picks his toe-nail and smells the pickings, and buys soft porn for his wife before being cuckolded by her later that afternoon. Upon returning to Ithaca, Odysseus, assisted by Telemachus and two servants, killed Penelope's 108 suitors, appearing afterward "caked with blood like a mountain lion when he has gorged upon an ox," and had his house washed and purged with sulfur before he could settle into it. In contrast Bloom is "reluctant to shed blood" and upon entering his usurped home burns incense to clear the air. When he looks at the bed in which Molly has had sex with Boylan, he finds Boylan's form still impressed on the sheets and simply brushes away the crumbs of potted meat that the two had been eating. One post of Odysseus's solid bed that symbolizes his solid marriage he carved out of a living olive tree, while the brass quoits of Bloom's jiggly bed squeak "jigajiga" in his mind throughout the day as a reminder of his cuckoldry. Before getting into that bed next to Molly, he kisses "the plump mellow yellow smellow melons of her rump" (604). Bloom's marital status is particularly degraded in contrast to that of Odysseus, whose wife waited for him to return and became the prototypical faithful wife of Western literature.

But Bloom is no mere anti-hero. He is a new kind of hero with new
valued qualities. He is sensitive to the feelings of others such as a blind
stripling, an old woman wandering the streets, and a woman who has been
in labor for three days. He goes out of his way to comfort Paddy Dignam's
widow and is saddened by the starving Dedalus children. He spends much
of his day trying to protect and be fatherly to Stephen Dedalus and come to
terms with the death of his own infant son Rudy. He is imaginatively
responsive to the sights and sounds of Dublin and to being Irish even as
he is repeatedly treated as an outsider. Even one of his critics admits that
"he's a cultured allroundman, Bloom is . . . there's a touch of the artist about
old Bloom" (193). He ponders the meaning of life, the instability of personal
identity, and the temptations of self-deception and hypocrisy. His mind
swirls with a smattering of ideas about reincarnation (metempsychosis),
botany (language of flowers), chemistry (drugs), death (funerals and cof-
fins), optics (parallax), and journalism (especially advertising). He has
emphatically ordinary credentials with an inelegant job and a circle of
friends who make insensitive remarks about his father's suicide and his
wife's sex appeal; and yet he is related allusively to Moses, Jesus, and
Odysseus and emerges as an exceptional but still ordinary person. When
he sees the "conquering hero" Boylan leave a bar to have sex with Molly, he
remains an "unconquered hero," a description suggesting resiliency, specifically the equanimity that eventually displaces his gnawing jealousy. That
such a historical break in conventions about the traditional hero was Joyce's
intention is evident from a letter to his brother Stanislaus in which he
maintained that "the whole structure of heroism is, and always was, a
damned lie."[31]

Joyce captures Bloom's neo-heroic character with puns, neologisms,
anagrams, lyricism, local wit, slang, foreign languages, songs, poems, classical allusions, parodies, stylistic imitations, stream-of-consciousness technique, a lexicon of rhetorical devices, and a dazzling deployment of
metaphor. Bloom is the most fully realized character in modernist fiction,
crafted with formal techniques that represent a sea change compared to
those that prevailed in the preceding age.

PURPOSE: *BILDUNGSROMAN* TO *KÜNSTLERROMAN*

In realist novels characters either have a strong sense of purpose or are
struggling to find one as are Pip, Dorothea Brooke, and Daniel Deronda.
For realist characters purpose is grounded in the idea that individuals
develop in accord with an organic model, as a tree grows from a seed,

through stages toward a goal. For some realist characters that teleology is directed by a providential spirit or deity who cares for his creatures and directs their lives. Thus a number of early realist novels are governed by a "providential aesthetic" and interpret coincidences as evidence of an overriding destiny.[32] Christianity demanded singularity of purpose, modeled after Jesus who claimed that he was "the way." Modernists challenged these views. In place of a continuous organic unfolding in life, they saw discontinuity, wrong turns, and dead ends. They viewed the organic model as romantic biology and interpreted the idea of an ultimate purpose in life as naive idealism. Coincidences were evidence not of providential design but of life's inherent flukiness. Singularity of purpose in the search for Christian faith or a nation's history was a myth. Modernists also rejected conceptions of personal progress as cumulative and viewed it rather as a process of repeated self-criticism and reconstruction. Thus Nietzsche in *Thus Spoke Zarathustra* emphasized self-overcoming, an endless self-questioning analogous to an artist's repeated self-corrections. His overman is the most fully realized self, a product of endless self-renewal.

The literary genre that realists used to dramatize the purposive development of characters was the *Bildungsroman,* typically the story of a young man who clashes with his family, leaves his home in the country for the city where he learns professional and social skills, overcomes difficulties in love, cultivates his sensibilities, and finally returns to his rural home prepared for mature adulthood, marriage, and social integration.[33] After Goethe's *Wilhelm Meister's Apprenticeship* (1795) other *Bildungsromane* followed: Dickens's *David Copperfield* (1850), Adalbert Stifter's *Indian Summer* (1857), and Gottfried Keller's *Green Henry* (1855). Modernists replaced the youth who aspires to assume responsibilities of adulthood with one who is suspicious of conventional adult institutions. They did not render early romance as evolving into conventional love but rather rendered love and urges for sexual fulfillment as strongly physical and sometimes a failure or traumatic or even comical. They replaced concluding reintegration into family and society by chronic alienation from public values, and crafted characters who meander through a life of new undertakings and discoveries but no ultimate purpose.[34] Every main character in Dos Passos's *Manhattan Transfer* (1925) wanders the streets of the city, enacting various destructive scenarios including divorce, suicide, abortion, alcoholism, bankruptcy, and murder. At the novel's end, the reporter Jimmy Herf leaves Manhattan and in response to a question how far he is going answers, "I dunno ... Pretty far."

Modernists resisted a strong sense of purpose because they were skeptical about the institutions that directed lives toward shared goals: especially marriage, family, school, community, and religion. World War I further eroded the authority of the national and imperial narratives that interpreted the lives of the men who fought in it as stories with an overall purpose. Modernist characters sought in these institutions rather partial fulfillment in limited projects with short-term goals. As the purposes of the courtship, family, national, imperial, capitalist, liberal, and religious narratives were challenged and recast, personal lives had to be reconstituted with different values and goals as well as new narrative strategies. The one undertaking that offered modernists an unambiguous purpose in life was art. While some modernists parodied the *Bildungsroman*, others replaced it with the *Künstlerroman* about the development of an artist as the model of a meaningful life.[35]

Thomas Mann's *The Magic Mountain* (1924) parodies the *Bildungsroman* with a story about an "ordinary" young man, Hans Castorp, who is orphaned at age seven and so does not have any primary family conflict to resolve. His *Bildung* begins not in the country but in a city, Hamburg, from where he retreats from society and his engineering studies to travel to a rural sanatorium in the Swiss Alps to visit his tubercular cousin Joachim and plunge into a society obsessed with disease and death. He falls in love with Clavdia Chauchat, whom he meets outside an x-ray room, and keeps as a memento a photograph of her tubercular lungs. Hans's high point is an epiphany in the Alpine snow when he resolves not to let the forces of death preside in his life, but for the remaining third of this long novel he stays at the sanatorium obsessively taking his temperature and doting on death. The purpose of the sanatorium is to make people get well, but he gets sick, and many of the inmates, including Clavdia and Joachim, die. He remains there from 1907 to 1914, as his life becomes increasingly devoid of purpose. The ultimate irony is that while the traditional *Bildungsroman* concludes with the hero learning to lead a meaningful and productive life, Mann's ends with his hero facing a meaningless and unproductive death, lost in the smoke and fire of World War I.

In *Jacob's Room* Woolf also parodies the *Bildungsroman* and the idea that life has some overall purpose. Formally, she uses the omniscient narrator of the conventional *Bildungsroman* who is capable of entering the mind of all characters, but at times she shifts to another narrator who is limited to guessing at Jacob's words and thoughts and who announces twice that "It is no use trying to sum people up" (*JR*, 31, 154). The novel's content further blocks teleology in Jacob's life. His father has died and his mother always seems to be elsewhere, so he does not originate from an explosive family situation that sets his life's course. He moves to London but acquires no urban wisdom. Thus, early portents lead nowhere. The direction of his life is symbolized by the pathetic, circular motion of the crab in the bucket. Jacob has the opportunity of a fine education at Cambridge, but the dons are inadequate, and he makes little of the university. Jacob studies history and travels to Greece to see ancient sites, but when he tries to write out his thoughts he begins to draw a nose. Such non-sequiturs abound in this novel that repeatedly subverts any clear sense of Jacob's purpose and includes numerous sentences that stop in the middle with incomplete thoughts.

In a diary entry of January 26, 1920, Woolf noted a technique she used to achieve "looseness and lightness [and] . . . a gaiety – an inconsequence."[36] By reducing Jacob's motivation and purpose Woolf was free to explore the richness of his immediate everyday experience. She not only abandoned conventional motivations and explanations but rendered them useless, suggesting that one cannot explain even a single character, let alone a war. And if one cannot explain a war, then perhaps one might not fight it or, next time around, start it. Focusing on immediate experience allows her to reinterpret how family, school, work, love, and travel impact on characters free from the oversimplified scenarios of cause and effect as well as the values that underlay the major master narratives, in particular the national narrative and the "liberal rationalism" that unraveled in the war. Her novel undermines not just the content of the master narratives but the unexamined idolatry of the rational thought processes that sustain them.[37] Woolf assails the national narrative explicitly with a few images of sailors drowning and soldiers blasted to bits and with her final image of Jacob's mother holding up his shoes, suggesting that Jacob was lost in the trenches; but the most historically significant subversion and reworking of the national and other master narratives is the novel's parody of the *Bildungsroman* as a genre that falsified life as having a transcendent purpose, especially heroic sacrifice in the trenches for Country, King, and God.

Amid all the breakdown of Western values and institutions included in the subversion and reworking of the master narratives, one narrative remained unequivocally celebrated by a majority of modernists – the story of a life devoted to art. The *Künstlerroman* recounted such a purposeful life. Modernists produced a good number of them and projected their personal struggle into characters: Mann into Aschenbach in *Death in Venice*, Lawrence into Paul Morel in *Sons and Lovers* (1913), Gide into Edouard in *The Counterfeiters*, Hesse into Goldmund in *Narcissus and Goldmund* (1930), and Joyce into Stephen in *A Portrait of the Artist as a Young Man*.[38]

The name of Joyce's protagonist, Stephen Dedalus, references the artistic vocation that shapes his life. *Dedalus* recalls *Daedalus*, the mythic "old artificer" who invents wings to flee his prison. The novel ends as young Stephen takes over from the third-person narrator with a first-person journal where he makes his final announcement that he has found purpose in life – "to forge in the smithy of my soul the uncreated conscience of my race." On the way to that end Stephen encounters many restraints, as he explains to a friend: "When the soul of a man is born in this country there are nets flung at it to hold it back from flight. You talk to me of nationality, language, religion. I shall try to fly by those nets" (*PA*, 179). That formulation reveals the dialectic between prison and escape that structures Stephen's artistic evolution. His art will enable him to fly by, that is, fly past, those nets, but it will also take shape as he learns to fly by means of them.[39] Stephen pushes to become an artist by refusing to serve the ensnaring institutions of the Irish nation, the Gaelic language revival, the Catholic Church, and (elsewhere) the family that the nets signify. While Joyce addresses the nationality issue in heated discussions about Charles Parnell and Irish Home Rule, the central institutional target is religion.

The grip of religion tightens after Stephen goes to prostitutes, and a priest prompts him to renounce his sinful ways and consider joining the priesthood. To terrify Stephen about the punishment for sins of the flesh, Father Arnall presents a series of lengthy sermons on hell. The unrepentant sinner, Arnall threatens, is thrust into the grave to rot and be devoured by rats. Each of his senses is assaulted: sight, by eternal darkness, hearing by howls and execrations, smell by a reeking sewer that produces an intolerable stench "multiplied a millionfold" with rotting human fungus, taste by nauseating foul matter and suffocating filth, and touch by the fire of hell that burns furiously in absolute darkness. Blood boils in the veins; eyes flame like molten balls. Arnall's sermons are the most forceful literary assault on religion in the modernist canon. By having a priest ask young boys to imagine such torment for eternity, Joyce has his readers consider what kind of a religion could think up such a scenario of eternal damnation, elaborate it with such vivid detail as a moral compass, and pound it into young minds at their most impressionable age. At the end of the sermons, Stephen reconsiders the meaning of his sexual desire, which soon becomes the mainspring for his vocation as an artist.

The argument of this book is that modernism was a subversion and reworking of nine master narratives and an unqualified celebration of a tenth, which together embodied the values and institutions that defined the history of the early twentieth century. The artistic narrative was the only one that emerged with its stature fully intact, aside from stories of failed artists such as Otto Kreisler or successful artists who failed for other reasons such as Aschenbach, and the single instance of the dadaists' assault on artists who produced war propaganda during World War I. Most *Künstlerromane* told of success, or at least potential success, such as the one Joyce portrayed in *Portrait* as essentially a struggle between a dispiriting religious narrative that recruited followers by instilling fear of hell and an inspiring narrative that led Stephen to resolve to become an artist.

CHAPTER 2

Event

In 2002, I taught a history seminar on modernism that included a survey of formal innovations in the novel. One student questioned what those innovations had to do with important historical developments such as imperialism and World War I. He was puzzled by my attaching such importance to formal aspects of novels and especially to the seemingly trivial events that were sometimes their main subject. After some reflection, I decided that his question warranted a lengthy response, which became this book. I do not treat how modernist novels impacted historical developments directly, but rather how they engaged those developments and how they differed from realist novels in that engagement. This chapter explores modernists' recalibration of the scale of events including the trivial ones that troubled my student as well as the way novelists integrated them causally, or otherwise, into increasingly weak plots in works that also addressed historical developments of the master narratives.

SCALE: RECALIBRATING THE SMALL AND THE LARGE

In accord with science's powerful model of knowledge based on empirical evidence, realists emphasized objective observations, and so characters in their novels are significant primarily for the actions they perform. As a precursor of modernism, in "The Art of Fiction" (1884) Henry James rejected the primacy of action over character by linking the two, as he asked, "What is character but the determination of incident? What is incident but the illustration of character?" In substituting subtler *incident* for more dramatic *action* he suggested the direction his novels were tending, as his next sentence revealed. "It is an incident for a woman to stand up with her hand resting on a table and look out at you in a certain way."[1] He had already created such a subtle but telling incident in *The Portrait of a Lady* (1881), with Isabel Archer's fireside meditation (Ch. 42). In the 1908 Preface, James explains that the scene, his favorite in the novel, "is a representation simply of her motionlessly *seeing*, and an attempt withal to make the mere still lucidity of her act as 'interesting' as the surprise of a caravan or the identification of a pirate." Isabel's reflection "throws the action further forward than twenty 'incidents' might have done."[2] In this moment she sees simply but tellingly that her husband resents "that she had too many ideas and that she must be rid of them," a "motionless" incident that James believed is more powerful than a robbery or piracy. In shifting high value from noisy, seemingly important events to quiet, comparatively simple ones, James inaugurated a revision of the scale of importance in fictional events.[3]

While nineteenth-century novels include numerous ordinary events, many center on extraordinary events: Ahab harpooning Moby Dick, Jean Valjean's flight through Parisian sewers, Edmond Dantès's revenge, Emma Bovary's suicide, Anna Karenina's suicide, Tess d'Urbyfield's rape, Hetty Sorel's infanticide, Raskolnikov's ax murders, and the deadly flooding of the river Floss. Impatience with such high drama was expressed in 1896 by the Belgian mystic Maurice Maeterlinck who celebrated simple events: "I have grown to believe that an old man, seated in his armchair, waiting patiently, with his lamp beside him, giving unconscious ear to all the eternal laws that reign about his house, interpreting, without comprehending, the silence of doors and windows and the quivering voice of the light . . . does yet live in reality a deeper, more human and more universal life than the lover who strangles his mistress, the captain who conquers in battle, or the husband who avenges his honor."[4] Modernists found richness in such moments. They made small events big, and big events small, or at least off-center, in reworking the scale and significance of human experience so that the master narratives crafted around those events underwent analogous re-evaluation.

The prime example of this focus on the seemingly trivial, which ultimately proves to be huge, is Proust's *Remembrance of Things Past*. The narrator Marcel recalls how his most vivid memories of Combray, where years earlier his family vacationed at his Aunt Léonie's house, were centered on the parlor, staircase, and door to his room through which his mother would enter to kiss him goodnight. He could have conjured up other parts of the town but only by a *voluntary memory*. But those places were dead, because "the past is hidden beyond the reach of intellect, in some material object, in the sensation which that material object will give us" (*RP*, 47–48). One such trivial sensation triggers an *involuntary memory* that underlies the entire novel. Years later in Paris his mother served him some tea with *petites madeleines*, and the combination of tastes made him feel exquisitely happy and immortal. This joy led him to wonder, "Whence did it come? What did it mean? How could I seize and apprehend it?" (1, 48). After a few more sips he realized that the source was a similar experience he had had years earlier when his aunt had given him a bit of madeleine dipped in her tea. The meaning of his joy is that such involuntary memories give him back time lost, the time that vanished when his mother, seeing how desperately he wanted a goodnight kiss, stayed with him the entire night.

The events that trigger such involuntary memories are not incidentally unimportant but necessarily unimportant. Important events register vividly in the mind at the time of their occurrence and are recalled regularly over the years and therefore lose their force from repeated volitional recollections and readily accessible classification in memory. Only unimportant events lie dormant for years of forgetting and so are able to burst into consciousness unexpectedly with associated memories that intensify their emotional force and expand their experiential reach. Marcel illustrates that process with the memory set off by the taste of tea and madeleines, which he initially takes several pages to unpack, beginning with his first detection of it: "Undoubtedly what is thus palpitating in the depths of my being must be the image, the visual memory which, being linked to that taste, is trying to follow it into my conscious mind. But its struggles are too far off" (I, 49). Indeed. It will take over 3,000 pages for Marcel to fully experience and explore the event. When in the end he returns to explain its force and that of other similarly trivial events, his convoluted prose replicates the complex experiential scenario that each one of them embodies: "the slightest word that we have said, the most insignificant action that we have performed at any one epoch of our life was surrounded by, and coloured by the reflection of, things which logically had no connection with it and which later have been separated from it by our intellect which could make nothing of them for its own rational purposes, things however in the midst of which . . . the simplest act or gesture remains immured as within a thousand sealed vessels, each one of them filled with things of a colour, a scent, a temperature" (III, 902–03).

The key to sustaining the pleasure from an involuntary memory becomes clear at the end of the novel when Marcel returns to Paris after the war and is invited to a party given by the Princess de Guermantes. Then he has several more involuntary memories sparked by trivial events. The first comes from the feeling of an uneven paving stone underfoot as he steps out of his cab. It recalls a similar sensation he had had years earlier at St. Mark's in Venice, a city of art that anticipates how he will ultimately make this pleasure last by incorporating it into a work of art. The second involuntary memory is the ting of a spoon hitting a plate that recalls a similar sound that a railwayman made with his hammer on a wheel when Marcel's train stopped, and he observed the sun streaming magnificently through some trees but felt no inspiration to write about them and despaired of realizing his literary vocation. On this later occasion, however, the sound motivates him to preserve the joy of such moments by writing. A third involuntary memory occurs when he sees in the Guermantes' library George Sand's novel, *François le champi*, which his mother read to him as a boy and which further underscores his resolve to write. These trivial events, all related to art, inspire Marcel to sustain the joys they engender by embodying them in art, which Proust made into the most important French *Künstlerroman* of the modernist period.

Joyce also underscored the importance of trivial events. In 1900 he addressed complaints that the modern age was one of "nerveless unheroism." Dramatic heroism and chivalry were central to the national and imperial narratives that were losing their moral luster. He countered that "out of the dreary sameness of existence, a measure of dramatic life may be drawn. Even the most commonplace, the deadest among the living, may play a part in a great drama."[5] He found a way to mine the commonplace in an autobiographical novel, *Stephen Hero*, written between 1904 and 1906, that named such events epiphanies and defined them as "a sudden spiritual manifestation, whether in the vulgarity of speech or of gesture or in a memorable phrase of the mind itself . . . of the most delicate and evanescent of moments."[6] The word refers to the manifestation of God in a human form in the person of Jesus Christ, which is celebrated on January 6, the Feast of the Epiphany. Joyce used *epiphany* in a secular sense to mean a sudden insight triggered by a trivial, everyday event such as a snatch of conversation overheard on the street.

Epiphanies differ from the sudden illuminations in realist novels that follow the disclosure of momentous truths such as Angel learning about Tess's previous pregnancy (*Tess of the d'Urbervilles*, 1891), Pip finding out that Magwitch is his benefactor (*Great Expectations*), or Jane discovering that her fiancé is married (*Jane Eyre*, 1847). Modernist epiphanies center on events that would appear trivial to anyone else but have enormous emotional impact on the person who experiences them. They draw their force not from conventionally recognized mental processes but from unique personal associations. While it would be absurd to argue that modernist novels as a whole are more subtle than realist novels, one can make such a judgment about the different scale of the pivotal events on which these respective novels turn.

The most important epiphany in *Stephen Hero*, a snippet of conversation Stephen overhears between a man and a woman, has no direct significance for Joyce personally but still moves him deeply and inspires him to write a "book of epiphanies." He never published it but did collect and deploy around twenty-five of them in subsequent works.[7] Two historically significant epiphanies in *A Portrait of the Artist as a Young Man* identify the institutions against which the young Joyce will rebel and the art he will embrace in their place. The first is based on an actual traumatic event in Joyce's childhood.[8] It begins without preparation as a guilty young Stephen hides under a table and his mother asks him to apologize but does not say for what, and Dante (Mrs. Riordan) chimes in that "if not, the eagles will come and pull out his eyes." The text then repeats the following verse:

> Pull out his eyes,
> Apologise,
> Apologise,
> Pull out his eyes.

The ambiguity of the voice uttering these words (Dante? the narrator? young Stephen? or an older Stephen?) suggests that this threat resounds throughout Stephen's life. This disturbing memory is not in itself trivial but is out of scale in that it portends the major developments of Stephen's entire artistic career. Later the narrator explains that "his strange name seemed to him a prophecy ... of the end he had been born to serve and had been following through the mists of childhood and boyhood, a symbol of the artist forging anew in his workshop out of the sluggish matter of the earth a new soaring impalpable imperishable being" (*PA*, 148). To become an artist Stephen must reject the constricting forces of family, nation, and church that are symbolized and defended by his mother (family and church) and Dante (nation and church) and, of course, *not* apologize for it.

The other major epiphany occurs shortly after he declines a proposal that he become a priest. He is walking along the beach and notices a beautiful girl. After gazing out to sea, she turns to look at him and blushes. He cries out and crosses the beach with his body aglow, limbs trembling. "Her image had passed into his soul for ever and no word had broken the holy silence of his ecstasy. Her eyes had called to him and his soul had leaped at the call. To live, to err, to fall, to triumph, to recreate life out of life!" (150). Joyce parlays this simple epiphanic moment into a turning point in Stephen's resolve to become an artist, far beyond the scale of the original incident.

Woolf subordinated the very big to the exceptionally small in her early story "The Mark on the Wall" (1917), a recollection that the unnamed female narrator makes of her meditation on the nature of a black mark on a white wall. Her speculations whether the mark is a nail, a rose leaf, or a shadow also take her to conventionally important subjects including the war and how society is governed hierarchically according to the peerage of the United Kingdom. Her streaming thoughts show how looking at the mark leads her to "contempt for men of action – men, we assume, who don't think," the sort of men who make war. Her recalibration of scale concludes with the non-sequitur of an anonymous interlocutor saying to the narrator: "Curse this war; God damn this war! . . . All the same, I don't see why we should have a snail on our wall," to which the narrator replies in a final illumination, "Ah, the mark on the wall! It was a snail." By beginning and ending with a seemingly trivial inquiry about a tiny mark, which slides repeatedly into conventionally important matters such as social rank and warfare, this story shows how such trivial matters may embody unsuspected significance.

Two years later in "Modern Fiction," Woolf proposed: "Let us not take it for granted that life exists more fully in what is commonly thought big than in what is commonly thought small." She criticized over-estimating conventional "comedy, tragedy, and love" and urged rather a close reading of the trivial. "Examine for a moment an ordinary mind on an ordinary day. The mind receives a myriad impressions – trivial, fantastic, evanescent." Her novels dramatize the rich humanity of seemingly trivial events such as a woman preparing for a party and a family planning to visit a lighthouse. In *To the Lighthouse* Woolf revels in ordinary minds pursuing small projects that brim with larger significance, as the artist Lily Briscoe explains: "The great revelation had never come. The great revelation perhaps never did come. Instead there were little daily miracles, illuminations, matches struck unexpectedly in the dark" (*TL*, 249). Woolf made art out of such little miracles, which she referred to as "moments of being."[9]

In recalibrating conventional scales of significance, modernists also made big events seem small. Alec's rape of Tess is the dramatic high point of *Tess of the d'Urbervilles*, and it ruins her life. By contrast, in Lewis's *Tarr*, Bertha is raped by Kreisler but quickly moves beyond it. In contrast to Tess's beloved Angel, who immediately after their marriage abandons her when he learns of her rape and pregnancy, Tarr marries Bertha even though she is carrying Kreisler's child. This modernist rape is indeed traumatic for the victim but is not her tragic destiny as it is for Tess. Elsewhere in the novel, Lewis scales down the significance of other climactic moments: a duel fails to come off, a murder is an accident, and a suicide results from a game.

While Lewis travesties such melodrama, Dorothy Richardson marginalizes it. The suicide of Miriam's mother in *Pilgrimage* occurs in a blank space between sections (*P*, 1, 489). The reader might well miss the account of Miriam's seduction by Hypo Wilson (based on H. G. Wells), which is described briefly as "an instant's sudden descent into her clenched and rigid form" (IV, 257). Richardson moves past it not out of concern about censors but because it is not important. Her subsequent pregnancy and miscarriage are also easy to miss.

In addition to personal crises, many modernists also de-centered *the* crisis of their age – World War I. While realist novels are concerned primarily with domestic matters, a few deal with war, and when they do, they treat it head-on as a defining event of their time. Tolstoy's *War and Peace* (1865–69) has war in its title and details at length the Battle of Borodino and Napoleon's retreat from Moscow that prepare the emergence of modern Russia. Zola's *The Debacle* (1892) recounts with the thoroughness of a historian the Battle of Sedan in the Franco-Prussian war of 1870 and the Paris Commune, including soldiers' poor training, rampant illness, mindless maneuvering, horrific combat, and grisly deaths. Stephen Crane's *The Red Badge of Courage* (1895) focuses on the war experience of a private in a Civil War battle who works his way from naive bravado through an initial cowardly act of desertion to a final defining role as a courageous flag bearer leading a charge. Vivid war reporting continues in popular, realistic World War I novels such as *Under Fire* (1916), which earned Henri Barbusse a reputation as "Zola of the trenches." It describes the stupidity, hopelessness, and killing of war from beginning to end with brutal realistic detail.

Modernists had to avoid the powerful clichés of men marching bravely into battle and dying heroically to defend their glorious country. They also had to avoid the strong pull of journalistic realism that such enormously important events enlisted. They were horrified by the war but generally treated the fighting in the margins of their novels, obliquely, or not at all. Joyce wrote *Ulysses* between 1914 and 1921 but set it in 1904 and made few hints that might refer to the war.[10] Mann wrote *The Magic Mountain* between 1912 and 1924, but the story occurs during the seven years leading up to the war and ends with Hans setting off for the front. Richardson's first fourteen volumes of *Pilgrimage* (totaling 2,000 pages) were published from 1915 through 1938 but cover the years 1893 to 1912. Lawrence wrote *Women in Love* in 1916, shortly after the bloody battles of Verdun and the Somme, but situated the action before the war. The novel hints at an era of disregard for human life but nothing specifically military, and his two couples cavort across Europe from England to the Alps in a journey that would have been impossible during the war. Forster set *A Passage to India* in 1912, but wrote it between 1922 and 1924. *The Counterfeiters* also has a pre-war setting. Musil set *The Man Without Qualities* in 1913. Ford Madox Ford's *Parade's End* (1924–26) follows Tietjens to the front lines, but Ford's interest is more on adapting his techniques of literary impressionism and time shifts than depicting the war's gory details. The third volume of Hermann Broch's *The Sleepwalkers* set in 1918 gets no nearer to combat than the activities of a deserter, an insane shell-shock victim, and an alcoholic ambulance driver.

Leading American modernists were motivated by having missed the war more than by having participated in it, and they located it in a shadowy prehistory in major novels such as F. Scott Fitzgerald's *The Great Gatsby* (1925), Ernest Hemingway's *The Sun Also Rises*, and William Faulkner's *The Sound and the Fury* (1929).[11] Hemingway's *A Farewell to Arms* (1929) takes place during the war, but the protagonist, an ambulance driver, is often away from the front and eventually deserts in this senseless war in which Italian Battle Police execute Italian officers during a retreat because they are not with their troops. Hemingway's *In Our Time* (1925) treats the war in interchapter vignettes of the fighting that avoid full engagement. Dos Passos's *Manhattan Transfer* goes from 1898 to the early 1920s and repeatedly references current events such as the assassination at Sarajevo and the declaration of war but displaces actual fighting to the blank space between Section Two and Section Three that begins with an Armistice Day parade.

In March 1914, Woolf wrote, "We do not like the war in fiction . . . The vast events now shaping across the Channel are towering over us too closely and too tremendously to be worked into fiction without a painful jolt in the perspective."[12] Her postwar novels treat the war with indirection. *Jacob's Room* levels war and the everyday with Jacob's mother equating concern about men blown up by artillery, which she could hear across the English Channel, with everyday matters: "Far away, she heard the dull sound, as if nocturnal women were beating great carpets. There was Morty lost, and Seabrook [her husband] dead; her sons fighting for their country. But were the chickens safe? Was that some one moving downstairs? Rebecca with the toothache? No. The nocturnal women were beating great carpets. Her hens shifted slightly on their perches" (*JR*, 175). Thus does she merge the big and the small, dead soldiers and the safety of chickens, the sound of artillery and Rebecca's toothache. The death of loved ones is certainly more important to her than the chickens' safety, but her mind still processes these events together. Jacob's death no doubt devastates his mother, but at the end of the novel she is concerned with what to do with his shoes.

Sometimes under great stress the small entirely effaces the big. Most of the characters in *Mrs. Dalloway* do not think about the war, while Septimus cannot think of anything else, an obsession that drives him to suicide. One implication of these contrasting responses is that the only way to remain sane in postwar England was to keep the war out of one's mind. In *To the Lighthouse* (1927), the narrator hints that the Ramsay house is shaken by "ominous sounds" that rattle dishes – a thematic preparation for the interruption in Woolf's account of the house with an announcement of the death of Mrs. Ramsay's son Andrew. An earlier version of the "Time Passes" middle section that spans the war years reveals that Woolf reduced explicit references to the war and muted identification of it with male violence and sexual brutality as she worked that section into the novel.[13] Proust marginalized the war by having Marcel devote only one sentence to his visit to Paris in August of 1914, the month when war was declared. Marcel discusses wartime Paris for a mere forty pages of the last volume, following his report of having returned there at the beginning of 1916. He undercuts the inflated rhetoric of the war propagandists by depicting shirkers and hypocrites posturing as patriots who in fact lead meaningless lives. He further reduces the heroic stature of the war by focusing primarily on several homosexuals in a Parisian brothel funded by the Baron de Charlus. The only blood during wartime that Proust described is from the masochistic sessions that Charlus, chained to a bed, has when a male prostitute whips him with a nail-studded whip. One courageous soldier whom Marcel admires, Robert de Saint Loup, is also a homosexual and longs to die inspiring the love of his men. He is awarded the *Croix de Guerre* for bravery but loses it in Charlus's brothel.

During the war dadaists declared war on art itself. They expressed their iconoclasm by demolishing the conventional hierarchy of values, specifically notions about the importance of artistic subjects, with works such as Marcel Duchamp's "readymades." He elevated an ordinary urinal into a work of art by mounting it on a pedestal and titling it *Fountain* (1917); while in 1919 he lowered the stature of Leonardo Da Vinci's *Mona Lisa*, by drawing on a cheap postcard reproduction of it a mustache and goatee on the figure's face and titling it *L.H.O.O.Q.* When pronounced in French those initials sound like "Elle a chaud au cul," which translates as "she has heat in the ass," meaning colloquially that she is horny.

Major modernists set their novels before the war or approached it obliquely and looked away from the headline stories to avoid its horrific magnitude. Henry James was devastated by the outbreak of the war as he wrote in a letter on August 5, 1914, the day after Germany invaded Belgium: "The plunge of civilization into this abyss of blood and darkness by the wanton feat of those two infamous autocrats [German and Austrian] is a thing that so gives away the whole long age during which we have supposed the world to be, with whatever abatement, gradually bettering, that to have to take it all now for what the treacherous years were all the while really making for and *meaning* is too tragic for any words." The war quashed his writing so that when on August 8 he dipped his pen into the inkpot, he wrote, "it's as if there were no ink there, and I take it out smelling gunpowder, smelling blood."[14] Three months into the Battle of the Somme, Ford wrote "A Day of Battle," explaining why he cannot write about the war: "but as for putting [war scenes] into words! No: the mind stops dead."[15] Ford's artistic paralysis is part of a general condition that Samuel Hynes characterizes as "the imaginative vacuum" that prevailed in 1916, from the war having narrowed soldiers' imagination and presented a phenomenon too vast and too horrible to imagine, let alone put into conventional false imagery of courage, self-sacrifice, and patriotism.[16] Disgust was no doubt behind William Butler Yeats's explanation in the preface to the *Oxford Book of Modern Verse* of 1936 as to why he omitted war poems from his anthology: "Some blunderer has driven his car on to the wrong side of the road – that is all." Head-on collisions of automobiles or armies are headline stories that do not offer a suitable subject for serious art. Modernists' indirection in treating the war is further indication of their commitment to re-evaluating the purpose of art. Their love of it was energized in reaction against a war that thrust senseless killing into their lives.

By 1934, Stein could see the broader historical perspective on this formal shift when she announced that in "the Twentieth Century ... events have lost their interest for people." In fact, people lost interest in conventionally important events but found interest in others as she herself went on to argue. During the war "the average dough-boy standing on a street corner doing nothing ... was much more exciting to people than when the soldiers went over the top." This shift of interest extended to novelists looking for a story, and so, she continued, "in *The Making of Americans*, Proust, *Ulysses*, nothing much happens."[17] Stein's overstatement contains a qualified truth: that modernists questioned conventional values embodied in the national narrative that was indelibly subverted by the war.

By making supposedly small events seem big and vice versa, modernists recalibrated the values attached to gender roles, courtship practices, patriarchal families, the progress of nations, imperial might, and liberal justice. This recalibration was especially effective in diminishing the prominence of World War I by Woolf's bracketing (literally in the case of Andrew's death), Proust's indirection, and Joyce's, Mann's, Gide's, Musil's, and Lawrence's displacing of the war by setting their major postwar novels before it. Dimming the bright light generated by the war made visible seemingly unimportant objects in the surroundings the way a solar eclipse makes visible stars that appear close to the sun.[18] By refocusing away from the war's massive violence, modernists could explore subtle yet deeply revealing experiences such as the involuntary memory of a childhood experience in time lost, the epiphany of seeing a girl on a beach, or the revelatory moment of seeing a mark on a wall.

Modernists also challenged the religious narrative and the value attached to the sacred space and time of holy events, which in turn devalued the religious sanction of royal political authority and any social, if not legal, rights accorded to royally anointed hereditary aristocracies. This democratization of politics and society transformed attitudes toward ordinary events in non-holy places and times. One manifestation of these developments in literature is the subject of Morris Beja's *Epiphany in the Modern Novel*, which argues that "as men have found themselves putting less and less trust in the truths and absolutes of the past, they have more and more come to stress the *trivia* of existence. They have sought meaning in what they could see, all around them, in the apparently inconsequential objects and events of everyday life."[19] Beja's "apparently" is ironic. Far from inconsequential, Joyce's epiphanies and Proust's involuntary memories offered modernists the richest sources of meaning as opposed to the "apparently" consequential public events of imperialism and war. This recalibration of what is important aligned with a growing resistance to the deterministic causal integration of events that made plots strong and led to the development of new ways to integrate narrative.

CAUSALITY: CAUSAL SKEPTICISM, MYTHIC PARALLEL, SPATIAL PATTERNING, CHANCE

In 1927, Forster defined the link between events, causality, and plot: "We have defined a story as a narrative of events arranged in their time-sequence. A plot is also a narrative of events, the emphasis falling on causality. 'The king died and then the queen died' is a story. 'The king died, and then the queen died of grief' is a plot. The time-sequence is preserved, but the sense of causality overshadows it."[20] In 1961, Wayne Booth underscored the driving power of causality: "When we see a causal chain started, we demand . . . to see the result. Emma meddles, Tess is seduced, Huck runs away – and we demand certain consequences."[21] That demand sustains reader interest. This section tracks modernists' resistance to a strong deterministic causality, the alternative integrating techniques they used to replace it, and the master narratives those techniques engaged.[22]

Realists such as Tolstoy posited multiple causes for human affairs and saw them operating deterministically. The high point of strong determinism was Zola. He was tagged a naturalist after the natural causal forces that governed his characters, such as the body's need for heat (satisfied by coal in *Germinal*), for food (satisfied by grain in *The Earth*), and for sexual pleasure (satisfied by a beautiful female body in *Nana*). To these causal factors Zola added heredity, which he believed caused character traits such as alcoholism and homicidal mania, as well as social forces such as capitalist greed and commercial acquisitiveness.

Modernists resisted strong deterministic explanations of behavior which governed the master narratives that held together the nineteenth-century world. Stein's attack was the most fundamental, because it aimed at the causal structure of conventional syntax. Her use of repetition and beginning again broke the causal action and explanation of characters in her early novel *Melanctha* (1909). She assailed causal reasoning itself in *Tender Buttons* (1914). In this collection of bewildering short prose poems, some causal actions cannot cause their effects: "a curving example makes righteous finger-nails."[23] Some *because* phrases do not explain: "there is a shadow in the kitchen because every little thing is bigger" (480). W*hy* questions seem unanswerable ("Why is there so much resignation in a package") or make no sense, "why is there no necessary dull stable" (502, 503). Some lines question the function of *why*: "Let us why, let us why weight, let us why winter chess, let us why why" (403). With "real is only, only excreate, only excreate a no since" she suggests that causal explanations might be nonsense or a nuisance or a creative excrement. She follows that mystifying comment on causality with a string of phrases that make no sense at all: "A no, a no since, a no since when, a no since when since, a no since when since a no since when since" (496). For Stein causality is nonsense or a nuisance or at best a creative waste product of language, vital to survival but not a sufficient account of behavior.

Woolf provoked skepticism in *Jacob's Room* by using causal explanations that are incomplete or non-sequiturs. The narrator refuses to complete an explanation: "Captain Barfoot liked [Jacob] best of the boys; but as for saying why . . ." (*JR*, 71). Her ellipsis dots frustrate causal understanding about Barfoot's attitude and question whether it is possible ever to know why people judge others. Jacob's girlfriend Clara explains in her diary that she likes Jacob, "though he's frightening because . . ." (71). These ellipsis dots indicate Woolf's refusal to clarify whether Clara could not explain to herself or whether the narrator withheld her explanation. Jacob refuses to question his motives for action, and when the narrator suggests why, the answer is a non-sequitur: "'What for?' Jacob never asked himself such questions, to judge by the way he laced his boots, shaved himself" (161). Less radically than Stein, Woolf still uses a similar strategy of setting up a reader's expectation of a causal explanation and then frustrating it as the syntax takes an unexpected turn that is grammatically correct but logically nonsensical to shock readers into realizing that the tidy explanations of human behavior they have come to expect are bogus. She writes as if to challenge readers: You expect me to explain Jacob's behavior? Well think again, because at bottom human behavior is inexplicable. Woolf questions the possibility of understanding why people are what they are and suggests how explanatory gaps interfere with human relations, especially in courtship and family narratives.

Faulkner grounds his critique of causality by spinning a dense network of motives for his characters and ultimately questioning the possibility of explaining any behavior. He takes this approach in *Absalom, Absalom!* (1936), which subverts the family narrative in the context of the national narrative with the story of Thomas Sutpen's dynasty set in the American South. Sutpen came to Mississippi in 1833 to establish a family, which required that he marry well to secure a reputable name, earn money to buy slaves and build a mansion, and sire children who will carry on his name. He achieves these preparatory goals, but the ultimate goal of the family dynasty is imperiled by the prospect of his daughter Judith's marriage to Charles Bon. Her brother Henry murders Charles, because the marriage would involve five acts that would undermine the Sutpen dynasty: incest (because he is Judith's half-brother), bigamy (because Charles is already married), miscegenation (because his mother was part black), homosexual incest (because Henry loves Charles and wants to fulfill that love by sharing his sister with him), and transsexuality (because Henry fantasizes about metamorphosing into his sister). Thus, Henry harbors a cluster of scandalous desires to be metamorphosed into his own half-black half-brother to despoil the virgin bride, his own sister (and somehow also be metamorphosed into her), and thus achieve a "pure and perfect incest."[24]

With such destabilizing impulses, Henry is open to his father's urging him to kill Charles and save the Sutpen dynasty and the Southern national narrative based on white racial supremacy. But Henry's cluster of motives still do not fully explain the murder, as Mr. Compson tells his son Quentin. "It just does not explain. Or perhaps that's it: they don't explain and we are not supposed to know. We have a few old mouth-to-mouth tales; we exhume from old trunks and boxes and drawers letters without salutation or signature, in which men and women who once lived and breathed are now merely initials or nicknames out of some now incomprehensible affection which sound to us like Sanskrit or Chocktaw; we see dimly people ... performing their acts of simple passion and simple violence, impervious to time and inexplicable" (*AA*, 80). The surviving documents that read like foreign languages cannot explain behavior. Faulkner dramatizes the erratic nature of causal explanations of individuals, families, and nations by disclosing the ingredients of Henry's homicidal motives to the internal narrators, to the reader, and to Henry himself at different moments throughout the novel with different degrees of completeness and authority. The more characters probe the causes of the murder, the Sutpen family decline, or the Civil War, the murkier their understanding becomes.

Faulkner's tangle of complex causes captures the tortured psychodynamics of the Southern family narrative, subverting also the Southern national narrative and the dehumanizing institution of slavery upon which it was based and for which it fought a self-destructive Civil War.

The causal skepticism of Conrad, Musil, Kafka, and Camus centers on the liberal narrative, especially its legal system that relied on cause-and-effect to explain crimes and achieve justice. In realist novels, murders are caused by such specific emotions as greed (Dickens's *Martin Chuzzlewit*, 1844), family strife (Dostoevsky's *The Karamazov Brothers*, 1880), jealousy (Tolstoy's *The Kreutzer Sonata*, 1889), or revenge (Zola's *The Human Beast*, 1890), and these authors do not seriously question the possibility of understanding the causality of single criminal acts. The central drama of *Crime and Punishment* (1866) is Raskolnikov's learning to accept responsibility for his crime, which is grounded on his causal understanding of it. In contrast, modernists doubt the possibility of causal understanding itself as they doubt the legal causal reasoning at the heart of the liberal narrative.

Lord Jim centers on why Jim jumped from the *Patna*, which a maritime court attempts to determine. The jump was indeed caused, but Conrad's purpose is to show that no one knows how. The court sought the impossible: "a directing spirit of perdition that dwelt within" (*LJ*, 31). And even if there were a directing spirit, we could not know it. "They demanded facts from him," Marlow explains, "as if facts could explain anything!" (29). Jim is forced to answer questions *yes* or *no*, which could not possibly reveal the truth. Why he jumped he cannot explain to the court or to Marlow who is so moved by the court's failure to understand Jim's act that he begins an inquiry that takes up most of the novel but concludes resoundingly that "it is impossible to see him clearly" (339).

Musil's skepticism in *The Man Without Qualities* begins with a frontal assault on causality as a foundation of nationalism when Ulrich, in reply to bank director Leo Fischel's question about the nature of Austrian patriotism answers, enigmatically, "the Principle of Insufficient Cause." Ulrich elaborates: "in our personal lives, and in our public-historical lives, everything that happens happens for no good or sufficient reason" (*MQ*, 1, 140). Musil applies that principle to the liberal narrative embodied in the Austrian legal system that judges and eventually executes the killer Moosbrugger. In a moment of panic, Moosbrugger knifed to death a prostitute who was clinging to him and threatening his weak sense of identity, but the court insists on finding sinister intentions, which he is too disorganized mentally to possess. His confusion highlights the absurdity of the court's demand for causal explanations. The judge's questions "Why did you wipe the blood off your hands?" and "Why did you throw the knife away?" seek to establish Moosbrugger's rational intentionality and therefore criminal responsibility. But while the judge sees those actions as a coherent whole, Moosbrugger sees them as separate incidents each with a "different cause that lay outside him." For the judge, Moosbrugger is responsible for these acts, while in fact "they had perched on him like birds that had flown in from somewhere or other." Incapable of expressing himself, he is found guilty and sentenced to death. The court's confident judgment contrasts with Ulrich's skepticism about causal reasoning generally: "Nothing in him was moved by cause, purpose, or physical desire, but everything went rippling out in circle after ever-renewed circle" (1, 131). Ulrich's view of causality grounds his larger view of history; its course is not that of a billiard ball but "the path of a man sauntering through the streets, turned aside by a shadow here, a crowd there, an unusual architectural outcrop, until at last he arrives at a place he never knew or meant to go to" (1, 396).

The causal reasoning behind liberal justice is savaged by Kafka in *The Trial*, where the accused Josef K. seeks in vain to discover the authority of the law and the rationale for its application to him. People act unpredictably against K. without logical preparation or rational explanation. He never learns his crime or who has accused him. His lawyer is incompetent, the court system is an inaccessible bureaucratic labyrinth, and myriad misunderstandings prevent him from learning the law. The novel ends with a travesty of legal causal reasoning when one of his executioners looks into his eyes "to observe the verdict" (*Entscheidung*, i.e. judgment, sentence) just before carrying out the execution. In a liberal society, carrying out the sentence is supposed to be based on the verdict, but here the verdict is only disclosed (we never know for sure) as the sentence is carried out. Kafka runs the causal arrow both ways simultaneously and leaves the reader wondering whether K. is executed because he is guilty or guilty because he is executed.

In *The Stranger* Camus makes over seventy references to the sunlight and heat, to Meursault's throbbing temples and stinging eyes, and, just before he fires his gun, to the blinding light off the Arab's knife; but during the trial the causal action of these circumstances is questioned. The examining magistrate insists on learning why Meursault fired not just once, but then four more times at a body lying on the ground. "Why? You must tell me. Why?"[25] Meursault cannot answer because he does not know. Before passing sentence the judge insists on an explanation, and Meursault narrates his own response: "Fumbling a little with my words and realizing how ridiculous I sounded, I blurted out that it was because of the sun" (103). This outburst does not offer nearly enough explanatory punch for the court conditioned to expect strong deterministic explanations required by conventional law.[26] With this "ridiculous" courtroom explanation Camus joins Conrad, Musil, and Kafka in devaluing deterministic causal explanations that were the basis for legal judgments about right and wrong and provided the ideological foundation for liberal society.

The power of Proust's involuntary memories is precisely that we are unable to trace their origins causally because they radiate through space and time erratically, gaining emotional strength along the way like a hurricane over warm water. In place of conventional causality, modernists devised new ways to integrate experience through mythic parallel, spatial form, and probabilistic causality.

In 1923, Eliot announced that Joyce's use of myth to organize *Ulysses* by "manipulating a continuous parallel between contemporaneity and antiquity ... has the importance of a scientific discovery."[27] Joyce based most of his episodes on incidents in Homer's *Odyssey* translated into Dublin life on June 16, 1904. The episode that best captures contemporary history at the time Joyce was writing the novel, "Nestor" is named after Homer's old warrior Nestor (Mr. Deasy), who relates to Telemachus (Stephen Dedalus) the siege of Troy and celebrates war. Parallel to Nestor, Deasy is a militarist and pro-English Unionist, the type who in 1914 would welcome the war and continue to revere military values throughout the slaughter. "Nestor," written in 1917, shortly after the Battle of the Somme, captures the anarchy and futility of the war with parallels to classical myth as well as to a current game of football. As Stephen teaches a lesson on the Battle of Asculum and his student recalls the Greek general Pyrrhus's remark, *"Another victory like that and we are done for,"* Stephen's thoughts include imagery of the impact of modern warfare on buildings and men – "shattered glass and toppling masonry" and "a corpse-strewn plain" (*U*, 20). As Deasy celebrates the military prowess of Unionist heroes, and Stephen's students play football nearby, Stephen conjures up the destruction of war throughout history: "Again: a goal. I am among them, among their battling bodies ... Jousts, slush and uproar of battles, the frozen deathspew of the slain, a shout of spearspikes baited with men's bloodied guts" (27). When Stephen remarks to Deasy that history "is a nightmare from which I am trying to awake," Deasy counters, "All human history moves towards one great goal, the manifestation of God" (28). By caricaturing Deasy as a long-winded, chauvinistic version of Homer's famous charioteer, Joyce impugns the national and religious narratives that Deasy cherishes.[28]

While Joyce's mythic method was well suited to address war and the values embodied in the imperial and national narratives, his spatial patterning was particularly well adapted to capture the simultaneous events in different locales of the modern big city. A few modernist writers attempted to adapt the new conception of painting as non-narrative and non-representational patterns of colored forms into its own medium of language as an arrangement of verbal images and phrases. This way of integrating literary texts was identified in Joseph Frank's essay, "Spatial Form in Modern Literature." In times of crisis, he argued, artists turn away from naturalistic, causally ordered depictions of the world and produce non-naturalistic, non-causally ordered art of formal patterns. This art is based not on a will to reproduce reality but "a will-to-art, or better still, will-to-form." The spatial forms produced "are always characterized by an emphasis on linear-geometric patterns, on the disappearance of modeling and the attempt to capture the illusion of space, on the dominance of the plane."[29] Frank sees this change in Joyce, Barnes, and Proust, who tried to create a harmonious formal order in a disharmonious age in which sequential narratives led to disorder and destruction.

Ulysses depicts Dublin, Frank continues, not as a sequence of causally related events but as a pattern of simultaneous events made up of cross-references that only make sense artistically when conceived as a whole by "reflexive reference" (27). The result is a fragmented narrative, and for that reason, "Joyce cannot be read – he can only be reread" (19). *Nightwood* is another modernist novel built on a spatial form. Barnes captures modern urban anomie with the character Felix, who, as a wandering Jew, embodies "the predicament of modern man himself, bewildered and homeless in a mechanical wilderness of his own creation" (36). The novel is integrated not temporally or causally but by "a pattern arising from the spatial interweaving of images and phrases independently of any time-sequence of narrative action" (49). Proust likewise subverts naturalistic time and causality by capturing moments when past and present combine in involuntary memories. To Frank's example from Proust, I would add Proust's affirming spatial form with metaphor as the key to truth, life, and art. The writer, Marcel exhorts, must connect immediate sensations, and "truth will be attained by him only when he takes two different objects, states the connection between them – a connection analogous in the world of art to the unique connection which in the world of science is provided by the law of causality – and encloses them in the necessary links of a well-wrought style; truth – and life too – can be attained by us only when, by comparing a quality common to two sensations, we succeed in extracting their common essence and in reuniting them to each other, liberated from the contingencies of time, within a metaphor" (*RP*, III, 924–25). For Proust, metaphor, and not causality, links disparate experiences spatially, temporally, and experientially to enrich life and offer the highest truth in art.

In addition to myth and spatial form, modernists also integrated novels with probabilistic causality or chance, which reflected the changing ideas of their time. The kinetic theory of gasses, Darwin's theory of evolution, Mendel's theory of hereditary transmission, and sociological studies of suicide involved probabilistic calculations. Such developments were consolidated in "the probabilistic revolution" of statisticians who in the generation around 1900 devised techniques for calculating probabilities including standard deviation, the chi-square, analysis of variance, and the t-test and its distribution.[30] These techniques made it possible to assign magnitudes to a variety of causal factors and determine the statistical probability of their respective causal roles. Nineteenth-century physicists conceived of probability as dealing with phenomena that ultimately, at least in principle, could be reduced to deterministic processes. In the early twentieth century, quantum physicists theorized that some phenomena were irreducibly indeterminate and therefore ultimately explicable with only a probabilistic causality, at least at the subatomic level.

Realists typically believed that coincidences were evidence of the causal action of chance. Some held that chance events were directed by a metaphysical force in the form of providence or destiny, if not a personal God. In *Crime and Punishment*, for example, Raskolnikov coincidentally overhears two conversations that convince him that there is "something fateful and fore-ordained" about his killing the pawnbroker.[31] In the novels of Dickens, Charlotte Brontë, and even Eliot, providence offers an ultimate meaning to coincidences.[32] In modernist art coincidences are generally not evidence of a directing fate but of life's fundamentally random nature. Recognitions of the probabilistic nature of life and art in chance appear in dadaist soirées and found objects or readymades. Surrealist automatic writing and objective chance target the deterministic causality of conventional aesthetics as well as the means-end rationality of modern warfare and capitalism.

The critic Leland Monk relates the increasing role of chance in the novels of Conrad and Joyce to developments in the new probabilistic sciences of genetics and quantum mechanics. But as Monk shows, it is impossible for any novelist to introduce true chance in a work that is governed by the author who determines every word. Still, even though "no novelist actually manages to represent chance in narrative, there is a history of the ongoing attempt to do so."[33] In the mid 1920s, surrealists celebrated chance encounters on the streets of Paris that energized their surreal vision, in particular Louis Aragon's *Paris Peasant* (1926) and André Breton's *Nadja* (1928).

The most explicit attempt to capture chance was by Gide, whose *Lafcadio's Adventures* (1914) dramatize a probabilistic causality to subvert the sort of deterministic causality that structures Zola's novels. Lafcadio attempts to break the conventional path to murder by killing without a conventional motive such as jealousy or revenge. While sitting in a train, he realizes that to kill the stranger in his compartment, he has only to release the door latch and push the man to his death. Inspired by the prospect of committing a "motiveless crime," he does just that. In contrast to Zola's crazed murderers, who kill because of strong biological, psychological, or social forces, Lafcadio kills for the sole reason of killing without a reason.

After the murder Lafcadio explains to another character, the novelist Julius, that he wanted to kill without a reason to affirm his free will and creativity. In a gesture toward that freedom, Lafcadio paradoxically lets his act be "determined" by chance, within certain limits, by deciding that if he can count to ten before a light appears outside, the stranger will be saved. In a realist novel a light might shine before he counted to ten, or not, depending on destiny or providence, but in Gide's godless world no such agency exists. Lafcadio takes charge of chance by slowing his count, although he still relies somewhat on chance in the light that finally shines allowing him to give his victim a fatal push. By meddling with chance Lafcadio detaches himself from faith in some transcendent guiding force and undertakes a murder for which he alone is responsible.

Gide more directly challenges Zola's explanatory mechanism through another character, Julius, who wants to write a novel about a motiveless crime. In expressing to Lafcadio his goal Julius states Gide's own approach. "I mean to lead [my character] into committing a crime gratuitously – into wanting to commit a crime without any motive at all."[34] Here Gide overstates his case, because Lafcadio's murder is not entirely gratuitous. It is indeed motivated, but the motive is, as Gide subsequently explained, not subject to the "ordinary psychological explanations" of naturalist novels. "I personally do not believe in the gratuitous act, an act motivated by nothing. That is essentially inadmissible. There are no effects without causes. The words '*acte gratuit*' are a provisional label that seems convenient to designate acts which escape ordinary psychological explanations, the gestures not determined by simple personal interest, and it is in this sense, in playing with words a little, that I can speak of *disinterested* acts."[35] Gide's "motiveless crime" highlights his goal to dramatize the capriciousness of action in contrast to the way the characters in naturalist novels act when governed by overwhelming external circumstances or irresistible inner compulsions.[36]

Lafcadio's Adventures impugns the religious narrative formally with a probabilistic causality that contradicts the determinism of divine providence and impugns it substantively by being set in a world where the deterministic logic of religion and miracles is fraudulent. Believers are duped and faith is shallow. The novel's French title, *Les caves du Vatican*, refers to labyrinthine caves under the Vatican as a metaphor for the underlying tangle of conspiracy that sustains the Catholic Church. At the outset Anthime is a vehement atheist. In an angry gesture he breaks the arm of a statue of the Virgin Mary made out of a fake marble. That night he dreams that Mary appears with a broken arm and strikes him with her empty sleeve. He awakens miraculously cured of his rheumatism and so impulsively converts back to Catholicism. The devious character Protos invents a story about a fake Pope in Rome and solicits money to fund a bogus conspiracy to restore the "real" Pope. To recruit the believer Amédée to bring money to Rome, Protos disguises himself as a cleric. While returning from Rome, Amédée is murdered by Lafcadio, an event that comes as close to a truly gratuitous act as Gide is able to craft. Anthime becomes disillusioned with religion once again and resumes his criticism of the Church, suggesting to Julius that when Amédée gets to heaven he might find "that his Almighty isn't the real God either" (230).

In the modernist period, struck billiard balls moved just as they did in the realist period, and human behavior continued to be caused just as regularly by the many causal factors that impinged upon it. What changed was causal knowledge. In an earlier study, I showed how in the modernist period causal understanding in physics, genetics, and physiology as well as in psycho-analysis, linguistics, sociology, and forensic psychiatry became increasingly specific, multiple, complex, probabilistic, and uncertain.[37] As thinkers sharpened causal knowledge in their respective sciences and systems of thought, they disclosed new appreciation of what they did not know and new uncertainties about what they did know or at least thought they knew. They came to see causal knowledge as increasingly probabilistic and uncer-tain. Analogous developments took place in crime novels where answers to the question why someone committed murder are explicit and crucial to the plot. While popular writers cultivated the genre of detective fiction (the whodunit), high modernist novelists avoided detective stories as well as crime novels (the whydunit) that were plotted around discovering the cause of a murder. Faulkner, Musil, Gide, and Camus, who did write about murders, depicted them as poorly or incompletely explained, if not unex-plainable. Most modernists avoided murders in accord with their rejection of dramatically pivotal events and clear causal explanations, a strategy that obliged them instead to use myth, spatial organization, or probabilistic causality to integrate events.

PLOT: ANTI-NARRATIVE

The plot of a story links significant events causally through time toward a meaningful goal. It includes events and causality and other elements such as beginnings and endings, which I explore in Chapter 5. Here I trace how modernists viewed plot as a whole. Their rejection of the strong plot is the most significant formal innovation of the period because it struck at the overall structure of fictional narratives more than any other, and by implication subverted the purposeful dynamic of the master narratives.

Realist novels typically have strong plots. In *Anna Karenina* events are linked by irresistible love that motivates Anna toward her tragic end. Jealousy dominates the plot of Tolstoy's *The Kreutzer Sonata*, revenge dominates *Moby Dick*, ambition dominates Anthony Trollope's *The Eustace Diamonds* (1871), and greed dominates Frank Norris's *McTeague* (1899). Dickens uses triumphant heroism (*A Tale of Two Cities*, 1859), poetic justice (*Oliver Twist*, 1838), and the concealment and exposure of damaging secrets (*Bleak House*, 1853) to structure his intricate plots.

Already in 1852, Flaubert registered his intention to resist strong plotting and write a novel "about nothing . . . which would sustain itself by the inner force of its style." He added, presciently, "I believe the future of Art lies in this direction."[38] *Madame Bovary* (1857) is punctuated by dramatic content with adultery, disappointed love, botched surgery, and a gruesome suicide, although these events are muted in the overall ordinariness of Emma's life and rendered in Flaubert's restrained style. His whisper of intention became a chanted chorus among modernists who challenged strong plots in the novel, because they did not believe that life is formally plotted or ends with a resounding closure and clear meaning. In 1907 James insisted that the germ of *The Portrait of a Lady* was the idea that "it must have consisted not at all in any conceit of a 'plot,'" which he characterized as a "nefarious name" for any set of relations that fall "into movement, into a march or a rush, a patter of quick steps."[39] In 1908 T. E. Hulme noted that "where the old [artist] endeavoured to tell a story, the modern attempts to fix an impression."[40] Lewis's spokesman in *Tarr* defined art as "life with all the humbug of living [i. e. plot] taken out of it."[41] In 1927 Forster complained: "Yes – oh, dear, yes – the novel tells a story . . . That is the highest factor common to all novels, and I wish that it was not so, that it could be something different – melody, or perception of the truth, not this low atavistic form."[42] In *Nadja* Breton celebrated the fact that "the days of psychological literature with its fictional plots are numbered."[43] In "Journal of *The Counterfeiters*," Gide announced, "I should like to avoid the artificiality of a 'plot.'" "Why," he wondered, "so much searching for a motivation, a development, the forming of a pattern around a central plot?" He aspired to create a novel in which "there would be unnecessary characters, ineffectual acts, pointless remarks, and the action *would not* get under way" (*C*, 409, 414).

In a similar vein, although overstated, Stein argued that "in the three novels . . . that are the important things written in this generation, there is, in none of them a story. There is none in Proust in *The Making of Americans* or in *Ulysses*."[44] In *The Making of Americans* she weakened the plot by giving away the life history of Martha Hersland in a single sentence: "This one was then once a very little one, a baby and then a little one and then a young girl and then a woman and then older and then late there was an ending to her and that was the history of this one" (*MA*, 386). Then Stein varied that simple plot, beginning again and again, weakening the cohesive dynamic of the plot in a story that repeatedly turned back on itself and got nowhere.[45] That spirit Musil captured in the first chapter of *The Man Without Qualities* titled "From Which Remarkably Enough, Nothing Develops." Six hundred pages of his novel are in a section titled *Seinesgleichen geschieht* (The Same Kinds of Things Happen) (*MQ*, 1, 83–725). In the text Ulrich complains that history follows worn-out plots, which authorities use to manipulate people. The strongest plots on the political level are conspiracies based on stereotyping and scapegoating that governments use to foment antisemitism, patriotism, imperialism, and war (1, 559–60).

The most pointed challenge was by Woolf, who in "Modern Fiction" insisted that "if a writer were a free man and not a slave, if he could write what he chose, not what he must, if he could base his work upon his own feeling and not upon convention, there would be no plot, no comedy, no tragedy, no love interest or catastrophe in the accepted style."[46] In *Jacob's Room* she weakened the plot with unfinished sentences, unanswered questions, disruptions in causality, and non-sequiturs. Free from the requirements of a strong plot, she could explore other experiences with simultaneous juxtaposition and capture the world going to hell in war, a moment of unfulfilled love, and Jacob failing to understand history, all at the same time as in the following scene. After a brief description of the deadly fate of men in battle at sea and in the trenches, Woolf switched to Jacob in Athens, running into Sandra Williams who invites him to visit the Acropolis. A comparison of drafts of the scene in Athens reveals how Woolf removed explanations of Jacob's behavior to capture the frustrations of love and the inability to communicate in a war-torn world. In an early draft Woolf attempted to render a revealing moment between Jacob and Sandra – a shared reality, a passion, and a kiss. The next draft explained what the couple sought: "something that should happen so definitely that there it would always be." Finally Woolf cut the motivational explanation, the lasting memory, and the line "She kissed him" and wrote simply that "Sandra's veils were swirled about her head."[47] That single image was all that remained of the plotted elements of earlier drafts as Woolf ruled out any explanation of what the couple achieved: "As for reaching the Acropolis who shall say that we ever do it, or that when Jacob woke next morning he found anything hard and durable to keep for ever?" (*JR*, 160). By stripping this scene of a conventional love plot, Woolf suggested the failure of relationships to reach any ultimate goal, especially something as iconic as the Acropolis was for Western civilization.

Joyce also eliminated the strong plot. His early *Stephen Hero* spells out details of character, motivation, and action that the later *Portrait* mutes. In *Stephen Hero* Joyce described Emma Clery as an attractive, middle-class girl who studies Gaelic, flirts with priests, and is disturbed by Stephen's sugges- tion that they spend one night together and then depart forever. *Portrait* describes her only as a dress, a sash, and fine black stockings, adding that "her fresh warm breath flew gaily above her cowled head" (*PA*, 60). The Gaelic lessons appear only as an Irish phrase book, the flirtation focuses on Stephen's anger against the Church, the rejection scene is transformed into a moment when he failed to take hold of her as she came up a tram step, and her name is abbreviated as "E-----C-----". The next day, as Stephen attempts to put their exchange into verse, the narrator explains, "all those elements which he deemed common and insignificant fell out of the scene. There remained no trace of the tram itself nor of the trammen nor of the horses; nor did he and she appear vividly. The verses told only of the night and balmy breeze and the maiden lustre of the moon" (*PA*, 61). Although verse calls for concision, one can read Joyce's explanation as a comment on the larger direction his writing was taking, as is evident from his carefully constructed but weakly plotted *Ulysses*. Bloom's day does center on a dramatic act of adultery, and in the course of the day he struggles with his son's death and his father's suicide, but the surface action of Joyce's novel is the quintessential weak plot of modernist fiction – Bloom travels around Dublin, meets with Stephen and others, thinks about many things, and returns home to sleep.

In addition to novels, an analogous development occurred in poetry and painting – their rejection of narrative, which in turn had a direct influence on rendering of plot in the novel. As Brian McHale argues, "modernist aesthetics effectively deprived poetry of the most valuable of its traditional resources for organizing extended texts, namely narrative."[48] That challenge is evident in the signature modernist poem, Eliot's *The Waste Land* (1922). Typescripts of early versions of the poem from 1921 engaged substantive historical narratives of that time: alienation from sexual irresponsibility and marital stress, inhumanity from colonial abuse, alienation from city life, death and destruction in World War I, and spiritual desolation from growing secularism. Eliot's solution to the dilemma of how to address these powerful historical developments with an art form that explicitly rejected narrative was a collage poem made up of imagistic fragments and a series of vignettes expressed by multiple voices that largely resisted traditional meter and rhyme.

His first draft of the poem begins not with "April is the cruelest month" but with the following lines about romantically adventurous young men.

> First we had a couple of feelers down at Tom's place,
> There was old Tom, boiled to the eyes, blind, . . .
> Then we had dinner in good form, and a couple of Bengal lights.
> When we got into the show, up in row A,
> I tried to put my foot in the drum, and didn't the girl squeal,
> She never did take to me, a nice guy – but rough;
> The next thing we were out in the street, Oh was it cold![49]

Eliot cut these lines, most likely in response to the criticism of Ezra Pound, along with many other lines with strong narrative content or explicit moralizing.[50] The imperial narrative was subdued with Eliot acquiescing to Pound's suggestion to cut the original epigraph to the poem, which was the passage from Conrad's *Heart of Darkness* when Kurtz realizes the spiritual desolation of imperialism – "The horror! the horror!" While the final version retained the "unreal city" of contemporary London, Eliot cut from his earlier version an address to London personified as a destructive force, which Pound characterized in the margin as "B-----S."[51] Although Pound never formally explained what he intended in editing the poem, he generously described it as "the justification of the 'movement,' of our modern experiment, since 1900."[52]

Painting produced its own rejection of narrative, which is the artist's analogue to plot. In the late seventeenth century, the French Academy formulated a hierarchy of genres with history painting at the top, followed, in decreasing status, by genre painting, portrait, landscape, and still life. History painting had strong narrative content of religious, mythological, historical, or literary subjects. This hierarchy influenced subject matter well into the nineteenth century, although by the end of the century artists began to resist its authority with impressionism, symbolism, and post-impressionism. Whereas the title of John Hadfield's book on Victorian painting, *Every Picture Tells a Story*, is overstated, it is close to the mark, especially in comparison with modernist painters who became emphatically anti-narrative.[53]

Illustration 1. Pablo Picasso, *Medical Student, Sailor, and Five Nudes in a Bordello (Composition Study for "Les demoiselles d'Avignon")*, March–April 1907. Graphite pencil and pastel on paper, 18¾ x 25 in. Öffentliche Kunstsammlung Basel, Kupferstichkabinett. Bequest of the artist to the city of Basel.

During nine months of 1906–07 Picasso made over 400 preparatory works to find the right composition for what became *Les demoiselles d'Avignon*. That investment of time and energy suggests the importance of this image for his own development and ultimately for art generally. His early sketch with seven figures includes a seated sailor surrounded by five prostitutes and at the left a medical student (in some sketches modeled by Picasso himself carrying a skull) – an image that suggests a strong narrative of sexual desire, venereal disease, and death (Illustration 1). In this sketch the crouching prostitute at the lower right has her legs spread, exposing her genitals to the sailor as he makes his choice. In the final image the two men are gone, so the nudes are not showing their bodies to a desiring male and cannot be identified as prostitutes, nor can the setting be construed as a bordello with its obvious narrative associations (Illustration 2). The five remaining figures create what Leo Steinberg calls an "anti-narrative counter

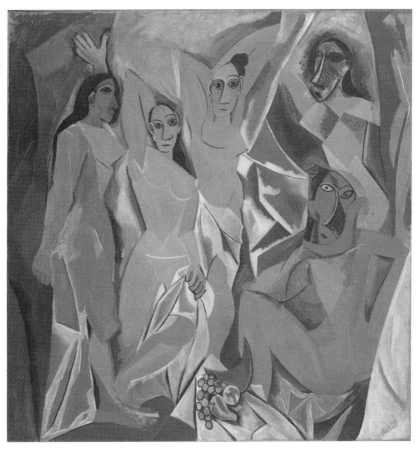

Illustration 2. Pablo Picasso, ARS, NY, *Les demoiselles d'Avignon (The Young Ladies of Avignon)*, 1907. Oil on canvas, 8 ft x 7 ft 8 in. Acquired through the Lillie P. Bliss Bequest (1333.1939). The Museum of Modern Art, New York. Digital Image Copyright The Museum of Modern Art/Licensed by SCALA/Art Resource, NY. Copyright 2006 Estate of Pablo Picasso/Artists Rights Society (ARS), New York.

principle: neighboring figures share neither a common space nor a common action, do not communicate or interact, but relate singly, directly, to the spectator."[54] The head of the crouching figure is rotated 180 degrees to confront the viewer and is replaced by an African-styled mask with distorted features, further confusing any conventional narrative reading. The dominant lines of vision and implied action within the painting rotate from the earlier strong narrative of the seated prostitute toward the entering male in the sketch to a non-narrative confrontation of all the figures with the viewer.

Demoiselles underscored the primacy of form over content, because its most significant feature was not its subject, which had been painted many times before, but the way Picasso painted it in a style quite inconceivable fifty years earlier. The final painting's formal features efface the sexual component of the narrative. Like novelists who reduced dramatic plots to explore other aspects of everyday experience, Picasso eliminated narrative imagery to explore other aspects of visual experience such as multiple perspectives and light sources, reduction of pictorial depth and flattening of the picture surface, simplification and distortion of form, and multiple styles within a single image. These innovations that opened the way to cubism and collage also allowed him to challenge, albeit ambiguously, Eurocentrism and racism. Modernists saw African "primitivism" as an exotic paradise of spontaneity and directness, a healthy corrective to a repressed modern society that had lost touch with the childlike innocence and basic instincts that African society supposedly embodied; but they also viewed it as a savage and backward society that worshiped strange gods. They viewed "primitive" art as simple and direct but crude. Although Picasso leaned toward the positive estimate of "primitive" culture, which he shared with the anticolonialist left wing of his own Parisian anarchist circle, he also harbored colonialist prejudices.[55] *Demoiselles* subverted and reworked the forms of Western art as well as the content of the national and imperial narratives as it celebrated the bold distortions, inventive contours, and directness of African aesthetics.

Picasso's subversion of narrative shows how his formal innovation addressed racism and imperialism. As with the modernist novelists, he was not just an iconoclast but offered positive alternatives to the strongly plotted sense of narrative art. His substantive interpretation of the world with innovative formal techniques, although vivid and powerful, was limited to a single moment in time and point of view and so was not as fully elaborated as were the interpretations of novelists who traced these developments at length and in the extended time frame that is the dimension of literary narratives.

In place of strong plots modernist writers used a variety of alternative strategies to address in particular the courtship, family, national, and liberal narratives. Woolf criticized the tyranny of plot directly and proposed to write lyrical novels structured by rhythm more than plot in subverting the hegemony of courtship narratives based on the legal, emotional, and artistic subordination of women. Some realist plots center on the family and affirm its social function. *David Copperfield* rotates around David's family and loyal friends; Victor Hugo's *Les Misérables* (1862) centers on Jean Valjean's efforts to protect his adopted daughter Cosette; and Zola's twenty-volume series of novels is built around the fortunes of the Rougon-Macquart family. Modernists who produced weak plots repeatedly assailed the institution of the family. *Ulysses* subverts the family narrative with a husband, Leopold, who has not had complete intercourse with his wife in over ten years, possibly because he is afraid to father another fatally sick child; a son figure, Stephen, who resists Bloom's attempt at fathering and himself theorizes that the true center of a family and the source of art is ultimately the woman; and a wife, Molly, whose consciousness is a plotless and achronological swirling of imaginative creativity that includes sexual fantasies about men other than her husband and recollections of her adulterous affair. Woolf travesties the patriarchal family plot in the thinly plotted *To the Lighthouse* with an insensitive father, who bullies his children who are strongly ambivalent about him, and a wife who loves him but is unable to say so. Faulkner uses multiple character-narrators to confuse the potentially strong plot of *Absalom, Absalom!* about tyrannical and murderous impulses that leave the Sutpen family narrative in a shambles.[56]

The plot structure of the national narrative ran aground with a war that was not about the progress of nations toward greatness but about stagnation, boredom, and routine interrupted by cataclysmic slaughter. Trench warfare was a chronic condition more than a sequence of climactic events. Battles stretched for miles and lasted months with little to show for them but at best a few thousand yards of shell-holes, poison gas puddles, and putrefying bodies. The epic plot of larger-than-life heroes fighting bravely for national glory behind a brave flag-bearer came apart in this war of attrition and shell shock when nobody really won, and defensive strategies based on trenches and barbed wire negated individual acts of courage.[57] Those novelists who did write war stories were unable to achieve enough aesthetic distance to produce great works. In 1923 the American critic Helen McAfee inquired why "the years since the Armistice have yielded no imaginative masterpiece of war literature." She explained that "we are still so much under the sway of the overwhelming emotions aroused by the newspaper reports of the Marne and Gallipoli that we are not quite open-minded toward their treatment in fiction." The war had been "too useful to novelists in turning a dangerous corner of the plot," and she concluded that the war "has certainly hurt more plots than it has helped."[58]

Modernists also weakened plots in targeting the liberal narrative as they questioned the possibility of a knowing subject making his way progressively through mappable space in a continuous public time to realize the liberal ideals of liberty and equality. As Philip Weinstein argues, the modernist novel crafted instead a process of "unknowing" that was the bankruptcy of plot. "Rather than tweak that familiar plot of knowing and mastery, modernist practice liberates narrative from the blandishments of plot" with characters who struggle through "unmastered space, discontinuous time, and unfamiliar objects."[59] Some modernist characters become increasingly baffled as they attempt to expand their knowledge and make their way through the world as enlightened liberal subjects, especially Kafka's Josef K. and K. and Faulkner's Quentin and Shreve. In place of strong plots modernists devised alternative unifying strategies: in Woolf, Sandra's veils swirling about her head instead of her motives for kissing or not kissing Jacob; in Joyce, Emma's fresh breath radiating above her cowled head instead of her shock over Stephen's sexual proposition; and in Picasso, iconic female forms confronting the viewer instead of desperately poor prostitutes trying to attract a drunken sailor. In unpacking such simple experiences modernists revealed a wealth of riches that also allowed them to craft master narratives in innovative ways, although in devising those ways, they never lost sight of how powerfully those narratives and their attendant values governed their characters' lives.

CHAPTER 3

Space

The physical space of the realist period is that of Euclidean geometry and Newtonian physics that affirmed two fundamental ideas – that there is only one space and that it is empty and inert. Euclid defined the properties of the one and only space and of the points, lines, and planes in it. Objects occupy different spaces, but the overarching framework of space itself remains uniform and unchanged by their presence. Newton also held that there is only one space and that it is uniformly extended and unchanging. During the nineteenth century mathematicians suggested non-Euclidean geometries, but the main assaults on the notion of a single and inert space gathered force in the modernist period. In 1901 the French physicist Henri Poincaré defined a multiplicity of visual, tactile, and motor spaces with non-Euclidean and non-Newtonian properties.[1] In 1909 the German biologist Jacob von Uexküll probed the distinctive space-worlds of different animals, further undermining belief in a single space.[2] The social foundation of space was elaborated in 1903 by the French sociologist Émile Durkheim, who explored spaces in different societies that vary according to the social structures established within them and that therefore are not singular or inert.[3] Such plural social spaces subverted the Eurocentrism of the national, imperial, and religious narratives that were based on the presumption that the singular space of Euclid and Newton prevailed during the entire sweep of human history and throughout the universe. In 1910 the Spanish philosopher José Ortega y Gasset introduced his theory of perspectivism – that there are as many spaces and realities as there are points of view. He applied that philosophy to politics in his journal *El Espectador* in 1916, which argued that World War I was caused by the narrow-mindedness of nations that lacked a broader outlook of multiple perspectives.[4]

Modernist novels also subverted these defining features of the space of classical geometry and physics (singular and inert), as they explored textured spaces that are actively constitutive or are located in multiple ways in the inner space of the mind or in the outer space of the city.

TEXTURE: DYNAMIC VOIDS

Art critics describe the subject of a painting as positive space and the space around it as negative space. Similarly in sculpture the marble is positive space, and the space around it is negative space. The term "positive negative space" implies that conventionally negative elements have a positive, constitutive function. In the late nineteenth century, dynamic voids all across the arts took on such a positive function. The inventions of electric lighting (1879), reinforced concrete (1892), and air-conditioning (1903) liberated architects from restrictions imposed by the requirements of illumination, load-bearing walls, and ventilation and enabled them to think more freely in terms of creative interior spaces rather than conventional rooms. Frank Lloyd Wright characterized his Larkin Soap Company building in Buffalo (1904) as "the original affirmative negation" that showed "the new sense of 'the space within' as reality."[5] Starting in 1907 cubists gave the space between objects as much pictorial substance as the subjects and backgrounds of their paintings. Georges Braque identified that generative function: "The fragmentation [of objects, space, and background] enabled me to establish the space and the movement within space, and I was unable to introduce the object until I had created the space."[6] Sculptors crafted the space around pieces as part of the work, sometimes substituting empty space for crucial features such as the face. Poets made the white paper part of their poems along with freely lined words. The framework of the poem, wrote Stéphane Mallarmé, is present "in the space that separates the stanzas and in the white of the paper: a significant silence, no less beautiful to compose than the lines themselves."[7] At the end of a page, he added, "the blanks unfailingly return; before, they were gratuitous; now they are essential."[8]

These constitutive spaces subverted and reworked the institutions of Western culture that were based on hierarchical distinctions between valued and degraded spaces – between the sacred spaces of religion where God was present and other profane, godless ones; between the privileged sanctuaries of the upper classes, especially those of the hereditary aristocracy, and the vulgar locales of the masses; and between the locus of sovereignty among those who could participate in government and that of the disenfranchised masses. These spatial rehierarchizations accelerated a broad cultural leveling that I refer to metaphorically as the democratization of space, in that what formerly did not count (or vote) now had a constitutive function.[9] Gertrude Stein made explicit that connection between politics and space in the arts. In contrast to traditional paintings in which the subject was more important than the background, she argued, in Cézanne "each part is as important as the whole." Stein's work adapted this formal shift in art to literature. She rejected aristocratic hierarchy in explaining that "to me one human being is as important as another human being." She affirmed democratic politics in explaining how she "threw away punctuation" to level out the importance of words in sentences and achieve "this evenness of everybody having a vote."[10] Hierarchies of creative accomplishment were to be celebrated, but those based on religious dogma, aristocratic privilege, or political oppression were anathema to her. She sought to demolish their authority by undoing the way conventional syntax was used to sustain traditional hierarchies.

This rehierarchization is evident in the modernist novel where an increasingly textured space takes on a dynamic function that resituates authorities based in privileged locations of churches and parliaments. In the realist novel, spaces are rendered most concretely as rooms that reflect the events that take place in them. Thus, for several pages Dickens inventories the many halls, staircases, rooms, furnishings, nicknacks, and wall-hangings in *Bleak House* that mirror the network of confusing social, legal, and family dynamics among those whose lives are affected by it (Ch. 6). Charlotte Brontë creates a red room for Jane Eyre that imprisons her as a girl and recurs to her when she feels trapped. Realist exterior settings focus on atmosphere and weather that suggest, or even determine, the actions that occur in them such as the stormy night that facilitates Jonas's committing murder in *Martin Chuzzlewit* (Ch. 46). Menacing weather implying divine anger is frequently a portent of evil in realist novels, but underlying this profusion of things, rooms, and atmospheres, space itself remains unthematized and invisible, a literary version of the empty and inert space of classical physics.

Modernists continued to write of events in meaningful rooms and evocative exterior settings, but they also had a more explicit focus on the nature of space itself in novels about darkness, night, caves, rooms, a court, or a castle. These positively textured voids represent spiritual or moral vacancies that play a constitutive role especially in imperial, courtship, personal, liberal, and religious undertakings.

The blank space on the map in *Heart of Darkness*, which had been a white patch in Marlow's boyhood, became in his adulthood a multivalent symbol of darkness and emptiness: the mystery of Africa, the empty stomachs driving the cannibalism of starving natives, the "dried, sunken" heads on stakes surrounding Kurtz's hut, and the figure of Kurtz who in the end becomes "a shadow darker than the shadow of the night." Conrad's Congo is the initial positive negative space of modernism that subverts the imperial narrative with sketches of morally degraded Europeans abusing powerless Africans.

Traveling into darkness was not new. Odysseus' journey to Hades and Dante's journey to hell are early examples, with the darkness defined by myth and religion. In Dickens's *Oliver Twist*, Bill Sikes spends his life in darkness and shadows defined by the London slums in which he lives and the nights when he robs and kills. Conrad's exploration of darkness is historically distinctive in an obvious sense because it addresses the imperialism of its time. But it is more significantly modernist in that it evokes darkness formally with its progressively confusing framed narratives beginning with the man on board a ship at the mouth of the Thames who begins what seems to be a straightforward sea tale but quickly turns the story over to Marlow's first-person narration that is pieced together from sketchy reports on Kurtz told by odd characters Marlow had met on his journey. They in turn have partial and unreliable information about Kurtz, who is unable to express himself because he is sick and dying and is tormented by memories of dark actions that he is hiding from everyone including himself. Marlow's journey into darkness is as much the story of his increasingly obscured telling as of his travels into increasingly obscure terrain and ominous atmospherics.

In *Nightwood* Barnes also captures darkness formally with a bewildering narration that makes the reader grope through the story as if blindfolded.[11] If Conrad's narrative is shadowy, Barnes's is pitch black. She gives the emptiness of darkness substance by making night the story's theme, form, and title. Just as one must learn to navigate through darkness by repeated effort, in this novel one can understand who characters are and where and why they act only by re-reading, and then only partially. The yield of such groping, Barnes believed, is a truer vision of reality that is obscured, ironically, by the clearly motivated actions of popular novels. The one character who sees best in this midnight of experience is Dr. O'Connor, a "god of darkness."[12] Night time effaces superficial appearances and loosens the hold of conventional values; in it people can be themselves, or reconstitute themselves, more freely than in daylight, in particular their gender roles and patterns of loving. The novel was based on the forbidden lesbian love between Barnes and Thelma Wood, possibly a source for the wood in *Nightwood*.[13] By setting the novel at night and creating a night time of reader confusion, Barnes gives formal substance to the opaque space of darkness where unconventional gender roles and courtship scenarios are less vulnerable to the judgmental gaze of others and more open to free expression.

In E. M. Forster's *A Passage to India* (1924) the dynamic space of the Marabar Caves is the setting for Adela Quested's hallucination of a rape with which she charges her host, the Indian Dr. Aziz, which occasions a trial that dramatizes the chauvinism and injustice of the British Raj. The echo that the caves make ("ou-boum" – no matter what sound triggers it) is not merely a matter of acoustics. It signifies the inability of language to express important matters such as friendship, love, and religion – "poor little talkative Christianity."[14] The darkness of the cave is also not merely a matter of optics. It draws attention to the power of empty space, its terrifying symbolism of loneliness and death. Adela is vulnerable to such associations with empty space, because on the hike to the cave she unintentionally insulted Aziz by asking whether he had more than one wife. That faux pas triggers the realization that she does not love her fiancé Ronny and cannot marry him. With friendship, love, marriage, and Anglo-Indian relations in ruins, the darkness and emptiness of the Marabar Caves plus their mind-numbing echo trigger Adela's hallucination and mental breakdown, because although she was physically untouched, her core values had indeed been violated.

The Marabar Caves continue to shape the narrative after Adela rescinds her charge because she remains haunted by the echo that obliterates any clear analysis of her life. She goes on hearing it until charges against Aziz are dropped, but it still continues to resound throughout the novel. Its sound is subsequently magnified and transformed into the din of insurgent crowds that erupt in protest after the trial when Aziz decides not to bring charges against Adela. The significance of the caves can be seen in comparison with a realist literary spot where love is also compromised. In George Eliot's *The Mill on the Floss* (1860), the Red Deeps is an exhausted stone quarry where Maggie Tulliver meditates alone. During one such meditation Philip Wakem reaches out to her for love. After several meetings, she decides to forsake love and devote herself to making happy the physically unappealing and unlovable Philip – a commitment that eventually leads to tragic conflict with her true love, Stephen Guest, and ultimately to her death. The Red Deeps remains memorable and important to Maggie, but Eliot does not explore the constitutive function of the space itself. It is a charming romantic spot, not a life-defining space. In contrast, Forster's Marabar Caves symbolize the most pressing questions about life and the impossibility of satisfactory answers. While his own narrative does not break down into a monotonal echo, the emptiness of the echo signifies the difficulty of human communication and the impossibility of a fulfilling connection between a colonizing and a colonized culture.

Modernists also attend to the generative function of rooms. Empty rooms are the subject of Woolf's novel *Jacob's Room*, as she noted in a diary entry of April 15, 1920 about her main formal intention in the novel – "that the

Room will hold it together." Throughout the twelve volumes of Richardson's *Pilgrimage*, Miriam is variously greeted, disowned, crushed, mocked, and haunted by the many rooms she inhabits. Proust affirms the power of important as well as seemingly unimportant rooms. When Swann is tormented by jealousy, the volatile rooms where Odette might be with others forcibly keep him away. Marcel's innocuous hotel room, he reports, "was full of things which did not know me, which flung back at me the distrustful glance I cast at them." The distances are wrong, the objects unfamiliar. He is tormented by the strange bookcases and shut out of the "conversation" between the clock and the curtains (*RP*, 1, 717).

The most menacing modernist spaces are in Kafka. In *The Trial* hallways are interminably long and confusing, stairways are dark with excessively narrow walls and long flights, doors do not fit right, windows do not let in light and air but allow for threatening surveillance, walls do not divide space rationally but either open unexpectedly or constrict movement, ceilings are too low or too high, and rooms are vacant or overcrowded. Josef K. is frequently lost in buildings, and in one of them he spends eight pages searching anxiously for an exit. In the room for his first interrogation the ceiling is so low that observers have to crouch and put cushions on their heads so as not to rub their scalps raw on the ceiling. The law-court offices are in the attic of a rundown apartment building. Josef K.'s most reliable source of information about the courts comes from a man who makes a living painting portraits of judges in a tiny garret in which the bed is in front of the door to his room, and the judges have to climb across his bed to enter for their sittings. The interior space of the local cathedral is equally threatening with a vaulted roof and overall size that "seemed to border on the limits of human endurance."[15] The labyrinthine complexity of Kafka's spaces mirrors the labyrinthine impenetrability of the law that confounds him.

While castles ring with vitality in historical novels, they are largely absent from realist novels, the very definition of which tends to exclude them. When they do appear, they are at the margins of action and in decline. In Zola's *Nana* (1880), Count Muffat has access to the court of Emperor Louis Napoleon, but that proximity only underscores the depths of his degradation in the hands of the prostitute Nana. Against this background, the prominence of the castle in Kafka's novel *The Castle* (written in 1922) is historically significant for its un-castle-like role. But its larger significance is the ambiguity of the space it occupies in the life of the villagers. It dominates everything in the village but apparently nothing in particular, from a space that is the center of action but impossible to access. Even the people who work in it or for it are not certain what it is or where it is. Its appearance shifts from moment to moment, but unlike Monet's Cathedral that changes perspectivally in different seasons and light, Kafka's castle changes ontologically in its very nature because it is nothing specific, rather a projection of the villagers' need for regulation by an authority that has no legitimate ground and therefore occupies no clearly identifiable space. It does not so much exist in space as float in it, and in that manner generates the forms, distances, and directions of space that structure village life.

The potent inaccessibility of Kafka's castle is emblematic of the changing function of space itself in the modernist novel. His evanescent castle dominates the villagers just as a variety of constitutive negativities rework the spaces of master narratives. By revising the hierarchical distinction between the sacred space of God and the profane space of man, for example, modernists put a crowbar to the ironwork of the religious master narrative. Henceforth, valued spaces would be determined by creative human endeavors, not by traditional institutions or sacred texts. In identifying the constitutive function of space itself, modernists opened the entire range of values and institutions associated with the hierarchically structured master narratives for creative revision, one that artists were exceptionally well trained and highly motivated to undertake.

MENTAL SPACE: IMPRESSIONISM, FREE INDIRECT DISCOURSE, STREAM OF CONSCIOUSNESS

Three major philosophical developments of the modernist period – Bergsonism, pragmatism, and phenomenology – shared a commitment to focusing on how human consciousness directly experiences the world. Henri Bergson concentrated on such inner experience, as indicated by the title of his doctoral dissertation, *Essay on the Immediate Data of Consciousness*.[16] The pragmatist William James called his philosophy radical empiricism to underscore its exclusive focus on the empirically given. Martin Heidegger's phenomenology focused on existence as always immersed in the surrounding world in opposition to the radical separation of self and world in Cartesian philosophy. We do not open the visor of consciousness, peer out, and lo! – discover others. We are primordially and necessarily with others.[17] While Heidegger focused on authentic and inauthentic modes of being-with, modernist novelists envisioned a variety of ways individuals experience the larger world they inhabit and help constitute.

Realist narrators, third or first person, rendered the consciousness of their characters objectively. Take Dickens's depiction of Lady Dedlock in *Bleak House*. Throughout the novel she seems bored and apathetic. When the first-person narrator Esther Summerson finally discloses the dark secret behind her demeanor and reveals her to be passionate and impulsive, she describes these emotions from without. The climax of that revelation comes as Dedlock is overwhelmed with shame when she is on the brink of exposure as the mother of an illegitimate child and believes herself about to be accused of a murder she did not commit. Summerson presents Dedlock's shame first as it would appear to others: "So! All is broken down. Her name is in these many mouths . . . her shame will be published – may be spreading while she thinks about it . . . she is denounced by an invisible accuser as the murderess of her enemy." The final account of her shame is also from an external perspective: "The complication of her shame, her dread, her remorse, and misery, overwhelms her at its height; and even her strength of self-reliance is overturned and whirled away" (Ch. 55). Readers are notified that she is ashamed but have no direct access to how she experiences that emotion from within. The anticipated judgment of others, also external, drives her to suicidal despair. Dickens questions the destructive pride of aristocratic families such as the Dedlocks that guarded family secrets at all costs, but he does so without letting readers directly into his characters' inner perspective.

When realists offered direct, first-person accounts of a character's consciousness as in *David Copperfield*, this consciousness is readily comprehensible. David expresses his emotions clearly, and they are logically connected to the events he experiences. While Lucy Snowe in *Villette* (1853) is more opaque, Brontë still portrayed her as a psychologically coherent character. As Nicholas Dames has shown, Victorian novelists generally sought to "transform the chaos of personal recollection into what is useful, meaningful, able to be applied to the future – into what *works*."[18] For realists, all of consciousness possessed similar qualities of logic and external orientation.

E. M. Forster's narration is transitional in that it allows readers a glimpse into psychic interiority when the narrator in *Howards End* (1910) explains how Margaret Schlegel desired that "public life should mirror whatever is good in the life within" in contrast to the outer life that governs public events.[19] That distinction is articulated with unintended self-mockery by Henry Wilcox, who, to apologize for a clumsy first kiss he lands on Margaret, explains, "I am not a fellow who bothers about my own inside." Henry is a caricature of the unreflective English gentleman who does not notice things in the world because he is ignorant of what is within himself. He blunders into a marriage that is salvaged by Margaret who understands both Henry's and her own "life within." While Forster showed how ignorance of that inner perspective limits courtship and family life, he still kept readers outside. Other modernists rendered interiority more directly with three distinctive techniques: impressionism, free indirect discourse, and stream of consciousness.

Ford applied the term impressionism to a technique that novelists used to recreate how characters process experience from inner and outer sensations as well as memories and associations. This technique contrasts with the way experiences are conceptualized by the realist narrator before they occur. In 1924, following the death of Conrad, with whom Ford had co-authored three novels between 1901 and 1909, Ford explained what literary impressionists must avoid, namely, reporting. "Life does not say to you: In 1914 my next-door neighbour, Mr. Slack, erected a greenhouse and painted it with Cox's green aluminum paint." In that scenario the erecting and painting are conceptual end-products of an experiential sequence that is actually presented to the mind as an unfolding of fragmentary impressions. He and Conrad sought rather to recreate how confusing impressions form into logical events in consciousness. "We accepted the name [Impressionists] because . . . we saw that life does not narrate, but made impressions on our brains."[20]

The novels of Ford and Conrad use literary impressionism to capture events of more historical significance than erecting and painting a greenhouse. In the preface to *The Nigger of the "Narcissus,"* Conrad announced his goal "to make you see." In fact he wanted his readers not just to see, but to see something significant. In *Heart of Darkness*, that significance was imperialism and its links to nationalism, capitalism, liberalism, and religion, because in pursuit of ivory Kurtz had to destroy local political institutions to gain power, kill elephants for profit, crush Congolese human rights to get workers, and invest himself with godlike authority to exact slavish obedience.

Conrad's impressionism captures how Marlow experiences such historically marked institutions from an interior perspective. As Marlow's boat draws near Kurtz's station, he has two puzzling impressions of his poleman dropping his pole and his fireman sitting down. Next Marlow checks a snag in the river and then notices that "sticks, little sticks, were flying about." At that moment he does not know what the sticks are. The river and shore are quiet, and the boat clears the snag. Finally he grasps the meaning of the sticks: "Arrows, by Jove! We were being shot at!" He comes to understand the source of the arrows as he looks into the woods on shore and sees "naked breasts, arms, legs, glaring eyes – the bush was swarming with human limbs." The sequence of initially puzzling impressions continues.

"Something big appeared in the air." At that instant Marlow does not know that it is a spear. Then his helmsman steps back, looks at him, and hits his head on the wheel. Something like a long cane knocks over a stool. As Marlow turns to check the river, his feet feel warm and wet. The helmsman is on his back staring at him, and, Marlow reports, "both his hands clutched that cane. It was the shaft of a spear that, either thrown or lunged through the opening, had caught him in the side just below the ribs . . . my shoes were full [of blood]" and the helmsman was "gripping the spear like something precious, with an air of being afraid I would try to take it away from him" (*HD*, 45–47).

This sequence of impressions obliges the reader to live through Marlow's confusion and gradual dawning awareness. The remainder of the story elaborates the historical circumstances behind the attack. The frantic movement of the "savages" in the woods was motivated by the threat to their way of life that Marlow's steamboat signified, especially fear of losing Kurtz, who had installed himself as a god and sanctioned dehumanizing practices that include, we soon learn, head-hunting. That symbol is revealed in another use of impressionism. Nearing Kurtz's station, Marlow looks through his binoculars at a decayed building and identifies what he guesses to be fence posts topped with "round carved balls." Several pages later he takes a closer look at what he now knows to be Kurtz's hut, and something makes him jerk back his head. He finally realizes what he has seen: "heads on stakes" (52, 57). Here impressionism recreates the immediacy of Marlow's shock of recognition that the imperial enterprise has been not a civilizing mission but a degenerative one.

Ian Watt's term for Conrad's impressionism is *delayed decoding*, which emphasizes how sequential events are interpreted as meaningful events after their initial recording in consciousness.[21] Ford's observation of the erection of a greenhouse is a logical sequence of purposeful events constructed subsequent to and out of a disjoined sequence of impressions with seemingly unrelated associations. The innovative nature of Ford's use of impressionism to capture World War I in *Parade's End* can be seen in contrast to Zola's objective narration of the Battle of Sedan in *The Debacle*. Zola described the horrors of war with 150 pages of events as soldiers witness others being blown apart by artillery. He inventoried what these witnesses saw and felt but did not take readers inside their minds, and those descriptions focus on the fighting alone – no errant mental associations to other places and times, as if to include them would distract from and degrade the significance of the fighting. In contrast, Ford made a novel out of such associations. He defined impressionism in formal essays that explain his "indirect, interrupted method." He noted further that "a great many novelists have treated of the late war in terms solely of the war," but those who lived through it know "how infinitely little part the actual fighting itself took in your mentality." Aside from long stretches of boredom, even during battles, the mind is on other things, as Ford phrased it, "on your daughter Millicent's hair, on the fall of the Asquith Ministry, on your financial predicament, on why your regimental ferrets kept on dying, on whether Latin is really necessary to an education."[22]

Parade's End is about Britain's decline and tenuous rebirth during and after the war. One impressionistic battle scene captures Christopher Tietjens's disarrayed thoughts when a soldier named O Nine Morgan stumbles into his hut and says "Ere's another bloomin' casualty." Already dead, Morgan falls onto the knees of another soldier, and blood streams over them both and onto the floor, reminding Tietjens of the blood that ran over a horse from a cut which he had bandaged with a girl's petticoat. He then wonders how another soldier could know an uncle of his and what his girl back home, who is a pacifist, would think of him now with his hands sticky with blood, "Disgust, probably!" He recalls having sent a runner to the orderly room and Morgan's half blown-away face grinning at the roof, and then wonders why it is grinning and whether Morgan had spoken after he was dead with a final reflex as the last air ran out of his lungs. Tietjens then remembers that he has had no letters from home except circulars from furniture dealers and wonders if his bowels will turn over if he thinks of the girl. She reminds him of a primrose, which recalls Heine's line "*Du bist wie eine Blume*" and an outburst, "Damn the German language!"[23] That leads to thoughts of a Jew he met and that his girl smelled like a primrose, then back to Morgan and whether, if he had given him a leave, he would still be alive.

For several pages Ford probes Tietjens processing the death of this soldier in a way that is symptomatic of Ford's larger treatment of the war as a desperate last gasp of a dying aristocratic society. The associated ideas that surge through Tietjens's mind mirror his judgments about the unraveling rationale of the British Empire, the "swine of the corridors" of Whitehall, the incompetent ruling classes that started the war, and the officer corps that commanded it. Ford does not just describe the irrationality of the nationalist narrative objectively, as Zola had done, but dramatizes it repeatedly as in this impressionist rendering of Tietjens's mixed-up thoughts.[24]

Modernists used another technique for rendering inner experience – free indirect discourse, which fuses the voice of the narrator with that of a character. That technique had been used by Goethe, Austen, Büchner, Dickens, Thackeray, Eliot, Flaubert, and Zola, but not as systematically or centrally as in modernist novels.[25] Woolf employs it to show an inner perspective on the world with special vividness in Clarissa Dalloway's mind after she receives some roses as a token of love from her husband, Richard, a conservative Member of Parliament, and they chat for five minutes before he leaves for a committee vote.

> "Some committee?" she asked, as he opened the door.
> "Armenians," he said; or perhaps it was "Albanians." (*MD*, 119)

After the word "said," Woolf shifts puzzlingly from external narration about Richard's farewell word to Clarissa's inner thoughts as she confuses the people of two countries suffering for vastly different reasons. The continuing action remains in Clarissa's mind as she thinks about where Richard is going, what people will say about her, and the unfortunate people who live in one of those countries that begin with the letter *A*.

> He was already halfway to the House of Commons, to his Armenians, his Albanians, having settled her on the sofa, looking at his roses. And people would say, "Clarissa Dalloway is spoilt." She cared much more for her roses than for the Armenians. Hunted out of existence, maimed, frozen, the victims of cruelty and injustice (she had heard Richard say so over and over again) – no, she could feel nothing for the Albanians, or was it the Armenians? But she loved her roses (didn't that help the Armenians?) – the only flowers she could bear to see cut. (120)

The Armenians were Christians in a Muslim area between Turkey and Russia who had been colonized and persecuted since the eleventh century. Albanians lived 1,200 miles to the west with considerably different problems. The Treaty of San Stefano of 1878 proposed to put Armenians under Russian authority, but Britain, concerned about its influence in the region, forced a revision to keep Armenians within the Ottoman Empire in exchange for pledging to protect them from Turkish abuse. But Britain failed to protect the Armenians; the abuse continued, culminating in massacres of up to a million of them in 1915, accompanied by crucifixions, mutilations, and rapes. The day of Woolf's novel in June 1923, Richard was on his way to a committee meeting on the Lausanne Treaty, which was in fact signed on July 24, 1923. It turned out to be another betrayal, because with it Britain ignored Armenian independence and established the state of Iraq to strengthen its influence in the region.

Woolf vents her contempt for upper-class women who invite the ruling classes to their parties (the Prime Minister would come to Clarissa's) by remaining within Clarissa's surprisingly self-centered mind. Having Clarissa confuse the two countries after Richard had told her that the Armenians were "maimed, frozen, the victims of cruelty and injustice" underscores the indifference of the British ruling class and the tacit complicity of its privileged women like Clarissa who is more troubled by cut flowers than by crucified Armenians. Even her confession of indifference is darkened by ignorance – "no, she could feel nothing for the Albanians, or was it the Armenians" (119–20).[26]

Woolf's anger over British imperialism is magnified by her presenting it through the mind of a protagonist who is otherwise acutely sensitive to others and her surroundings. Modernists generally learned to capture the outer world focused through individual psyches where it is personalized and thereby made more vivid. Woolf also used free indirect discourse to capture the depression and panic of shell-shocked Septimus Smith in the throes of suicidal despair as another way of assailing the national narrative that led Britain into war. Readers are not just told about the horrors of the war; they share Smith's panic as battle scenes recur to him in the moments before he commits suicide. When later during her party Clarissa learns of that suicide, we follow how she is overwhelmed by empathy with his suffering and admiration for his courage. Feelings she was unable to muster for millions of anonymous Armenians erupt in her compassion for an unknown young man who killed himself. The most powerful action in *Mrs. Dalloway* occurs in the minds of characters captured by free indirect discourse that reveals their perspective on the circumstances of their time.

Modernists also rendered inner space with a stream-of-consciousness technique that may include memories, expectations, emotions, judgments, fantasies, stimuli from five senses, bits of overheard or recalled speech, fragments of syntax, even parts of words or invented words that simultaneously course through the mind and make up a moment of consciousness. The metaphor of stream, which comes from the psychology of William James, is inappropriate because it suggests continuous uniform motion through time and in a stable stream-bed, whereas consciousness moves erratically in multiple directions both temporally and spatially with no fixed path.[27] In a lecture of 1899 on "Stream of Consciousness" James proposed alternative metaphors: "a succession of states, or waves, or fields . . . that constitute our inner life."[28] I retain the term because it has become standard.

Realists experimented with stream of consciousness but used it less often than did modernists and in more restrictive circumstances. Tolstoy used it in a few paragraphs to render the frantic workings of Anna Karenina's mind just before her suicide. Desperate because Vronsky no longer loves her, she projects her inner anguish onto an outer world of indifference and hate. During a carriage ride she reads advertising signs ("Office and Stores . . .

Dental Surgeon") amid her agonizing ruminations about Vronsky and reacts to the smell of paint as she anticipates how he will react to her note (Pt. 7, Ch. 28).

Modernists used stream of consciousness more extensively. Edouard Dujardin developed the technique from the beginning to the end of a work in 1887.[29] By 1900, Arthur Schnitzler used it throughout his novella *Lieutenant Gustl*, but still for a sustained moment of emotional intensity as a man outraged over a public insult is driven to contemplate suicide.[30] Starting in 1915, Richardson was the first to use it throughout a long work of fiction, the series of novels that make up *Pilgrimage*. In 1918 the novelist May Sinclair estimated its historical significance in a review of the first three volumes: "In this series there is no drama, no situation, no set scene. Nothing happens. It is just life going on and on ... In identifying herself with this life, which is [the narrator] Miriam's stream of consciousness, Miss Richardson produces her effect of being the first, of getting closer to reality than any of our novelists who are trying so desperately to get close."[31]

Richardson's stream-of-consciousness technique ranges through countless impressions, memories, and ideas. It also violates conventional syntax with ellipsis dots to suggest the gaps between impressions, as in the following passage, where she excavates the inner working of Miriam's mind while commenting on female gender roles:

... women stopped being people and went off into hideous processes. What for? What was it all for? Development. The wonders of science. The wonders of science for women are nothing but gynecology – all those frightful operations in the *British Medical Journal* and those jokes ... the hundred golden rules ... Sacred functions ... highest possibilities ... sacred for what? The hand that rocks the cradle rules the world? The Future of the Race? What world? What race? Men ... Nothing but men; for ever. (*P*, II, 221)

Richardson elaborates on such female concerns in recurring stream-of-consciousness passages of her protagonist-narrator: living alone, earning a living as a dentist's assistant, rejecting conventional religion and politics, enhancing her knowledge of science and the arts, attending lectures and meetings of literary groups, enjoying cigarettes in public, learning to ride a bicycle, exploring cities on her own, visiting the dying, and cultivating her sex life while avoiding seductions and marriage.

In *The Sound and the Fury* Faulkner's stream-of-consciousness passages capture the decline of the Compson family narrative as it is presented through the minds of the sons Benjy, Quentin, and Jason. The hypochondriacal mother wallows in self-pity and neglects all of her children except her cruelest son Jason. The father's alcoholism is fatal, and Jason's villainy disqualifies him to lead the family. The family sells "Benjy's pasture," part of the Compson family property, so that Quentin can go to Harvard where he remains morbidly preoccupied with desire for his sister Caddy, as is captured in a stream-of-consciousness fantasy of him replacing her lovers: *"you thought it was them but it was me listen I fooled you all the time it was me you thought I was in the house where that damn honeysuckle trying not to think the swing the cedars the secret surges the breathing locked drinking the wild breath the yes Yes Yes"* (*SF*, 149). This passage dissolves conventional grammar, syntax, and rational thinking to capture the unraveling of Quentin's mind and the decline of his family, as despondency over Caddy's promiscuity and marriage eventually drives him to suicide. She abandons her daughter and leaves the family to run off with a man. Benjy is sterile, castrated after he approached a young girl who reminded him of Caddy and was seen as trying to attack her. He is without speech and yet is the "idiot" who, in mute rumination, begins the sorry tale of his family that is full of sound and fury signifying not nothing but the Compson family's "Twilight" (the novel's original title) as well as the deterioration of an entire culture based on chivalric ideals, racism, aristocratic pedigree, old time religion, and the purity of Southern women.

Joyce used stream of consciousness in *Ulysses* to engage all the master narratives, but especially the courtship narrative, as throughout the day Bloom thinks about Molly's infidelity that he suspects is scheduled for 4 p.m. At that time he is in a bar with friends after Boylan has just left for his tryst with Molly. Simon Dedalus is singing a song about a man who first saw his beloved when he was "full of hope and all delighted" and then realizes that she is gone, a song with lines that trigger Bloom's recalling his own hopeful first meeting with Molly and now her imminent meeting with Boylan. The following passage is introduced by Simon Dedalus's singing voice in italics [SD] followed by Bloom's stream of consciousness [LB] including lines from Boylan's song *Those Lovely Seaside Girls* about girls who make his head swirl [TL], Boylan's speech [BB], Molly's speech [MB], lines from the soft-porn novel *Sweets of Sin* that Bloom has just bought for Molly and in which he reads key passages about a woman perfuming herself for a man and about hands feeling an opulent body [SS], and lines from Martha Clifford's letter to Bloom, which he had read earlier that morning, asking what perfume his wife uses [MC]. Bloom's consciousness includes thoughts about Boylan's past singing rewarded by flowers from fans and his upcoming meeting with Molly and how she might perfume her body and sweeten her breath in anticipation of the meeting, plus what Boylan and Molly might have said when they first arranged to meet and what they might say as they meet in Bloom's apartment.

[SD] – *Full of hope and all delighted* . . .
    [LB] Tenors get women by the score. Increase their flow [of sexual desire]. Throw flower at his feet. [BB] When will we meet? [TL] My head it simply. [LB] Jingle all delighted. He can't sing for tall hats. [TL] Your head it simply swurls. [SS] Perfumed for him. [MC] What perfume does your wife? I want to know. [LB] Jing. Stop. Knock. Last look at mirror always before she answers the door. The hall. There? [BB or MB] How do you? I do well. [LB] There? What? Or? Phial of cachous, kissing comfits, in her satchel. Yes? [SS] Hands felt for the opulent. (*U*, 225)

Bloom's sadness peaks as he listens to Simon's song and thinks about Boylan in his jingly car arriving at Molly's door and knocking, and then about her approaching the door, opening it, and exchanging a few words with Boylan before they have sex. Such passages capture the complexity of Bloom's experience as he feels simultaneously identification and competition with Boylan but also envy over what he is about to enjoy and jealousy over what Molly is depriving him of as well as compensatory naughtiness from his epistolary flirtation with Martha and the stimulation he felt while buying and reading parts of the soft-porn novel for Molly. Deeper still is the troubled marital prehistory of Bloom and Molly that the novel has already explored, including their shared grief over the death of their son Rudy, which, for some undisclosed reason, brought to a halt their normal sexual relations ten years earlier. The line from Boylan's song refers to Boylan's swirling head at the sight of seaside girls but also to Bloom's swirling head as he considers Boylan having sex with Molly. Bloom's thought "Jing. Stop. Knock." cuts off the word "Jingle," which refers to the sound Boylan's car makes, to enact syntactically his stop before knocking on Molly's door. The lines from the novel about perfume link Molly preparing to attract Boylan with Martha inquiring about how to attract Bloom. The line from *Sweets of Sin*, "Hands felt for the opulent," describes a man cuckolding a silly old husband by caressing an adulterous young wife who has "opulent curves" like Molly. The meaning of this moment for Bloom is accented by the next line of the song about a man realizing that his earlier hope and delight was "idle dreaming." Such stream-of-consciousness passages, difficult to understand at a first reading, gain significance as the novel proceeds, and they recall widely separated thoughts, memories, utterances, sights, sounds, and smells compressed into a moment of exceptional intensity. A few months after its publication in 1922, Ford proclaimed Joyce's historic role in probing interiority in stream-of-consciousness passages such as this one. "*Ulysses* contains the undiscovered mind of man; it is human consciousness analyzed as it has never before been analyzed. Certain books change the world. This, success or failure, *Ulysses* does."[32]

The historical significance of this passage is its formal innovation but also how it treats jealousy. In realist novels jealousy is an all-consuming emotion; its source is projected onto the unfaithful beloved, and so lovers learn little from it about themselves or their beloved. In *Wuthering Heights* Heathcliff's jealousy over Cathy is based on a misheard conversation. He runs away for three years, consumed by jealousy and convinced that his misery is caused entirely by her betrayal. Then he returns a rich man to wreak vengeance on her and her family. When he finds her on her deathbed, he learns how much she loved him but does not discover his responsibility for his jealousy. It rages for another eighteen years against everyone who, he continues to believe, did him wrong, until at the end he loses his mind and begins to talk with her ghost, convinced that he will be reunited with her in death. In *Jane Eyre*, Rochester does not see his own responsibility for jealousy deriving from his own fantasies and insecurities. He is jealous over his former lover Céline, but, he tells Jane, as soon as he realized that his rival was beneath contempt, "the fang of the snake Jealousy was instantly broken; because at that same moment my love for Céline sank under an extinguisher" (Ch. 15).

The history of jealousy is part of a broader historical shift in depictions of the courtship narrative that modernists subvert and rework in the direction of increasing authenticity as lovers become more aware of what it means to be jealous as well as in love.[33] As Simon's song is receiving applause, Bloom works through his jealousy as he prepares to reconstitute his relationship with Molly at a higher level of self-awareness that Joyce captures again with stream of consciousness: "Come. Well sung. All clapped. She ought to. Come. To me, to him, to her, you too, me, us" (*U*, 227). Bloom's private suffering is broken by a moment of shared love. Later he realizes that exclusive possession of a woman is a man's futile fantasy with "each imaging himself to be first, last, only and alone whereas he is neither first nor last nor only nor alone in a series originating in and repeated to infinity" (601). The progression of his specific feelings is sketched with a short list: "Envy, jealousy, abnegation, equanimity" (602). In the end he achieves equanimity from self-understanding. He is more fully aware of what jealousy means and of his responsibility for it than was Heathcliff or Rochester, and so his jealousy is more authentically experienced, more his very own.

The innovative use of impressionism, free indirect discourse, and stream of consciousness is evidence of a historical shift in the spatiality of the novel as it relocated toward the interior consciousness of characters in their experience of the world. In 1910 Rilke wondered: "Is it possible that despite our discoveries and advances, despite our culture, religion, and science, we have remained on the surface of life?" As a poet learning to see, his character Malte announced that "everything enters me more deeply and doesn't stop where it once used to. I have an interior that I never knew of. Everything passes into it now."[34] In 1934 Stein urged a similar interior probing: "I had to find out what it was inside any one . . . not by what they said not by what they did not by how much or how little they resembled any other one but I had to find it out by the intensity of movement that there was inside in any one of them."[35] In this period, action moved inside the mind where novelists registered outer experience in the most vivid, stable, and humanizing ways.[36]

The relocation to inner consciousness was not a "disintegration of the outer world," as Georg Lukács charged, but a way of accessing that world most directly and presenting it most vividly.[37] Woolf dramatized the decline of Western civilization in the war through the mind of Septimus Smith as he relived the trauma when his friend Evans was killed. Faulkner recreated the decline of the Compson family through the agitated mind of Quentin fantasizing about his sister. In *Fräulein Else* (1924) Schnitzler brought to life the economic, familial, and social pressures on a young woman in interwar Vienna with a stream-of-consciousness rendering of the protagonist who works herself into a suicidal frenzy from agreeing to pose naked before a rich old man in exchange for his agreeing to help her embezzler father out of a financial jam.

The mercurial realm of consciousness also emerged, ironically, as the most stable, or at least most centered, locus of experience. While realists located stability in the outer world of public institutions – marriage, family, respectability, justice, wealth, nation, and religion – modernists located stability where those institutions were constructed in the mind. As those institutions lost the authority of abiding, if not timeless, frameworks, they were replaced by the subjective frameworks of individual consciousness. Freud, Bergson, and Heidegger found the grounding source of chaotic outer experience in psychoanalyzed egos, immediate data of consciousness, and authentic being. They proposed living without public determinations of what "one does" and rather with inner experience that provides a subjective, authentic ground for the sensuous fullness of experiencing the outer world in one's very own way.

Modernists viewed the challenged and challenging institutions of especially family, church, and state as artificial constructions that limited life. They continued to represent these institutions but primarily as interpreted by individuals. They saw conventional homes as not private but public institutions, constructed out of traditions that did not serve family members' individuality. Interiorization offered a humanizing home within the psyche in a world where the comforts of publicly created homes were not as secure as they had been, or at least had been thought to be, in Austen, Dickens, the Brontës, and Eliot. Bloom's marriage has been usurped, and he repositions himself with respect to Molly more securely in his mind than in his marital bed. Marriages for the couples in Proust, Gide, and Ford are built on lies. In James's *The Golden Bowl*, the bowl itself, gilded on the outside but cracked underneath, is a symbol of the lie behind a marriage. Many modernist authors were periodically self-exiled from their countries: James, Hemingway, Fitzgerald, Stein, Dos Passos, Conrad, Ford, Joyce, Mann, Musil, and the entire postwar "lost generation." Modernists began to accept what Heidegger called the "thrownness" of existence, the notion that we exist in no special place for which we are destined, and that home is an illusory remnant of a lost childhood, a fantasy of a right place that never actually existed. They instead refashioned a more authentically humanized home in the recesses of consciousness as it sought fulfillment in whatever uncanny outer location it happened to be.

URBAN SPACE: WANDERING ROCKS

Modernists also set their novels outside the mind in the big city. While urban space changed historically from the realist period in an obvious way because it existed in a different time (Dickens's London versus Woolf's), it also changed more importantly because the experience of urban space itself was transformed by increasing populations. But the fact that the population of Dickens's London of 1850 was eight times greater than that of Joyce's Dublin of 1904 suggests that more was in play than mere population.[38] The pace, scale, variety, and intensity of urban experiences were transformed by new communication technologies such as telephones, movies, radios, and daily newspapers and new transportation technologies such as automobiles, busses, taxis, ambulances, and electric trams. In *Manhattan Transfer* Dos Passos even invokes a steamroller smoothing fresh tar to suggest how the city "crushes" the life out of its inhabitants.[39] Urban space as reflected in the novel changed historically in terms of its structure, directionality, centeredness, visibility, continuity, stability, and range.

The structure evolved from old cities that grew organically around farmers' markets to modern cities reshaped by urban renewal and zoning laws that created more rational plans conducive to large-scale capitalist production and consumption. Andrei Bely's *Petersburg* (1913–16) is about a plot to assassinate Senator Apollon Ableukhov, head of an unnamed Russian governmental institution, and topple his regime during nine days between the recently lost Russo-Japanese War in May 1905 and the Revolution of late October. The novel is, as the title indicates, about the city itself, and the senator's governing style is embodied in his strong sense of urban space – his fear of open space and preference for the symmetry of central Petersburg. He lives in a dehumanized ordered space of cubes and straight lines, and revolution threatens his rationally ordered government through seditious types who appear to him like dots and spheres. These violent "swarms" live on Vasilievsky Island, where, Bely narrates, "one of those dots broke loose from its orbit and hurtled at him with dizzying speed, taking the form of an immense crimson sphere."[40] Ironically, Petersburg's design was not from a modern planner but from Peter the Great, who admired enlightenment reason. Still, to Bely it embodied an odious grid distinctive to the modern age, which he satirized with Ableukhov's passion for parallelepipeds.

Upward glances in the nineteenth century were directed at birds and clouds, occasionally at God and the heavens. In the twentieth century gazes turned up to skyscrapers and airplanes. Balzac and Dickens wrote about the city with sweeping panoramas as if they saw it from above, while modernists wrote about urbanites who looked up at structures and technologies that functioned above the earth's surface. In *Manhattan Transfer* Jimmy Herf is obsessed by "a grooved building jutting up with unaccountable bright windows falling onto him out of a scudding sky."[41] Skyscrapers both dwarf and elevate the experience of Manhattanites scurrying around in the canyons they create. Herf's inability to find an entrance to one skyscraper underscores the inaccessibility of the towering building as well as the city itself. In *Mrs. Dalloway*, looking up unifies and uplifts Londoners who struggle to decipher the letters from a skywriting airplane. Woolf situates Clarissa enthusiastically at home with the new transportation technologies including airplanes that reconfigure London's spatiality. "For heaven only knows why one loves it so, how one sees it so, making it up, building it round one, tumbling in it, creating it every moment afresh . . . in the bellow and the uproar; the carriages, motor cars, omnibuses, vans, sandwichmen shuffling and swinging; brass bands; barrel organs; in the triumph and the jingle and the strange high singing of some aeroplane overhead was what she loved; life; London; this moment of June" (*MD*, 4). Proust describes German aircraft over Paris during the war with awe, as the beautiful aeroplanes climbing into the night appear to Marcel like Wagnerian Valkyries pursued by searchlights illuminating the night sky (*RP*, III, 781). The ability to go up and look up also suggested the reverse direction as people in skyscrapers and airplanes could look down, transforming urban space into a living map on which human insects moved about with minuscule projects.

Dense interior networks and sprawling perimeters made modern city centers impossible to determine. *Manhattan Transfer* begins with Bud Korpening coming into Manhattan on a ferry and asking, "How do I get to Broadway? . . . I want to get to the center of things." He never finds the center, although he repeatedly asks for directions to it, because Manhattan has no center. The actress Elaine Oglethorpe gets to a quasi-center on Broadway as she boasts when her image appears on signs advertising her role in a play, but they are an illusory center. The novel's title refers not to the city or its center but to a transit station to Manhattan in New Jersey. Just as modernist novels typically have no clear originary moment in time, their cities have no precise center in space. Joyce's Dublin is a centerless labyrinth. City trams originate from Nelson's Pillar, but Joyce mocks its centrality by noting that at the top is a "onehanded adulterer," Admiral Lord Nelson, who symbolizes British imperialism, and by having two elderly women climb up it and spit plum pits on the people below (*U*, 121). In *The Second Coming* Yeats proclaims famously that "the centre that cannot hold," but in the city of the modernist novel it cannot even be located.

The visibility of realist urban space is sometimes obscured by particles: smoke in *Hard Times*, sawdust in *Our Mutual Friend*, and twelve kinds of fog in the opening of *Bleak House*, which is a metaphor for the obfuscation of the law by the Court of Chancery. In each of these novels, the particles indicate Dickens's faith that clarity of vision and understanding can be achieved; if the smoke, sawdust, and fog could be cleared away, the hidden would become apparent. Modernist urban space can be opaque and inaccessible even on a clear day, and visibility itself can be menacing. For Kafka, space is especially unknowable and unmappable. Josef K. repeatedly gets lost in cities where neighborhoods are eerie, streets are unfamiliar, and buildings are hard to find. Windows do not promote a humanizing visibility but allow threatening stares or remote gazes. His initial arrest is seen through his window by a woman standing ominously in the window opposite who is joined first by one strange man and then another each time Josef looks. His execution is observed by a vague figure who leans out of an open window but does nothing to help. His final thoughts are a flurry of questions about that figure of last hope; they are never answered. In *The Castle*, the castle itself dissolves under K.'s gaze: "the longer he looked, the less he could make out."[42] Its location is also uncertain even for locals who try different approaches without success. Kafka's Castle is an icon of the opaqueness and inaccessibility of space.

Realist urban space is continuous, and even when city life causes momentary confusion and disorientation, as in Dickens's novels, readers can rely on realist plots to restore order, so that the characters each end up living and working where they belong. That ideal of rational spatial organization was proclaimed by the Victorian moralist Samuel Smiles in 1859 – "A place for everything, and everything in its place."[43] Modernist urban space is more discontinuous and displaced, as meetings are more unpredictable, and it is less clear where anyone belongs. In the realist novel characters navigate urban space continuously as they walk or ride in horse-drawn vehicles. In the modernist novel they can travel by foot, carriage, bus, tram, automobile, or train. They receive information from telephone calls, wireless messages, multiple postal deliveries, advertising signs, newspaper headlines, movies, and chance encounters with an increasingly diverse population speaking a variety of dialects and languages. The increasing division of labor and levels of education further diversify urban space with personal interactions that therefore become less predictable. Boody Dedalus's mock prayer in *Ulysses*, "Our father who art not in heaven," although directed at her drunken father Simon, is a motto for modernist spatial dislocation as well as the loss of religious faith (*U*, 186).

Buildings and cities in realist novels stay put. Modernists occasionally move them to suit their narrative purposes, as space itself is relativized in the world where it is processed by consciousness. In *Petersburg*, buildings can be as spatially relative as the psychological framework that registers the city's dynamic activity, as when Bely locates the Ableukhov home in three different places. Proust moves Combray from southwest of Paris in the opening volumes of *Remembrance* to northeast of Paris in the last volume to situate it near Rheims, which enables him to transpose the Battle of Verdun into the Battle of Méséglise, named after a path where Marcel fell in love with Gilberte. She accentuates the madness of the war by juxtaposing it with their childhood romance along this same path, as she writes to him: "How often I have thought of you, of those walks of ours together which you made so delightful, through all this now ravaged countryside, where vast battles are fought to gain possession of some path, some slope which you once loved and which we so often explored together!" (*RP*, III, 778). Proust mocks the national narrative so shredded in the war by having great armies slaughter one another over "some path, some slope" where two children fell in love. Cities and things are as malleable as human consciousness, as he theorizes in the final lines of *Swann's Way*. "The places we have known do not belong only to the world of space on which we map them for our own convenience. None of them was ever more than a thin slice, held between the contiguous impressions that composed our life at that time; the memory of a particular image is but regret for a particular moment; and houses, roads, avenues are as fugitive, alas, as the years." Marcel's final involuntary memory is of the garden bell from his childhood at Combray, which informed him that Swann was gone and that his mother would be giving him a goodnight kiss. That sound still rings in him, and he resolves to recapture it in his novel that will "describe men first and foremost as occupying a place, a very considerable place compared with the restricted one which is allotted to them in space ... in the dimension of Time" (III, 1107). The important things do not occur in any fixed place so much as in the fluid consciousness of time.

In spite of continual construction in Dublin, buildings and the city itself remain stable in *Ulysses*. Joyce wrote the central episode of the novel, titled "The Wandering Rocks," using a map of Dublin, Thom's Directory of Dublin Businesses, and a stopwatch to calculate the precise time it would take for characters to make their way from point to point.[44] But in that fixed cityscape Bloom's consciousness wanders all about his past and future and the entire world to the far reaches of the universe. The name of the episode refers to the treacherous Wandering Rocks of Greek myth (probably the Straits of Bosporus) that supposedly shifted position in the mist and could sink ships. In *Ulysses* they are both the confusing signs that complicate Dubliners' activities and the formal techniques that confuse readers' comprehension. Joyce uses them also to integrate simultaneous activities in different places that were distinctive to the modern city.[45]

Simultaneity is spatial and temporal. It is the experience at one moment of two or more sensations from different places or times. Throughout history, people could always hear voices in a duet simultaneously but could not exchange spoken words between distant cities simultaneously. In the modern period new communication technologies made something like that possible for the first time in history as they detached communication from transportation and expanded the spatial range of instantaneous communication. In 1876 the telephone made it possible to hear and speak to a person instantaneously across many miles. By 1893 a telephone news service in Budapest sent "broadcasts" to 6,000 subscribers, unifying the city simultaneously. In 1895 cinema created new ways of representing visual simultaneity as quick-cut editing made it possible to show an action from several angles with such speed that viewers seemed to experience them all at once. In 1896 the wireless made it possible to send Morse code to many places simultaneously, including ships at sea. The goal of World Standard Time was established at an international conference in 1884 but was not fully activated until July 1, 1913, when the Eiffel Tower sent a time signal that was transmitted instantaneously around the world. Journalists celebrated the new simultaneity, noting that electronic communication had "annihilated" time and space. In 1913 the futurist Gino Severini wrote: "Today, in this epoch of dynamism and simultaneity, one cannot separate any event or object from the memories, the plastic preferences or aversions, which its *expansive action* calls up *simultaneously* in us."[46] The historian Pär Bergman, who researched simultaneity in France and Italy between 1909 and 1914, concluded, hyperbolically, that during these years "succession gave way to simultaneity."[47]

In realist novels, events occur only in one place at a time. Realists rendered simultaneity with new beginnings of alternate plots or with verbal directions introduced by "meanwhile" phrases. Flaubert experimented with more immediate simultaneity in *Madame Bovary* with quick cuts between Rodolphe's romancing of Emma and officials' announcing prizes for pigs and manures. Modernists devised a number of innovative ways to capture simultaneity in poems, plays, music, cinema, paintings, and sculpture, as new technologies provided the means by which the idea of simultaneity came into prominence and the experience of it became an everyday reality.[48] Joyce was especially responsive to these technologies: *Ulysses* references wireless twice, gramophones seven times, telephones eight times, newspapers eighteen times, and the telegraph twenty times. Oddly, the novel makes no reference to cinema even though Joyce was profoundly influenced by it. In *Ulysses* he adapted cinematic montage techniques to the written word to capture Dublin's riotous simultaneity.

His "Wandering Rocks" episode offers the most historically distinctive rendering of urban spatiality of the modernist period in ways that, as a set of techniques, were inconceivable fifty years earlier. There Joyce draws on various montage, collage, and stream-of-consciousness techniques to compress space and time in nineteen sections that focus on different individuals or groups. The most distinctive innovations are the interpolations or montage-like interruptions in the narrative that capture simultaneity in a variety of ways beginning with simple repetition of the same event that the narrative had sketched previously. Dislocative interpolations introduce simultaneous events that occur elsewhere in the city and have a similar function, such as Bloom buying soft porn for Molly while elsewhere at the same time Boylan buys her fruit. Many people observe the same thing simultaneously as two carfuls of tourists view the Bank of Ireland. Other groups hear simultaneously an ambulance speeding through Dublin or the last-lap bell of a bicycle race. The race is sequential but still suggests simultaneity as does the movement of the river Liffey. Joyce invokes its unifying function by charting the progress of a handbill that Bloom tosses into it as it flows through the city. Simultaneity spans space as well as time as street names and monuments conjure up the spatial source of English authority in Ireland and the historical origins of Dublin's colonial status.

Simultaneity is also suggested by journeys that begin and end the episode. While these are sequential, Joyce works to suggest the simultaneous interaction of the individuals making those journeys and Dubliners responding to them. At the outset Father Conmee's journey through Dublin by foot and tram suggests the ubiquitous role of the Church around the city as he exchanges perfunctory greetings with people. As the narrative describes him crossing Mountjoy square, it is interrupted with an interpolation (the first of thirty-one in the episode) about Dennis Maginni, a professor of dancing, who has nothing to do with Conmee and is walking at Dignam's Court on the other side of town. Joyce throws another rock or trap, as they are called, in the way of the reader with that use of *Dignam* that conjures up Paddy Dignam whose funeral Bloom attended earlier in the day, and whose son Patrick, now orphaned, is the purpose of Conmee's trip to an orphanage to secure a placement. The episode ends with the Viceroy's cavalcade through Dublin that occasions a sequence of simultaneous interactions between the Viceroy's carriage and many city inhabitants who register a spectrum of mainly disrespectful responses to this symbol of British imperialism as they forget to salute, can't see, smile coldly, just miss, gaze down, and offer the backside of trousers passing through a door. These two journeys unite the city with their variously deficient simultaneous exchanges regarding the all-embracing institutions they symbolize.

The three changes in the rendering of space I have surveyed responded to a variety of historical developments. The new sense of space's constitutive function was influenced by developments in physics, geometry, biology, sociology, philosophy, painting, sculpture, and architecture. In place of conventional narratives set in empty, inert space and based on hierarchized traditional spaces such as the metropole and the colony, modernists crafted narratives in dynamic spaces of a less Eurocentric world. *Heart of Darkness* signaled that space was no longer an empty container in which European hegemony could be played out, but a dimension of experience that actively challenged and reshaped the institutions and values of imperialism. Forster's Marabar Caves redressed British chauvinism with their potent darkness and unnerving "ou-boum" echo that absorbed and negated whatever insulting or dehumanizing words were uttered into them. Interiorization was achieved with impressionism, free indirect discourse, and stream-of-consciousness techniques, which modernists who were influenced by new findings in psychology and philosophy used to capture the workings of the mind. Interiorization dramatized how individuals experienced the chaotic outer world. The urban setting was a historically distinctive space reconfigured by crowding and new communication and transportation technologies along with structural transformations of growing governmental and economic bureaucracies. That new space included a more gridlike structure, redirection upward in response to skyscrapers and airplanes, obfuscation of a clear center, different sources of visual obstruction and different meanings of surveillance, greater spatial discontinuity and unpredictability, instability of buildings and cities, and an expanded range of simultaneity. These developments are substantive aspects of the modern city, and their presentation in novels enlisted a variety of innovative formal techniques including montage and collage.

The most historically significant aspects of the spatiality of modernist novels are the formal innovations used to craft those spaces. The substantive spatial changes are unmistakably historical in a trivial and obvious way by virtue of the fact that they existed in different times, while the formal changes with transformed spatialities are more significantly historical. Thus the modernist city could be depicted with realist formal techniques, as indeed it was in numerous formally conventional novels from the modernist period, but it is inconceivable that the space of any city could have been depicted in 1850 the way Joyce did it in his "Wandering Rocks" episode.

CHAPTER 4

Time

The story time of narratives is uniform and chronological. Text time is the modification of story time in the telling. Four major aspects of it vary in the modernist period – orientation, pace, continuity, and order.[1]

Realist novels situate events in a time that moves in a sequence of present moments that recede into the past and advance into the future. Past-tense verbs knit the story together as a completed and knowable history.[2] These novels pace events through considerable lengths of characters' lives with summaries and scenes, punctuated by gaps over time intervals and pauses that expand on moments. Although the summaries cover different time periods at different paces, and narratives are interrupted by gaps and pauses, their underlying time frames are continuous. Realist text time follows chronological order with occasional disordering analepses and prolepses.[3] Modernists rework these four main aspects of text time and in so doing rework the temporal foundation of the master narratives.

ORIENTATION: VALORIZING THE PRESENT

In contrast to the realists' fluid movement of stories from past to present to future, modernists often focus on the present.[4] In 1906, while writing *The Making of Americans*, Stein reconfigured realists' tracking of the story across the entire time span by replacing past-tense verbs with gerunds and present participles and by repeatedly returning to the beginning of story lines – as she put it, by "beginning again." The gerund in her title is ironic. The "making" of the Hersland family never has a chance to be completed because the text repeatedly returns to the beginning of each narrative line. For 925 pages Stein resisted allowing her characters to change substantially and instead repeats the narrative of their lives in the present moment rendered with gerunds and participles.

In *Melanctha* Stein adapted the continuous present tense and repetition of adverbials of time with the formula "always now" to capture how characters and marriages never get beyond their core nature as defined at some arbitrary moment. Melanctha's troubled marriage with Jeff cannot change significantly because it is, like the structure of Stein's narrative time, stuck in a continuous present, repeatedly beginning again. Thus, "Always now when Jeff was wondering, it was Melanctha he was doubting, in the loving ... Always now he did not know really, if Melanctha was true in her loving."[5] Jeff in his insecure relationship with Melanctha remains paralyzed, as is captured by dozens of sentences beginning with "always now" that underscore the predominance of now moments. The reader's frustration with such repetition mirrors the characters' struggles to free themselves from the pin of a character type that holds them in place as they wriggle about, endlessly repeating with slight variations the same predictable words and unproductive behavioral patterns.

In a lecture of 1935, Stein stated the purpose of this technique as to reject "the inevitable narrative of anything, of everything succeeding something ... in anything having beginning and middle and ending."[6] She avoided narrative succession because she saw individuals locked in repetitive patterns that went nowhere and were distorted by narrative conventions of cause and effect, beginning and ending, even temporal succession. Stein's signature phrase, "A rose is a rose is a rose," which she first published in 1922, paralyzed narrative progression and invited one to see a rose in the here and now undistorted by personal memory, botanical knowledge, or poetic tradition.[7] In response to a question at another lecture, she explained that "when the language was new – as it was with Chaucer and Homer – the poet could use the name of a thing and the thing was really there ... [but] after hundreds of years had gone by and thousands of poems had been written, he could call on those words and find that they were just wornout literary words ... Now the poet has to work ... to get back that intensity into the language ... I'm no fool. I know that in daily life we don't go around saying 'is a ... is a ... is a ...' but I think that in that line the rose is red for the first time in English poetry for a hundred years."[8] Stein valorized the present in both story time and text time. She believed that although people in fact and in story time live with present experiences passing into the past and moving into the future at the same rate as clocks tick, their subjective experience of movement through time is one of doubling back, repetition, and stultifying patterns chronically locked in the present.

Some characters have a sense of being locked in the present from repetition. In *The Magic Mountain* Mann's characters order their lives according to clock time but experience its passing subjectively, according to circumstance. Repetition at the tuberculosis sanatorium generates boredom that makes the present loom up as something that will last for a seeming eternity. "Someone brings you your midday soup, the same soup they brought you yesterday and will bring again tomorrow. And in that moment it comes over you – you don't know why or how, but you feel dizzy watching them bring in the soup. The tenses of verbs become confused; they blend and what is now revealed to you as the true tense of all existence is the 'inelastic present,' the tense in which they bring you the soup for all eternity" (*MM*, 217–18).

Other modernists rendered the present full of riches. Woolf, Joyce, Faulkner, and even Proust viewed the present as a vibrant locus of experience for the story time as it bulked up the text time of their novels. During a stroll in Westminster, Mrs. Dalloway is immersed in her immediate surroundings of people, buildings, and trees: "What she loved was this, here, now, in front of her" (*MD*, 9). A similar thought returns in Regent's Park: "life itself, every moment of it, every drop of it, here, this instant, now, in the sun" (79). The proximity of death in her thoughts, intensified after learning of Septimus's suicide, valorizes being alive in the present, which Woolf inventories with loving care as though every chance composition of persons and objects were a possibility of joy, an artistic masterpiece.

Joyce celebrates the present through Bloom, who brings himself back from a depressing reflection on the "grey horror" of a desolate past in ancient Palestine with the thought, "Well, I am here now. Yes, I am here now" (*U*, 50), and through Stephen who urges, "Hold to the now, the here, through which all future plunges into the past" (153). Joyce's characters open their eyes and ears to a vibrant present which overwhelms scraps of the past or wispy projections into the future. Several of his techniques evoke the here and now: epiphanies, interpolations, parallel cutting, and stream-of-consciousness reconstructions of what his characters experience minute by minute. *Ulysses* is a series of stops in Stephen's and Bloom's here and now, to watch a dog gambol across the strand or the silk-stockinged leg of a woman getting into a carriage, hear a familiar song or a distant train whistle, savor a glass of beer or a gorgonzola sandwich.

In an interview of 1956 Faulkner said that "there is no such thing as *was* – only *is*. If *was* existed there would be no grief or sorrow."[9] He underscored the daunting fullness and chaos of the present moment in the opening narrative of *The Sound and the Fury* through the mind of the mentally retarded Benjy, who is stuck in the present moment without any clear sense of the temporal ordering of past and future even as he is awash with memories stretching back thirty years. While Benjy remains overwhelmed by the present because of mental illness, other characters share the "radiant, violent, unmanageable" nature of present moments that also carry the potential of future interpretation into powerful and meaningful experiences.[10] Proust's famous exhortation, "the only true paradises are the paradises we have lost," suggests that the past is the repository of ultimate joy; but experiences first time around are flat compared with their re-emergence in subsequent present moments, which are the site of increasing richness every time they surface in moments of heightened awareness (*moments bienheureux*) during involuntary memories.

The valorization of the present in novels also challenges the time frame of the master narratives that are structured as a span of important periods of past, present, and future. Stein addresses the family and courtship narratives paralyzed by chronic repetition of past destructive patterns and led astray by self-deceiving illusions of progress. Mann critiques all the master narratives in dialogues between the sanatorium inmates Leo Naphta and Ludovico Settembrini, who remain locked in debates on love, justice, religion, politics, and history. Woolf and Joyce confound the predictable timetables of the tram routes of the city life by dwelling on their protagonists' unpredictable urban experiences.

The English vorticists affirmed the present in their journal, *Blast*, that first appeared on the eve of war in June 1914. The editor Wyndham Lewis announced that vorticists "stand for the Reality of the Present – not for the sentimental Future, or the sacrosanct Past." Vorticists want to "Blast years 1837–1900." The central image of their art, the vortex, is a meeting point of forces in the here and now that "plunges to the heart of the Present." Vorticists view everything absent – past or future – as a negation of life.[11] Pound underscored that same view in 1915, announcing, "We are 'vorticists' ... The past and the future are two brothels created by nature ... Art lives only by means of the present."[12]

Secular existential philosophy also prized the present. Absent a divine view from eternity, the present became an especially important locus of experience. Nietzsche was troubled by preoccupation with past sins that overload the present with guilt as well as nostalgia that overwhelms the present with fantasies of a lost golden age. The greatest drawback of the past is that it cannot be changed. In *Zarathustra* he theorizes that one must expropriate that burden and make the "it was" one's own. "To recreate all 'it was' into 'thus I willed it' – that alone should I call redemption."[13] His motto *amor fati* (love of fate) is not about resignation, but creation, making the here and now something to celebrate. "My formula for greatness in a human being is *amor fati:* that one wants nothing to be different, not forward, not backward, not in all eternity. Not merely bear what is necessary, still less conceal it ... but *love* it."[14] His frequently misunderstood doctrine of eternal recurrence is not so much a cosmology of cyclic history as a test for the fullness of existence. That is, *if* one knew that this present moment would recur eternally, would one feel despair or joy? The most fully realized person, the overman, would feel joy. Zarathustra concludes that one must take responsibility for one's present existence and affirm it joyfully, "pregnant with lightning bolts that say Yes and laugh Yes" and affirm wildly "the ring of recurrence."[15] Thus does Nietzsche substitute a human present for both the cosmic time frame of the religious narrative and the eternal now of the divine mind.

Modernists did not deny the influence of the past on the present but refused to have their characters overwhelmed by family tradition, social convention, national heritage, or religious guilt. They had hope but refused to be distracted from living fully in the present by dwelling on the future, let alone a heavenly afterlife. To those subversive ends, the text time of their novels paused to dilate the present of their characters by means of a continuous present tense, beginning again, the inelastic present, moments of being, and *moments bienheureux*.

PACE: FASTER, SLOWER, MULTIPLE

To vary the steady pace of story time, realists used gaps to jump over unimportant events and pauses to elaborate important events. Modernists frequently transposed those functions with gaps over crucial events and extensive pauses over seemingly insignificant ones. They also innovated formally with accelerated pacing, decelerated pacing, concurrent multiple pacing, and serial multiple pacing.

Life in the realist and modernist periods proceeded according to the same objective time frame with sixty minutes in every hour. The subjective sense of pace, however, accelerated in the modernist period from new technologies and techniques that sped up the movement of people and information across ever larger spaces. Ocean liners, bicycles, automobiles, and airplanes accelerated transportation; telephones, wireless, newspapers, and cinema accelerated communication; and time management, assembly lines, and vertical and horizontal integration accelerated production. While some were distressed by these changes, others were thrilled. By 1909 futurists celebrated speed as the defining feature of the age and the preferred subject of art. As Marinetti announced: "We say that the world's magnificence has been enriched by a new beauty; the beauty of speed.

A racing car . . . is more beautiful than the *Victory of Samothrace*."[16] Musil
documented that acceleration more ominously in *The Man Without
Qualities*, which begins with a sketch of modern big cities – "of irregularity,
change, forward spurts, failures to keep step, collisions of objects and
interests." Ulrich is introduced at home in Vienna, "ticking off on his
stopwatch the passing cars, trucks, trolleys, and pedestrians . . . timing
everything whirling past." Fast as pre-war Vienna had become, many
dreamed of a faster pace with "air trains, ground trains, underground trains,
and people mailed through tubes special-delivery" (*MQ*, 1, 4, 6, 27).

Some modernists accelerated syntax in response to the new technologies.
In 1913, Marinetti applied that new speed to language itself with a manifesto
that announced "words-in-freedom" that would "destroy syntax" by doing
without adjectives and punctuation, although he continued to use both.[17]
While his proclamations exceeded the ambitions of most novelists, one
novelist did accelerate syntax. Hemingway's reduction of modifiers, simple
declarative constructions, and spare punctuation was in part a function of
his job as a reporter for the *Kansas City Star*, sending messages over the
Atlantic cable that required concision and simplicity to save money and
avoid confusion. While he presented events in his novels with conventional
pacing, his lean telegraphic style suggested an accelerated pace. Mann's
acceleration in *The Magic Mountain* was conceived to capture the rigid
scheduling and monotonous life style of the sanatorium inmates. He
explained the acceleration of text time following Hans's first three weeks
in the sanatorium, which filled over 200 pages, while the next three weeks
would be dispatched in a flash. The acceleration of text time captures the
lived time of the inmates, which all but disappears in their repetitive daily
lives that rush by with increasing speed during the full term of Hans's seven
years there. As life is emptied of variety, Mann theorized, time seems to
accelerate (*MM*, 648).

Another historical variant in pacing is a deceleration in the shortened
story time of one-day novels such as *Ulysses, Mrs. Dalloway*, and Malcolm
Lowry's *Under the Volcano* (1947), set on The Day of the Dead in 1939.
Proust's focus on simple events also necessitated a retardation, which
prompted Genette to attempt to distinguish quantitatively between the
realist and modernist periods. By comparing the number of text pages to the
time span of *Eugénie Grandet* (1833) and *Remembrance of Things Past*, he
estimated that Balzac covers about 90 days per page in comparison with
Proust's 5.5. Thus Proust's novel is on average 16 times slower than
Balzac's.[18] Proust's deceleration also increases as the novel proceeds in ever
longer gaps separating increasingly long, slow-moving scenes, mainly 5

evening parties that together take up around 450 pages. Genette concludes that Proust's pacing involves "the almost total absence of summary in the form it had during the whole previous history of the novel" and that Proust's novel is made up almost entirely of scenes in which text time approximates story time.[19]

Proust's innovative slowing is illustrated early on when Swann comes for dinner, and young Marcel is sent to bed before he gets his mother's customary goodnight kiss. Proust extends the text time for twenty-two pages to track the slow pace of Marcel's anticipated "hours of anguish" waiting for her kiss – plotting to divert her to his room, the smell of varnish on the staircase that he slowly ascends to his room, composing a note asking his mother to come to his room, further delay as the cook decides whether to deliver the note, waiting for a reply, a long digression on an analogous waiting that Swann went through years earlier when he waited in anguish for an unfaithful lover, Marcel's excitement as he hears his mother coming up the stairs after Swann has left, the unexpected joy of her deciding to spend the entire night with him, and her selecting a book to read to him before they go to sleep. The scene provides central insights into his life and the novel – that her capitulation marked the end of his childhood innocence and that life is basically about loss of love and efforts to retrieve it. Proust slows the pace of that and other scenes to show the potential richness of certain key experiences in the personal narrative that realists such as Balzac and Dickens would pass over as trivial. He differs from Stein who does not claim such significance for the banalities she repeatedly present-tenses; on the contrary, she means them to be trivial.

The slow pace of long stretches of *Remembrance of Things Past* allowed Proust to delve deeply into seemingly trivial experiences that ultimately prove to be brimming with richness, as, for example, the intricate mix of attitudes expressed by Monsieur Legrandin's wink that includes friendship, secrecy, snobbery, and affectation.[20] Joyce probes the depths of Dublin life minute by minute in reconstructing the processing of everyday experience by his characters. Faulkner plumbs the abyss of Thomas Sutpen's obsession in *Absalom, Absalom!* by repeatedly retelling Sutpen's story through different character-narrators. Henry James's "incidents" are packed with nuances that a fast-paced story would not have the time to explore.

New sorts of depth analysis are also evident in other areas of modernist culture. Between 1900 and 1905 Edmund Husserl developed the signature feature of his rigorous philosophical method, the *phenomenological reduction*.[21] It involved bracketing off or excluding from consideration dubious aspects of complex experience, such as the existence of external objects or the knowing mind, in order to focus with scrupulous rigor and at unprecedented length on the most indubitable, simple experiences such as a white sheet of paper on a desk or a melody of seven notes. In 1910 Eugen Bleuler coined the term "depth psychology" to refer to analysis of unconscious mental processes pioneered by Freud, Pierre Janet, Carl Jung, and others.[22] The depth of Freud's psychoanalytic investigations is suggested by the sheer length of his long case histories, some running to over a hundred pages, which penetrate to unconscious layers of his patients' psyches back to the furthest recesses of childhood, protected by powerful forces of repression.[23] Modernists slowed the pace of fictional narratives as well as philosophical and psychiatric inquiries to delve ever deeper into human experience.

Modernists also used multiple paces running concurrently, as in Woolf's *The Waves*: the single day of the nine interludes from dawn to sunset that introduce each chapter, the sequence of time passing represented by the days of the week, the lifetimes of the characters, and the centuries of historical time which echo through her characters such as Louis who claims to have been a great poet in the time of Elizabeth.[24] Concurrent multiple paces suggest how the master narratives pulsate concurrently through the lives of individuals according to the different tempos of courtship scenarios, family genealogies, urban dynamics, and even the cosmic time frame of the religious narrative.

A multiplicity of rhythms runs serially in *Ulysses*. The pace of the text time varies from the relatively steady "initial style" of most of the earlier episodes to the varying rhythms of the other episodes. The "Aeolus" episode is set in a newspaper office and captures the pacing of journalism with the narration chopped up by headlines. The "Lestrygonians" episode follows the rhythm of peristalsis as Bloom watches others eating: "Gulp. Grub. Gulp. Gobstuff" (*U*, 139). "Sirens" is patterned after a musical fugue. The episode in which Bloom masturbates, "Nausicaa," throbs with the paces of sexual tumescence and detumescence. "Oxen of the Sun," about a woman delivering a child, replicates the paces of gestation and parturition by recapitulating the history of the English language in adulterated imitations of evolving literary styles from Anglo-Saxon to modern American slang. "Ithaca" is a series of questions and answers about Bloom and Stephen returning to Bloom's home. These pace changes capture the clashing tempos of individual lives and public commerce.[25] Joyce offers no logical order to the rhythms and suggests diverse experiential bases, mainly bodily functions (digestion, walking, sexual excitation, gestation) and mental activities (journalism, music, science, thought). Why these different paces? Because, recalling Woolf's insistent cry, life is like that.

CONTINUITY: BROKEN WATCHES IN CONTINUOUS TIME

Joyce begins the "Proteus" episode in Stephen's mind with the phrase, "Ineluctable modality of the visible." If Stephen closes his eyes, the world around him continues ineluctably. "Open your eyes now ... See now. There all the time without you: and ever shall be, world without end." Hearing reveals an "ineluctable modality of the audible" (31). We can shut our eyes or cover our ears but not stop the sights and sounds that mark the continuous passage of experience in public time. Joyce revels in the word *ineluctable* because it emphasizes the relentless continuity of experience.

William Everdell presents considerable evidence to show that "the heart of modernism is the postulate of ontological discontinuity."[26] In contrast to the temporal models of nineteenth-century thought based on "evolution, fields, seamlessness, and *Entwicklung*," he argues, modernists identified discrete entities such as neurons and genes that indicated discontinuities in nerve impulses and hereditary transmission where nineteenth-century scientists had presumed continuities. Modernist physicists theorized about quantized subatomic events, where classical physics had presumed continuous movement and energy levels. Modernist painters developed discontinuous techniques of pointillism and collage, presumably to replace traditional painterly techniques such as *sfumato* and atmospheric perspective. Everdell's examples, however, are of spatial entities and art forms and so do not address the fundamental continuity of time no matter how fragmented the entities or how disrupted the events that occur in it may seem. His reference to ontology suggests that modernists discovered the fundamental discontinuity of temporal existence, but ontological temporal discontinuity is impossible and so is not subject to historical change.

The time of experience remains fundamentally continuous throughout the realist and modernist periods, but novelists render time differently. For realists continuous time remains absolute and relatively unquestioned. Modernists question time more seriously by devising techniques to suggest discontinuity. The only way for time to be discontinuous is to stop, but such a stop must endure, and that enduring would take time. Modernist stops are seeming, not actual. Death ends lives, but time does not stop. Wars disrupt routines, but life even in the trenches proceeds in continuous time however traumatized the mind experiencing it may be. In *To the Lighthouse*, Mrs. Ramsay dies in what is arguably the single most historically distinctive and stunning sentence in the modernist novel:

[Mr. Ramsay, stumbling along a passage one dark morning, stretched his arms out, but Mrs. Ramsay having died rather suddenly the night before, his arms, though stretched out, remained empty.] (*TL*, 128)

Her death is historical in the way it disrupts the narrative in an adjectival phrase in a single sentence, about Mr. Ramsay stumbling along a passage with his arms outstretched, which suddenly erupts with an announcement of the death of the novel's protagonist half-way through the novel. This short, bracketed paragraph breaks into the narrative the way death often breaks into life, shockingly, with no seeming connection to what came before, analogous to what the war did to everyday life on a large scale. First-time readers no doubt read that sentence several times to make certain that Mrs. Ramsay was actually dead. Another bracketed passage breaks into the narrative with the announcement of a number of deaths in the war.

[A shell exploded. Twenty or thirty young men were blown up in France, among them Andrew Ramsay, whose death, mercifully, was instantaneous.] (133)

The blatantly ironic speculation that Andrew's death was, in the euphemistic language of the British War Office, "mercifully . . . instantaneous" contrasts with the merciless reality of front-line injuries that left uncounted men dying slowly and in agony, sometimes hanging alive on barbed wire for days. But neither Mrs. Ramsay's death nor the wartime slaughter could stop the continuous running of time. The section in which these passages occur, titled "Time Passes," creates an impression of discontinuity with abrupt interruptions in six such bracketed passages about the fate of the Ramsays' marriage and children but framed in an actual time that passes continuously throughout.

Modernists symbolized temporal discontinuity with broken watches. Hans Castorp's watch breaks, but he does not get it fixed because mechanical timekeeping has become irrelevant in the sanatorium. Bloom's watch stops coincidentally at 4:30, which he guesses is when Molly and Boylan had sex, marking an end to her commitment to marital fidelity. In *The Sound and the Fury* Quentin is introduced listening to the ticking of his grandfather's watch that his father gave him so that he would not remember time, but forget it. Even so, Quentin cannot forget the wedding of his sister Caddy two months earlier, which darkened his love for her. He wants not just to stop time but to turn it back to her virginal days. He steps through a doorway and then back inside to make his shadow retreat, as if that might magically reverse time. The failure of that pathetic gesture triggers another obsessive memory of her wedding. Then he twists off the hands of his watch's face, but it keeps ticking. Realizing the impossibility of stopping time, let alone turning it back, he ultimately commits suicide in a supreme effort to stop time. Although mechanical timekeepers stop for each of these characters, time itself remains continuous.

Another modernist effort to stop timekeeping technology is set on a world stage in a broad historical context. In Conrad's *The Secret Agent* (1907), the apprentice anarchist Mr. Verloc, to prove himself a reliable *agent provocateur,* undertakes to blow up the Greenwich Observatory, which made solar readings from which time signals were established and sent to the Eiffel Tower and from there beamed around the world as the source of World Standard Time. Verloc fails in his effort to stop the source and symbol of world time, a brilliantly symbolic anarchist objective, because on the way to the observatory his brother-in-law Stevie trips while carrying the bomb and blows himself up. Conrad's narrative, however, is as continuous as the story time that spans the episode.

World War I created a large-scale impression of discontinuity on the national level. In the foreword to *The Magic Mountain*, Mann wrote what many thought – that the war created "a rift that has cut deeply through our lives and consciousness." Discussions of the war among observers as well as later scholars abound with imagery of discontinuity with rifts, gaps, and cataclysms. Paul Fussell claims that World War I disrupted older notions of a seamless history running from past to future.[27] Samuel Hynes's interpretation of *Parade's End* offers a similar picture. In that novel Ford documented substantive disruptions during the war: "telephone connections don't connect, military communications fail, letters are not delivered." Ford also tried to capture the discontinuity formally with impressionistic fragments, time shifts, multiple perspectives, and ellipsis dots denoting breaks in individual thought. Hynes views the novel as quintessentially modernist, which he defines as "the forms that post-war artists found for their sense of modern history: history seen as discontinuous, the past as remote and unavailable, or available only as the ruins of itself."[28] The war indeed shattered notions of purpose in history and the sense of temporal continuity, but not its actuality, because those changes could not be intelligible unless public time ran continuously. It was precisely the contrast between the seamless running of public time and the disruptive events that took place in it that made the war experience so jarring.

Realists and modernists alike rendered lives interrupted by sudden events – inheritance and bankruptcy, love and loss, revolution and war. What does change is the way modernists suggested that time itself, sometimes symbolized by broken watches, was disrupted by the disrupting events that took place in it. The central irony here is that the modernists' success at suggesting such temporal discontinuity was only possible because the dimension of time in which those events took place continued to roll on ineluctably.

ORDER: ACHRONY, REPETITION, TRAUMA, EPIPHANY

Story time is ineluctably ordered chronologically (a, b, c). Text time can modify chronology with analepsis (b, c, a), prolepsis (a, c, b), and repetition (a, b, a). This section surveys modernist achronological orderings.

The compelling logic for making sense of history is chronology. As Wilhelm Dilthey noted early in the modernist period, autobiography is the foundation for knowing, because the things we know best are the events of our own lives that take place in strict chronological order.[29] Modernists' achronology was suggested by two developments beginning in 1896 when the first moving picture was publicly shown and Freud first used the word psychoanalysis, both suggesting unprecedented temporal possibilities. Montage editing enabled editors to cut a moment out of a film sequence and splice it elsewhere in the sequence, and projectors could run film backwards to make a flower turn back into a bud. Before cinema, no one had actually seen such a reversal. Freud viewed the mind at the unconscious level as functioning without regard to chronology. *The Interpretation of Dreams* surveyed how orderly sequences in conscious life are rearranged by the dreaming mind. In 1920 he explained that unconscious mental processes are "timeless," because "the idea of time cannot be applied to them."[30] He also integrated numerous temporal sequences in his case histories. They offered a composite narrative of at least seven competing orders in which events occurred in real life, became traumatic, manifested themselves as symptoms, were reordered in dreams and symptoms, were related to Freud during sessions, were dealt with in therapy, and were presented in a case history. Peter Brooks relates Freud's case histories to the modernist novel directly: "Like the modernist novel, Freud's case history of the Wolf Man shows up the limits of storytelling while nonetheless insisting that the story must get told. The plots of narrative have become extraordinarily complex, self-subversive, apparently implausible. They have been forced to abandon clear origins and terminations in favor of provisional closures and fictional inceptions; their causes may work by deferred action and retroaction; their connections are probable rather than logical."[31]

Modernists resisted the relentless organizational principle of chronology and with it the implied sense of purpose that chronology held together. Musil identified the importance of chronology through Ulrich, who thinks about its powerful appeal, its function in conventional novels, its absence in his own life, and how people cling to it in defiance of increasing public disorder. "It struck [Ulrich] that when one is overburdened and dreams of simplifying one's life, the basic law of this life, the law one longs for, is nothing other than that of narrative order that enables one to say: 'first this happened and then that happened' . . . It is the simple sequence of events in which the overwhelmingly manifold nature of things is represented in a unidimensional order . . . stringing all that has occurred in space and time on a single thread which calms us . . . Lucky the man who can say 'when,' 'before,' and 'after'!" Bad things may happen, "but as soon as he can tell what happened in chronological order, he feels as contented as if the sun were warming his belly. This is the trick the novel artificially turns to account." People love chronology because "the impression that their life has a 'course' is somehow their refuge from chaos." Ulrich realizes that "he had lost this elementary, narrative mode of thought to which private life still clings, even though everything in public life has already ceased to be narrative and no longer follows a thread, but instead spreads out as an infinitely interwoven surface" (*MQ*, 1, 708–09). Identifying chronology as an "impression" that salvages meaning out of chaos, a "trick" that novelists use to engage readers "artificially," Musil denies it to his protagonist and has him reflect on the huge efforts people make to sustain it in the face of chaos.

Realists varied chronology to fill in a back story, shift the point of view, or heighten expectations of the future. Modernists varied it for those purposes but also to capture how the mind ranges erratically about the temporal spectrum. Even as their characters celebrate the present, as with Clarissa's cry "this, here, now," they also recall the past and anticipate the future. Proust's narrator uses achrony as a way out of the inexorable order of time passing. Swann is trapped in time, forever chasing a love that is shut out of his life because he allowed it to be welded to the indelible memories of Odette's infidelities. Marcel succumbs to similar scenarios with Gilberte and Albertine but eventually finds relief in involuntary memories. Ultimately he frees himself actively when he discovers how to expropriate time by embedding it in a work of art about the recapture of time lost.

Proust's narrative of this effort is a profusion of achronological possibilities. It begins with an undated first period of Marcel's childhood when he "used to go to bed early" and suffered from insomnia. The second moment recounts an earlier period of his childhood including when his mother kissed him and spent the entire night with him. The third moment moves ahead to the madeleine episode, followed by a lengthy return to his childhood at Combray, then forward to his initial sleeplessness, followed by a long retrospective about

Swann's love for Odette before Marcel was born, and finally a seventh episode of Marcel's adolescent love for Gilberte in Paris. Thereafter the major sections follow chronology but contain countless analepses and prolepses, including prolepses within analepses and vice versa. These structure this novel, exemplifying the complex dimension of time that Proust held to be life's essence.

The most bewildering modernist achronology is the first narrative in *The Sound and the Fury*, which in seventy pages shifts back and forth over a hundred times among eight major moments between 1898 and 1928, sometimes in the middle of a sentence, as these moments merge in Benjy's disordered mind. As Faulkner explained, "To that idiot, time was not a continuation, it was an instant, there was no yesterday and no tomorrow, it all is in this moment, it all is [now] to him. He cannot distinguish between what was last year and what will be tomorrow, he doesn't know whether he dreamed it, or saw it."[32] Faulkner used italics, he explained on another occasion, "to indicate to the reader that this idiot had no sense of time. That what happened to him ten years ago was just yesterday."[33] Faulkner goes to such lengths with achronology to dramatize not just Benjy's pathology, but through it the unraveling of the Compson family built around the Cavalier and Victorian legacies that were losing their ability to sustain the values and temporal ordering of the Old South.[34] These thirty years of Compson decline include alcoholism, illness, deaths, funerals, cemetery visits, even buzzards devouring carrion, and most poignantly the end of Caddy's sexual innocence that drives Quentin to suicide and torments Benjy who registers it in noticing that she no longer smells like trees in the rain.

In recalling his work with Conrad, Ford explained the importance of their subverting chronology: "It became very early evident to us that what was the matter with the Novel, and the British novel in particular, was that it went straight forward, whereas in your gradual making acquaintance with your fellows you never go straight forward. You meet an English gentleman at your golf club ... You discover, gradually, that he is hopelessly neurasthenic, dishonest in matters of small change, but unexpectedly self-sacrificing, a dreadful liar but a most painfully careful student of lepidoptera ... To get such a man in fiction you could not begin at his beginning and work his life chronologically to the end. You must first get him in with a strong impression, and then work backwards and forwards over his past."[35]

Ford applied this technique in de-chronologizing the courtship narrative. The first-person narrator of *The Good Soldier*, John Dowell, shifts about in time to make sense of two flawed marriages that he comes to understand in stages, and never fully. Dowell concedes that "when one discusses an affair – a long, sad affair – one goes back, one goes forward. One remembers points that one has forgotten and one explains them all the more minutely since one recognizes that one has forgotten to mention them in their proper places and that one may have given, by omitting them, a false impression."[36] While the events occur chronologically, the characters become aware of the lies that confound their love stories, which necessitate repeated looping back and leaping forward to make sense of an itinerary that generates lies, betrayal, insanity, and suicide. Not all love stories are this choppy, but Dowell's repeated unsuccessful efforts to get the time straight implies that individual courtship narratives cannot be told straight but rather achronologically.

Conrad also used a strong opening impression for Lord Jim, whose story is told achronologically. In 1900 transportation and communication technologies across the British Empire generated conflicting time frames. Sea transport was carried on by a complex system of shipping routes, refueling stations, naval ports, and merchant ships that provided a historically unprecedented network of world merchant transport but one still highly unreliable. Communication went by electronic, written, and oral means. A number of British territories lacked submarine cable connections, and those that were in place were frequently broken as were overland telegraph lines. Mail service out of London took thirty-eight days to Sydney, seventeen to India, and eight to Ottawa.[37] Gathering the facts across vast oceanic distances was precarious because information went through these mobile, heterogeneous, and uncoordinated transportation and communication systems. The novel's frame narrator spent years at sea before embarking on the story, and Marlow traveled all over Australasia gathering disparate information about Jim, who also journeyed widely.

The novel captures the "disoriented" chronology of events under these circumstances. As Michael Valdez Moses notes, "Conrad's representational techniques, such as shifting and highly mediated narration, constantly shifting point of view, and his otherwise inexplicable alternation between oral and epistolary forms of storytelling, are *the concrete manifestations of the systems of social organization and communication that prevail at the peripheries of empire*."[38] Different time frames determine Jim's fate, beginning with his initial disgrace and punishment, because when he returns to port he is unaware that the authorities already know that he had abandoned the passengers and that the *Patna* had not sunk, so he feels safe in lying that it had. After authorities revoke his navigation certificate, he attempts to outrun the communication links to some place where his dereliction of duty is unknown. Eventually he settles in Patusan (based on an island in the Dutch Indies), which, as Marlow notes, is "far from the beaten tracks of the sea and from the ends of submarine cables" (*LJ*, 357). Conrad also makes readers experience this achronology of delayed information by withholding knowledge of the *Patna*'s survival until Chapter 12. His own narrative, the narrative that Marlow attempts to construct for Jim, and the narrative of the entire British Empire are all out of order.

While achronology breaks up the imperial narrative in *Lord Jim*, it subverts the national, imperial, and capitalist narratives in Conrad's *Nostromo* (1904). Those latter narratives are embodied in Señor Ribiera, a dictator of the imaginary South American Republic of Costaguana and a pawn of international capitalists interested in silver from the San Tomé mine. Ribiera's story is presented out of order, reflecting Costaguana's political disorder. He is introduced after the lost battle of Socorro, fleeing over mountains on a mule. The nation's vulnerability to revolution is revealed by the internal narrator Captain Mitchell, who explains that Ribiera's mule died under him "at the end of the Alameda, where the military band plays sometimes in the evenings between the revolutions."[39] Revolutions are apparently as frequent as, and no more significant than, band concerts. In the next chapter Conrad begins to work back in time until a hundred pages later he presents Ribiera's rise to power propped up by international capitalists (119). A hundred pages after that another character reports on Ribiera's overthrow as having happened "yesterday" (224). Conrad's time shifts, like the history of Costaguana, travesty any sense of progress in a country gripped by unproductive revolutions and ruled by intermittent dictators vying with imperialists for silver that winds up back in the ground buried where no one will find it. This looping narrative implies that any singular logic to national and capitalist development is illusory and that revolutions circle into political chaos just as greed circles into financial collapse.

Repetition is a mental process deeply rooted in life and the foundation of social behavior. Slogans sell products, mottos identify groups, traditions galvanize loyalties, refrains complete songs and poems, myths and legends accrue authority from retelling, rituals and incantatory prayers comfort believers, and obsessive-compulsives repeat thoughts and actions for symptomatic relief. The modernist theorist who identified the instinctual compulsion to repeat is Freud. The title of the volume in which he introduced his theory, *Beyond the Pleasure Principle*, refers to the dominant motivating principle of enlightenment psychology – that people are motivated fundamentally to seek pleasure and avoid pain. But Freud found many examples of people who repeat painful experiences in nightmares and neurotic behavior as well as destructive relationships. After a long struggle to explain such self-induced anxiety in accord with the pleasure principle, in 1920 he went "beyond" it and introduced a more primordial instinct, the "repetition compulsion," which drives people to repeat earlier experiences, no matter how painful they originally were, and thereby to reduce anxiety and restore psychic equilibrium. Modernists put repetition to use in innovative ways to capture this primordial instinct.

In the realist novel, characters recall past events, and narrators retell them, but those retellings do not significantly alter the fundamental chronological order of the narrative. Modernist novelists retell stories in ways that do alter chronology, sometimes making the retelling explicit or even the novel's subject. These innovations range from Proust's use of the iterative, narrating once what happened many times ("For a long time I used to go to bed early"), to Stein's use of repetition, narrating many times what happened once.

Proust's use of iterative narrative is the subject of fifty pages of close analysis by Genette, who generalizes about its historical significance. "No novelistic work, apparently, has ever put the iterative to a use comparable – in textual scope, in thematic importance, in degree of technical elaboration – to Proust's use of it in the *Recherche du temps perdu*."[40] Proust's retelling is thus compressed into iterative narratives about what Marcel did on Sundays, every week, "for a long time," and so forth. Proust's iterative narrative dramatizes how Marcel's love is the repetition of an earlier narrative that has become attached to some fantasized, but invariably ill-suited, woman. Long after he has become indifferent to Gilberte, for example, Marcel reflects on the repetitive nature of love. "Often, our life being so careless of chronology, interpolating so many anachronisms into the sequence of our days, I found myself living in those – far older days than yesterday or last week – when I still loved Gilberte, [and] the self that had loved her, which another self had already almost entirely supplanted, would reappear, stimulated far more often by a trivial than by an important event" (1, 691). Without actually retelling, Proust introduces an innovative way to use iterative narratives to capture the repetitive nature of habit and obsession in love, a dark version of the stock courtship scenario: one of incompatible lovers endlessly repeating past failures.

Throughout *Ulysses* both pleasurable and painful memories stream into Bloom's mind and disrupt chronology. He repeatedly recalls the pleasurable moment when he proposed to Molly, and they exchanged an exceptionally sensuous kiss: "Ravished over her I lay, full lips full open, kissed her mouth. Yum. Softly she gave me in my mouth the seedcake warm and chewed. Mawkish pulp her mouth had mumbled sweetsour of her spittle. Joy:

I ate it: joy" (*U*, 144). He recalls that day eight more times with increasing poignancy as the narrative retells that peak moment through Bloom's consciousness. Molly also returns to it in her interior monologue. In one schema Joyce gave no time for her monologue, and in another schema an infinity sign – ∞.[41] It is indeed both infinite and timeless, as her mind swirls about, reworking the courtship narrative from a linear story of girl meets boy to an assortment of moments churning achronologically about the span of her entire life from her girlhood in Gibraltar, through numerous erotic fantasies and experiences, to the novel's finale in her present consciousness.

A painful thought also disrupts chronology as Bloom contemplates the meeting of Molly and Boylan. Although none of the novel's sixty-two references to Boylan by name occur in Bloom's thoughts, he nevertheless thinks of Boylan throughout the day in disruptive flashes. One especially jarring flash occurs just after Bloom has masturbated while gazing at Gerty, and he notices that his watch stopped at 4:30 – "Was that just when he, she? O, he did. Into her. She did. Done. Ah!" (303). From the interior of Bloom's mind the narrative reworks what has happened and will happen, disordering the chronological movement of the story.

While Proust and Joyce dramatize characters recalling and anticipating events, Faulkner and Stein address the narrative technique of repetition. Faulkner announces his critical view of linear sequence in *Absalom, Absalom!* through Quentin who observes, "*Maybe nothing ever happens once and is finished. Maybe happen is never once but like ripples maybe on water after the pebble sinks*" (*AA*, 210). Faulkner creates that novel out of such ripples, with narrators retelling thirty-nine times the main dramatic event – Henry's murder of Charles.[42] In *The Sound and the Fury* Faulkner tells the main story four times through different narrators. As he explains, first he wrote Benjy's narrative, "and it wasn't right, so I wrote it again, and that was Quentin, that wasn't right. I wrote it again, that was Jason, that wasn't right, then I tried to let Faulkner do it, that still was wrong."[43]

The most emphatic modernist proponent of repetition was Stein. Up to around 1908, she was distressed over the way people's lives were stultified by repeated words and feelings, but while writing *The Making of Americans* she came to see subtle varieties in apparent repetition and invoked them as a source of beauty in art and of meaning in life. In 1909, she articulated her new artistic goal: "I believe in repetition. Yes. Always and always, must write the eternal hymn of repetition."[44] The novel's subtitle, *Being a History of a Family's Progress*, is ironic because her characters' repetition seems to fore- close progress, as the family unravels from failed businesses and flawed marriages. Stein exploits repetition formally with a vengeance as she repeatedly notes how repetition defines her characters. "In the middle of their living they are always repeating, everybody always is repeating in all of their whole living but in the middle of the living of most men and many women it is hard to be sure about them just what it is they are repeating" (*MA*, 139). Eventually she does become sure that each repetition is slightly different. She gives historically unprecedented attention to the minutest changes in the simplest acts. "Slowly every one in continuous repeating, to their minutest variation, comes to be clearer to some one," and she concludes resoundingly, "repeating is a wonderful thing in being" (284).

But repetition with slight variation is not actually repeating, as she eventually acknowledged. Her attention to the slightest variation in apparent repetitions led her in 1934 to clarify that "there is no such thing as repetition." She added that actual repetition is impossible and denied that she had used it. "If I had repeated, nobody would listen. Nobody could be in the room with a person who said the same thing over and over. He would drive every body mad."[45] Reading her nearly repetitive narratives reveals two insights about human experience: the pervasiveness of repetition with ever so slight variations in people's lives and how such variations are what life is about. Her "careful listening" to those subtle differences, as she described her method, is evidence of another modernist recalibration of the scale of importance captured by her innovative technique of repetition with slight variation. She not only wrote about ordinary events as did Proust, Joyce, and Woolf, but did so about the same events again and again. Her grand history of a family narrative over several generations boils down to subtle variations in the simplest experiences of unaccomplished individuals, which she varied slightly with unprecedented tenacity. Her subversion of the scale of that narrative applies to all the master narratives so forcefully that after reading Stein, calling them "master" seems overblown.

A particularly insistent impulse toward repetition is evident in novels about traumas and epiphanies. Traumas overload the mind and cannot be processed by normal psychological means. Epiphanies I have defined, following Joyce, as "sudden spiritual manifestations." They also overload the mind in a generally pleasurable way; however, they can be disturbing, as was Stephen Dedalus's childhood epiphany about refusing to apologize, although it eventually liberated him from the institutions of home and church and was therefore ultimately uplifting if not immediately pleasurable. Put schematically, traumas close off experience, while epiphanies open it out. Both alter the time orientation of characters toward the past and necessitate achronological ordering of text time as the narrative loops back to their origins and periodic re-surfacings.

Realist novels are full of traumas that are immediately recognized as of great importance and work their damage over the years continuously at the conscious level. In *Great Expectations* Miss Havisham is jilted on her wedding night and smolders in rage for many years, fully conscious of the meaning of her disappointment and resolved to get revenge. Captain Ahab loses a leg hunting Moby Dick, immediately recognizes the loss as catastrophic, and dedicates himself to revenge, "gnawed within and scorched without, with the infixed, unrelenting fangs of some incurable idea" (Ch. 41) A dozen times Melville refers to Ahab's fixed idea as monomania, which is "the direct issue of some former woe."

In contrast, a number of distinctively modernist traumas begin with more subtle incidents that originate in childhood and gain force over time to surface years later as fully traumatic by deferred action (*Nachträglichkeit*). That term is from Freud, who in 1896 explained this mental process: "Infantile sexual experiences . . . remain without effect to begin with and only exercise a pathogenic action later, when they have been aroused after puberty in the form of unconscious memories."[46] Deferred action plays a prominent role in Freud's case history of 1918 about a man who at a year-and-a-half presumably observed his parents having sex. That puzzling but non-traumatic observation evolved into an adult neurosis, Freud argued, only after it was intensified through deferred action by his sister's seduction of him at age four, followed by sexual rejection from his maid, religious instruction from his mother that exposed him to a frightening book illustration with wolves, a terrifying dream about wolves, and a reshaping of his emergent libido toward his threatening father. These events that stimulated retrospective fantasizing about the innocuous witnessing of the primal scene brought about the adult obsessional neurosis that involved animal phobia, castration anxiety, and a bedtime ritual of repeatedly kissing all the holy pictures in his room and making signs of the cross on himself and his bed.[47]

In realist novels children are traumatized, but such incidents are immediately recognized as traumatic and never have explicitly sexual content. In *Great Expectations*, Pip's earliest memory as a young boy is being shocked in a churchyard, just after he had identified the graves of his parents and five brothers, when a huge man dressed in rags jumped out and growled that he would slit his throat if he made a sound, said that he would like to eat his cheeks, and threatened further that he would have another man cut out his heart and liver if he did not bring him a file and some food, which Pip does. This unforgettable incident loses rather than gains force over the years, although it betokens Pip's lifelong conscience and kindness and sets up the decisive, surprising revelation years later when he learns that his benefactor is not Miss Havisham but the man he helped as a boy, the convict Abel Magwitch.[48]

In contrast, modernist traumas tend to emerge from comparatively simple childhood incidents that are initially disturbing but do not reach their full traumatic potential until years later. In *The Sound and the Fury* a minor incident of the Compson children mushrooms over the years into the originary moment of the family's decline. When Caddy was seven years old (Quentin was nine, Jason was five, and Benjy was three) she got her drawers muddy, and, as she climbed a tree to see inside her home where her grandmother's funeral was taking place, her three brothers gazed up at her dirty drawers. That vision, which Faulkner reported as being the inspiration for the entire novel and the most personally moving moment in all of his novels,[49] remains fixed in the brothers' minds and gains traumatic force over the years as Caddy becomes sexually promiscuous, conceives a child out of wedlock, marries, and leaves home – actions that progressively traumatize her brothers.

In *Absalom, Absalom!* Thomas Sutpen loses another kind of innocence in a traumatic boyhood experience. Faulkner's narrator Quentin spends six pages telling his listener Shreve McCannon all the things that young Sutpen did not know prior to his trauma, including where he came from and where he was, where his clothes came from and where his father got food, how some people had property and others nothing, what he looked like, his age (somewhere between eleven and fifteen), and his confusion about why whites alternately ignore and brutalize "niggers." The trauma is relatively trivial. His father sent him to a big plantation house with a message, and a black man in livery answered the door and told him to go around back. The shock of that rebuke sets up Sutpen's adult personality and determines his dynastic ambition to make certain that nothing like that ever happens to him again. In fact it ultimately leads to murder and the failure of his dynasty. Quentin identifies three aspects of this trauma for young Sutpen: "he was seeking among what little he had to call experience for something to measure it by, and he couldn't find anything," "he knew that something would have to be done about it in order to live with himself for the rest of his life," and "it finally told him what to do that night he forgot about it and didn't know that he still had it" (*AA*, 188–92). The episode thus conforms to Freud's theory of trauma by deferred action in three ways: Sutpen has little experience to process the initial incident by normal psychological means, it becomes a core of his emerging personality, and it is temporarily forgotten but subsequently resurfaces and remains active enough to determine his tragic fate.

Realist characters experience epiphanies over something important and with clear causes such as blind Rochester's realization that the woman at his side is Jane Eyre, as he exclaims, "Great God! – what delusion has come over me? What sweet madness has seized me?" (Ch. 37). The narrator Jane relates the incident once and continues chronologically. Modernist epiphanies are different. They can originate in something that is at first barely noticed, that would seem trivial to anyone but the person experiencing it, and they are slow to gain full strength. Like modernist traumas they reshape the sense of time for characters and necessitate achronology for narrators in telling the story.

Morris Beja defines an epiphany as "out of proportion to the significance or strictly logical relevance of whatever produces it."[50] That definition fits the central epiphany of *The Magic Mountain*. At the sanatorium Hans falls in love with Clavdia Chauchat, whose gray-blue eyes remind him of how at age thirteen he had been infatuated with Pribislav Hippe, who had eyes like Clavdia's. After a year of silent infatuation, in an epiphanic moment he asked Hippe for a pencil and used it in drawing class. Hippe left school, and Hans forgot about him until his passion for Clavdia reawakened those feelings, and the two moments and love objects fused. As he explained to her: "I knew you before, from days long past, you and your marvelously slanting eyes . . . when I was still just a schoolboy, [and] I asked you for a pencil, just so I could meet you at last, because I loved you" (*MM*, 406). This boyhood incident is indeed out of proportion to his feelings for Clavdia and is further magnified when it inspires Hans's climactic epiphany in the snow. As he pulls his ski poles out of the snow they give off a blue light that reminds him of "eyes seen long ago and ineluctably rediscovered" (566). On the verge of succumbing to the cold, Hans opts for life: "*For the sake of goodness and love, man shall grant death no dominion over his thoughts. And with that I shall awaken* . . . I've long been searching for that truth: in the meadow where Hippe appeared to me, on my balcony, everywhere" (588). Hans's original epiphany of borrowing a pencil ultimately determines far larger matters of his adult love life as well as his will to live.

Proust's epiphanies emerge from trivial sensations through all five senses, and his narrator largely ignores the original experiences behind them. They are triggered by the taste of the tea and madeleines, the smell of hawthorn blossoms, the sight of sunlight streaming through trees, the whistles of pleasure boats at Balbec, and the feel of a starched napkin against his face and of the uneven paving stones underfoot in the baptistry of Saint Mark's in Venice. Marcel was only vaguely aware of boat whistles and the starched napkin. He apparently took so little notice of the uneven paving stones the first time he felt them that he did not mention them. He barely registered the origin of his most important epiphany, the taste of tea and madeleines, in that he offers no comment on it until he recalls it later.[51] These original trivial events, barely noticed the first time around, ultimately trigger the *moments bienheureux* that so transform Marcel's life. Their recapture breaks him out of relentless chronology and for that reason generate a sense of immortality, because they are "outside time," beyond time's inexorable course leading to death.

While realist joy spikes suddenly, important modernist epiphanies manifest slowly as with Lily Briscoe in *To the Lighthouse*. Her ultimate moment of vision turns on what would seem trivial to anyone else – moving a tree to complete a painting – but in time it fills out to encompass far more important matters. The day the novel begins she starts to paint a "vision which she had seen clearly once and must now grope for among hedges and houses and mothers and children" (*TL*, 53). Lily's second moment of vision occurs later that day as she thinks about the gratification she gets from her art: "In a flash she saw her picture, and thought, Yes, I shall put the tree further in the middle; then I shall avoid that awkward space" (84). She puts a salt cellar on a flower pattern in the table cloth to remind her to move the tree. Later that day as she contemplates the cruelty of love, the epiphany continues to emerge. "For at any rate, she said to herself, catching sight of the salt cellar on the pattern, she need not marry, thank heaven: she need not undergo that degradation. She was saved from that dilution. She would move the tree rather more to the middle" (102).

The revelatory nature of that compositional insight becomes apparent ten years later when she returns to the house after Mrs. Ramsay has died and the epiphany resumes its generative course. "Suddenly she remembered. When she had sat there last ten years ago there had been a little sprig or leaf pattern on the table-cloth, which she had looked at in a moment of revelation. There had been a problem about a foreground of a picture. Move the tree to the middle, she had said. She had never finished that picture. She would paint that picture now" (147). The action crescendos as creative instincts spur her on. She sits where she had been ten years earlier – facing a wall, hedge, and tree – and imagines Mrs. Ramsay and her son in the composition. "She had borne it in her mind all these years. It seemed as if the solution had come to her" (148). The climax of her epiphany completes the painting and the novel and refers indirectly to Woolf's own artistic achievement: "With a sudden intensity, as if she saw it clear for a second, she drew a line there, in the centre. It was done; it was finished. Yes, she thought, laying down her brush in extreme fatigue. I have had my vision."

This paradigmatic modernist epiphany includes distinctly modernist features: the initial event is trivial (moving a tree in a painting), the final event is trivial (drawing a line in the center of a painting), it gathers strength over a long time (ten years), and it touches on other highly important matters (love, marriage, spiritual salvation, art). The long duration of its emergence and the wide range of its impact necessitate frequent returns to it in the text. Although such retellings affect all the master narratives, the personal, courtship, and artistic ones are the most frequent formats for modernist epiphanies as they are for Lily's.

Formal innovations in the orientation, pace, continuity, and order of text time reworked the time frame of experience manifest in the master narratives. Those narratives derived from Christian universal history that emphasized an overall time from past to present to future, moving at a steady pace, continuously, in chronological order from the creation to the everlasting hereafter. Replacing that narrative, historians postulated varieties of grand narratives that unified all of history, centered in the nations of the Western world. Against the "universal" or "grand" time span of these narratives, or even the more limited time spans of the master narratives, the modernists' celebration of present moments was notably original. Stein compressed *The Making of Americans* into a collection of single moments of the continuous present. "A rose is a rose is a rose" was a slogan for the continuous present, a meditation exercise to marginalize a cliché-ridden past and fanciful future and instead focus on the here and now. Woolf's love for "this, here, now" expressed the aspiration of all those modernists who, like Conrad, wanted to "make you *see*." By focusing intently on the immediate data of consciousness, modernists invited readers to find meaning in the simple present and not look for meaning that depends on vast master narratives of heroic love, family honor, national progress, or religious salvation.

Technological developments accelerated transportation, communication, and production, creating a culture of speed on which the futurists based their aesthetic credo. Modernists captured that acceleration, but the more historically distinctive features of their pacing were the decelerations of text time in novels about a single day as well as the concurrent multiple paces in Woolf and the serial multiple paces in Joyce. Those options governing the pace of experience subverted the single steady pace of the master narratives that increasingly seemed unable to frame the shifting and idiosyncratic tempos of human experience.

The distinctly modernist modes of orientation and pace aligned with actual disruptions in the course of events to create striking examples of apparent temporal discontinuity. Although the public time frame of the story time and of the master narratives rolled on continuously, incidents such as stopped watches and a plot to blow up the Greenwich Observatory reveal modernists working to capture a sense of temporal discontinuity. One master narrative in particular was subverted by disruptive public events. The continuity of the national master narrative was snapped by the disastrous role that nationalism played in the outbreak of World War I, which exploded the idea that the history of nations was ultimately a story of progress.

Chronology is the central metaphysical scaffolding of the master narratives. Achronology, like discontinuity, negates the root word. By themselves, these words convey a nihilistic message. But modernists' subversions always implied a positive reworking, and thus their resistance to chronology was complemented by an affirmation of techniques for ordering experience based on the workings of consciousness including stream of consciousness, spatial form, interpolations, numerous techniques to capture simultaneity, and Faulkner's way of creating aesthetic order by replicating ripples on water.

CHAPTER 5

Framework

In the Western world the idea of a first and last moment is embodied in the concept of God. Those paired features are implied in the line, attributed to God and Jesus, "I am Alpha and Omega, the beginning and the ending, saith the Lord" (Revelation 1:8). Alpha and Omega, the first and last letters of the Greek alphabet, designate the comprehensiveness of a God that is all that has been and will be. Thus the phrase in Revelation implies that God is the first and last moment in time and ensures the progression of history toward a meaningful goal. This chapter considers literary beginnings and endings that derive from these concepts.

BEGINNING: IN THE MIDDLE OF THINGS

Realist narrators are likely to begin at the beginning, or at least with confident knowledge of the beginning, often with a narrative of the protagonist's parents or even earlier family history, and then introduce clearly defined characters and events in specific places and times. For example: "In the year 1815 Monseigneur Charles-François-Bienvenu Myriel was Bishop of Digne" (Victor Hugo, *Les Misérables*); "It was the opening of the season of eighteen hundred and thirty-two, at the Baths of Wildbad" (Wilkie Collins, *Armadale*, 1866); "On the 15th of September 1840, at six o'clock in the morning, the *Ville-de-Montereau* was lying alongside the Quai Saint-Bernard, ready to sail, with clouds of smoke pouring from its funnel" (Gustave Flaubert, *Sentimental Education*, 1869).

Modernist narrators are increasingly unclear about the precise origin of a story or even the possibility of there being a clear origin, and they begin their narratives *in medias res* (in the middle of things). In contrast to classical *in medias res* beginnings such as that of *The Iliad*, which eventually disclose the point of origin with flashbacks, modernist novels leave ultimate origins undisclosed and unknowable. Far from revealing a clear beginning, some modernist novels have what Melba Cuddy-Keane calls "anti-beginnings" that block out or subvert any clear beginning.[1] *Jacob's Room* begins in the middle of a sentence in a letter Jacob's mother is writing: "'So of course,' wrote Betty Flanders . . . 'there was nothing for it but to leave.'" Readers do not know, and never learn, the addressee of the letter or why Betty and her sons need to leave. *To the Lighthouse* begins in the middle of a conversation with Mrs. Ramsay's answer to a question about a planned excursion from her son: "'Yes, of course, if it's fine tomorrow,' said Mrs. Ramsay." *The Notebooks of Malte Laurids Brigge* begins with the conclusion of a thought: "So this is where people come to live; I would have thought it is a city to die in." This contrast between realist and modernist beginnings is evident in stories that begin with accounts of creative writing, childhood, adulthood, courtship, family life, rural settings, urban settings, and religion.

The epigraph to George Eliot's *Daniel Deronda* (1876) challenges this historical argument by questioning the possibility of a true beginning. "Men can do nothing without the make-believe of a beginning," she writes. "Even Science, the strict measurer, is obliged to start with a make-believe unit, and must fix on a point in the stars' unceasing journey when his sidereal clock shall pretend that time is at Nought." The difference between Eliot and the modernists is one of degree. While realist novels may not begin at the "true beginning," they do have more confident beginnings than modernist novels as is illustrated by comparing the beginning of a characteristic modernist novel with Eliot's own earlier *Adam Bede* (1859), which begins with a bold statement of narrative intention.

With a single drop of ink for a mirror, the Egyptian sorcerer undertakes to reveal to any chance comer far-reaching visions of the past. This is what I undertake to do for you, reader. With this drop of ink at the end of my pen I will show you the roomy workshop of Mr Jonathan Burge, carpenter and builder in the village of Hayslope, as it appeared on the eighteenth of June, in the year of our Lord 1799.

This novel is opened by a confident narrator who knows everything she needs to know about the place and time of her story and communicates with a readership that shares her universal time frame in the unifying calendar of "our" Lord. In her epigraph to *Daniel Deronda* fifteen years later, Eliot appears to have questioned this earlier confidence. A half-century later the narrator of Conrad's *Under Western Eyes* (1911) shattered it with a beginning that reveals profound self-doubt.

To begin with I wish to disclaim the possession of those high gifts of imagination and expression which would have enabled my pen to create for the reader the personality of the man who called himself, after the Russian custom, Cyril son of Isidor – Kirylo Sidorovitch – Razumov. If I have ever had these gifts in any sort of living form they have been smothered out of existence a long time ago under a wilderness of words.

Conrad's narrator lacks confidence in his imagination and in words. This self-critical beginning reflects Conrad's personal depression and self-doubt but also articulates a general modernist skepticism about authorial command.

The history of beginnings is strikingly evident in the introduction of protagonists in early childhood. Dickens's first-person narrator in *David Copperfield* records his own beginning with the objectivity and tone of a public records office. "To begin my life with the beginning of my life, I record that I was born (as I have been informed and believe) on a Friday, at twelve o'clock at night." In contrast, Joyce's *A Portrait of the Artist as a Young Man* begins *in medias res* with a baby's subjective experience captured in an ambiguous time with a shifting mix of voices: a third-person narrator, baby Stephen's father Simon, and a narrated version of little Stephen's consciousness.

Once upon a time and a very good time it was there was a moocow coming down along the road and this moocow that was coming down along the road met a nicens little boy named baby tuckoo . . .

His father told him that story: his father looked at him through a glass: he had a hairy face.

He was baby tuckoo. The moocow came down the road where Betty Byrne lived: she sold lemon platt.

> O, the wild rose blossoms
> On the little green place.

He sang that song. That was his song.

> O, the green wothe botheth.

When you wet the bed, first it is warm then it gets cold.

Joyce begins the novel in the middle of Simon's direct speech, but Joyce does not introduce it with any conventional tag such as "he said," nor with quotation marks. Simon's opening narrative begins with a parody of a fairy-tale opening, "Once upon a time," but promptly shades into the consciousness and language of the "nicens little boy" Stephen. The narrator explains that Stephen's father told him that story, but it is not clear if the descriptions of his father looking at him through a monocle or with a hairy face are the narrator's or baby Stephen's. The explanation that he was baby tuckoo could come from the narrator or the father. Stephen sings "his song" with an infantile lisp that renders "*rose blossoms*" as "*wothe botheth*." The tactile sensations following bed wetting are little Stephen's, although the idiom of its description is that of a narrator with the perspective of a child. These multiple voices and viewpoints capture the confusion and rich complexity of the origins of human consciousness and make this passage of considerable historical significance. Hugh Kenner argues that "every theme in the entire lifework of James Joyce is stated on the first two pages of the *Portrait*."[2]

Joyce implies that all lives emerge out of the many impressions and voices that babies register before they have language and that continue to take shape as individuals struggle to identify and articulate them. Stephen's early effort to sing is a first stage in his development as an artist and thus portends the main subject of this pioneer *Künstlerroman*. The remainder of the beginning pages anticipate the substance of the novel in referring to a family with a patriarchal father and comforting mother, a plan for Stephen to marry, Irish history and politics, guilt for unnamed sins, and a poem (his first work of art) threatening that if he does not apologize, someone will "pull out his eyes." The early language of this child will mature throughout the novel into the more complex style of a young artist.

Novels about adult protagonists show similar historical differences between realist and modernist beginnings. The first sentence that Jane Austen devotes to her protagonist in *Emma* (1816) gives details of her name, appearance, character, wealth, home situation, and age.

Emma Woodhouse, handsome, clever, and rich, with a comfortable home and happy disposition, seemed to unite some of the best blessings of existence; and had lived nearly twenty-one years in the world with very little to distress or vex her.

In *Mrs. Dalloway*, Woolf presents one of the most strikingly modernist beginnings with a protagonist who is not handsome, clever, young, happy, or comfortable in her home. Woolf's *in medias res* beginning starts with indirect speech from an unidentified protagonist to an unnamed inter-locutor, then continues with narration that conflates events at two uniden-tified places and times in a diction that shifts ambiguously between that of the protagonist and that of the narrator.

Mrs. Dalloway [who?] said [to whom?] she would buy the flowers [for what?] herself.
    For Lucy [who?] had her work cut out for her. The doors would be taken off their hinges [why?]; Rumpelmayer's men were coming. And then, thought Clarissa Dalloway, what a morning – fresh as if issued to children on a beach.
    What a lark! What a plunge! [into what?] For so it had always seemed [tense shift here to past perfect the only indication that action moves back to unidentified

moment in time] to her, when, with a little squeak of the hinges [sound that links present with past], which she could hear now [when?], she had burst open the French windows and plunged at Bourton [where? later we learn it's her parents' summer home] into the open air. How fresh, how calm, stiller than this of course, the air was in the early morning; like the flap of a wave; the kiss of a wave; chill and sharp and yet (for a girl of eighteen as she then was) solemn, feeling as she did, standing there at the open window, that something awful was about to happen; looking at the flowers, at the trees with the smoke winding off them and the rooks rising, falling; standing and looking until Peter Walsh said, "Musing among the vegetables?" – was that it? – "I prefer men to cauliflowers" – was that it?

This beginning to a story about a woman buying flowers for her party that night quakes with instability in the relationships between characters, tension between the narrator and reader, and uncertainty as to what is going on. Woolf's title and first two words suggest Mrs. Dalloway's dependency in being married to Richard, but they contrast in the fourth sentence with her more independent self as Clarissa Dalloway. A few pages later she thinks about that dependency directly: "this being Mrs. Dalloway; not even Clarissa any more; this being Mrs. Richard Dalloway" (*MD*, 11). Something awful did happen when thirty-three years earlier Peter Walsh had interrupted "the most exquisite moment of her whole life" (35) as Clarissa kissed Sally Seton on the terrace at Bourton, here recalled with another memory, also on the terrace, when she was looking at flowers, trees, and birds and Peter made a sarcastic comment about her musing among the vegetables, followed by a supercilious pronouncement about his preferring men to cauliflowers. And we still do not know how long ago it was. *Emma* begins with the protagonist clearly defined and securely stationed in a world of heterosexual love pairings. *Mrs. Dalloway* begins with a protagonist conflicted about her marital dependency, fluctuating between past and present as if in a literary double exposure, and remorseful about a suppressed lesbian love. Realists might do something similar farther into a novel but not at the beginning, which they typically rendered clearly as to time, place, and the identity of characters. Realist novels are more readily intelligible on first reading, while this opening cannot be properly understood the first time through and begins to make proper sense only on a second reading of the entire novel.

    The beginning of courtship narratives also divides between realist epistemological confidence and modernist skepticism. Jane Austen's *Pride and Prejudice* (1813) opens with the most famous generalization about courtship in the nineteenth-century novel: "It is a truth universally acknowledged, that a single man in possession of a good fortune, must be in want of a wife."

This generalization of Austen's narrator is an example of what Wayne Booth calls stable irony, which presupposes that the reader will recognize it as irony.[3] In the second sentence the narrator identifies those characters in her story who miss the irony and elaborates the consequences of that generalization for their community: "However little known the feelings or views of such a man may be on his first entering a neighbourhood, this truth is so well fixed in the minds of the surrounding families, that he is considered as the rightful property of some one or other of their daughters." While the narrator distances herself ironically from such sweeping generalizations and exposes the naiveté of those who might accept them as valid, she appears confident that she understands the dynamics and conventions of the love story she undertakes to tell as well as how clear beginnings led to present circumstances.

Modernists did not always have such confidence. Ford's *The Good Soldier* begins with two claims about the narrator's knowledge followed by four confessions of ignorance, the first of sixty-eight variants of "I don't know" that appear throughout the novel. Although Ford allows his reader to know more than his first-person narrator John Dowell, he never offers the epistemological certainty that underlies Austen's novels, choosing instead to use a self-deluded narrator to highlight Dowell's partial knowledge about the beginning and course of human relationships.

This is the saddest story I have ever heard. We had known the Ashburnhams for nine seasons of the town of Nauheim with an extreme intimacy – or rather, with an acquaintanceship as loose and easy and yet as close as a good glove's with your hand. My wife and I knew Captain and Mrs. Ashburnham as well as it was possible to know anybody and yet, in another sense, we *knew nothing* at all about them. This is, I believe, a state of things only possible with English people of whom till today, when I sit down to puzzle out what I know of this sad affair, I *knew nothing* whatever. Six months ago I had never been to England and, certainly, I had *never sounded* the depths of an English heart. I had *known the shallows* [emphases added].

This beginning is deceptive from the outset. The title of the novel is wrong, because the soldier, Edward Ashburnham, is not good: he deceives his friend Dowell, is unfaithful to his wife Leonora, drives his mistress Florence to suicide, and drives his ward Nancy to insanity. The first sentence is doubly understated because the story is not merely sad but spectacularly tragic, and Dowell did not hear it but lived it.

The beginning paragraph sets up the novel's epistemological format of sweeping generalization followed by denials, self-corrections, and skepticism about understanding love.[4] Dowell announces that he and his wife had known the Ashburnhams with extreme intimacy, but that intimacy was true

only of his wife, who was having a secret affair with Edward. Dowell adds
that he and his wife had a loose and easy acquaintance with the
Ashburnhams, but it was actually tense and uneasy. He claims that they
knew the Ashburnhams as well as it was possible to know anybody but then
reverses himself, saying that they knew nothing about the Ashburnhams.
That concession itself turns out to be partly wrong, because, without his
realizing it, his wife Florence knew a lot about the Ashburnhams through
her affair with Edward. Dowell's reference to Florence as his wife is misleading, because he never consummated his marriage and for many years
believed that his wife could not have sex because of her supposed heart
condition that he now knows to be feigned. This first paragraph reveals
Dowell's ignorance about love relations that increases throughout the novel
as he subsequently wonders, "Who in this world knows anything of any
other heart – or of his own?", and he concludes toward the end, "I don't
know. I know nothing. I am very tired . . . I don't know. I leave it to you."[5]

Realist novels about families are structured around what Patricia Tobin
calls "the genealogical imperative" that infuses family histories with causality and purpose, rooted in a determinative origin from a first couple whose
authority is centered in a founding father.[6] Such novels begin with introductory sketches of parents or more distant ancestors. The first chapter of
Martin Chuzzlewit is titled, "Introductory, concerning the pedigree of the
Chuzzlewit Family," and, although the tone is ironic, the opening line
confirms that the family's pedigree was of "extreme antiquity," while the
remainder of the chapter elaborates the details of that ancient ancestry,
albeit of dubious authenticity. The narrator of Gottfried Keller's *Green
Henry* begins by explaining, "My father belonged to the peasantry of an
ancient Alemannic village." In "the passing of centuries . . . a feudal lord
adopted the name [of the race in that village] as his title and built a castle."
Tess Durbyfield's trouble is set in motion by her father's conviction that he
is "the lineal representative of the ancient and knightly family of the
d'Urbervilles."

Modernists rejected the genealogical imperative rooted in a knowable
originary moment, documented in family Bibles, legitimized by family
pedigree, and sustained by filial devotion. In *Lafcadio's Adventures* Gide
mocks reverence for family tradition by tracing Lafcadio's heritage to an
obscure ancestor "who in 1514 married his second wife Filippa Viconti, a few
months after the annexation of the Duchy to the papal States." Interrupting
this tedious family history, the narrator critiques himself: "it would be easy,
though not very interesting, to trace the family fortunes up till 1807."[7] So he
skips two centuries and resumes with equally tedious, more recent family

background that is still irrelevant to Lafcadio's character, because he was sired by an undeterminable one of the five "uncles" his mother kept about.

Turn-of-the-century novels abound with sons rebelling against fathers, while mother-son relations remain sacrosanct.[8] Lawrence subverts that convention in *Sons and Lovers* (1913) with the destructive relationship between Paul Morel and his smothering mother. In *Ulysses* the mother-son relationship suffers through Stephen's guilt about refusing his dying mother's wish that he pray for her. Filial disrespect in the form of surprising indifference is strikingly evident in the opening paragraph of Camus's *The Stranger*.

Maman died today. Or yesterday maybe, I don't know. I got a telegram from the home: "Mother deceased. Funeral tomorrow. Faithfully yours." That doesn't mean anything. Maybe it was yesterday.

Meursault's use of the intimate and childish *Maman* raises the expectation that he will be saddened over his mother's death, but he seems indifferent. The style of these sentences that include a telegram is itself telegraphic with short, disjointed sentences and an impersonal tone. That staccato style reflects an underlying philosophy, elaborated in Camus's *The Myth of Sisyphus* (1942), that human experiences do not have clear beginnings and cannot be explained causally, and so existence cannot be justified and is therefore absurd.

Beginnings also introduce settings that change from realist objectivity to modernist immersion. Hardy's *The Return of the Native* (1878) begins with a survey of a place "perfectly accordant with man's nature."

A Saturday afternoon in November was approaching the time of twilight, and the vast tract of unenclosed wild known as Egdon Heath embrowned itself moment by moment. Overhead the hollow stretch of whitish cloud shutting out the sky was as a tent which had the whole heath for its floor.

The heaven being spread with this pallid screen, the earth with the darkest vegetation, their meeting-line at the horizon was clearly marked. In such contrast the heath wore the appearance of an instalment of night which had taken up its place before its astronomical hour was come: darkness had to a great extent arrived hereon while day stood distinct in the sky.

The entire first chapter continues this God's eye view of the heath's terrain, vegetation, and variations in light and climate. In contrast to Egdon Heath losing out to the epic encroachments of advancing civilization, in the opening lines of *The Sound and the Fury* Benjy's pasture is lost to a golf course.

Through the fence, between the curling flower spaces, I could see them hitting. They were coming toward where the flag was and I went along the fence. Luster was hunting in the grass by the flower tree. They took the flag out, and they were hitting. Then they put the flag back and they went to the table, and he hit and the other hit. Then they went on, and I went along the fence. Luster came away from the flower tree and we went along the fence and they stopped and we stopped and I looked through the fence while Luster was hunting in the grass.

"Here, caddie." He hit. They went away across the pasture. I held to the fence and watched them going away.

This novel not only begins *in medias res* but in a thoroughly mixed-up mind. Confusion abounds in the first sentence regarding who is speaking, when these events occur, what the fence encloses, what are curling flower spaces, who is hitting, and what they are hitting. Gradually readers learn that Benjy is the first-person narrator, and the day the novel opens, April 7, 1928, is his thirty-third birthday, although his mental development is that of a three-year-old. The fence encloses what had been a pasture that Benjy viewed as his own. It had been sold to become a golf course to raise money to send his brother Quentin to Harvard, the curling flower spaces are landscaping, and the hitters are golfers hitting balls. The flag in the second sentence marks a hole. The third sentence introduces Luster, a black teenager who looks after Benjy and is hunting for golf balls he can sell to earn back a lost quarter in order to buy a ticket to a minstrel show. The call to a caddie, we eventually learn, agitates Benjy, because his emotional life centers on love for his long-gone sister Caddy.

Hardy's third-person narrator sees far across the horizon from the heavens to the earth and across time. Faulkner's first-person narrator is trapped in the present moment and behind a fence, trying to comprehend with the limited vision of mental retardation, confusing everything he sees in a landscape that is threatening because it is so bewildering. A pasture that he associates with an earlier sense of being at home in the world and loved by his sister is now desecrated by strangers who are hitting, mysteriously taking flags out of holes and then putting them back, calling out the name of his beloved sister who does not respond and is nowhere in sight. Egdon Heath is a place of beauty and tranquility, threatened by an encroaching civilization in a comprehensible process that Hardy's narrator understands, while the golf course is a confusing terrain desecrated by a group of strangers endlessly hitting and moving flags for no comprehensible purpose in ways that utterly mystify Faulkner's narrator. Both initial settings portend the disruption of human relations, but one is mappable and open to the public, the other a private labyrinth of confusion. Hardy's narrator records what he sees in an inviting, easily accessible world, like a camera panning across a scene. Faulkner's mute narrator is trapped in his deficient mind, unable to describe coherently a frightening world from which he is cut off by a fence.

Urban settings divide historically in analogous ways. *Bleak House* begins with an impersonal string of noun phrases listed like items in an almanac.

LONDON. Michaelmas Term lately over, and the Lord Chancellor sitting in Lincoln's Inn Hall. Implacable November weather. As much mud in the streets, as if the waters had but newly retired from the face of the earth . . . Smoke lowering down from chimney-pots . . . Dogs, undistinguishable in mire. Horses, scarcely better . . . Foot passengers, jostling one another's umbrellas.

Dickens grounds his story in a clearly articulated, objective survey of the essential framing information to enable the reader to understand the events as they occur: city, time, buildings, environment, animals, and people. In contrast, Rilke begins *The Notebooks of Malte Laurids Brigge* in the middle of a thought about where people live in Paris, followed by a string of partial observations, half-understood actions, and reference to a map with extraneous information.

So this is where people come to live; I would have thought it is a city to die in. I have been out. I saw: hospitals. I saw a man who staggered and fell. A crowd formed around him and I was spared the rest. I saw a pregnant woman. She was dragging herself heavily along a high, warm wall, and now and then reached out to touch it as if to convince herself that it was still there. Yes, it was still there. And behind it? I looked on my map: maison d'accouchement. Good. They will deliver her – they can do that. Farther along, on the rue Saint-Jacques, a large building with a dome. The map said: Val-de-grâce, hôpital militaire. I didn't really need to know that, but all right.

Dickens's information is systematic and aspires to comprehensiveness, while Rilke's is unsystematic and fragmentary. Dickens's city confuses his characters but not his narrator. His third-person narrator is fully informed, if not omniscient, while Rilke's first-person narrator emphasizes his apprenticeship at understanding a world he is "learning to see."

In an analysis of the beginning of Eliot's *Middlemarch* (1872), Alan Palmer posits a "Middlemarch mind" through which the opening pages of the novel are captured in passages such as "and how should Dorothea not marry? – a girl so handsome and with such prospects?" (Bk. 1, Ch. 1). While the gossip-driven, custodial mind of Middlemarch seeks to bring her into the fold, Rilke's less cohesive and less caring city populace gathers about a man who fell but does nothing to help, while the anonymous staff of a maternity hospital may or may not deliver the child of an unnamed pregnant woman dragging herself along a wall, uncertain whether the wall is actually there.[9]

Nineteenth-century literary consciousness from Austen to Eliot was dedicated to men and women marrying, and realist authors structured their works from beginning to end around that unifying plot. Modernists resisted that plot, as when Rilke opened his fictional diary with a presumably unmarried pregnant woman on the verge of delivery, alone in Paris where people come to die.

Modernists rejected clear beginnings and sought ways to start their novels *in medias res* to capture an increasingly secular world where belief in ultimate origins was becoming more and more difficult to sustain. Frank Kermode argues that "the rise of what we call literary fiction happened at a time when the revealed, authenticated account of the beginning was losing its authority ... There was a long-established opinion that the beginning was as described in Genesis, and that the end is to be as obscurely predicted in Revelation. But what if this came to seem doubtful? Supposing reason proved capable of a quite different account of the matter, an account contradicting that of faith?"[10] Such skepticism is evident in the opening lines of *Ulysses*.

The religious narrative provided *the* source for beginnings in the Judeo-Christian world, starting with the seemingly simple and deeply reassuring, but ultimately mysterious, explanation in Genesis that "In the beginning God created the heavens and the earth."[11] Of course God existed before the creation, before time itself was created, in a timeless eternal realm out of which God "separated light from the darkness," but the phrase "In the beginning" continued to provide a model for the ultimate origin of the universe as human beings came to know it. The New Testament complicated the notion of a beginning by holding that Jesus was begotten by God even before the creation of the universe but then was also born to Mary in a human form in the Incarnation. Christian theology added yet another originary moment with Jesus' Last Supper and Crucifixion, which inspired the most important rite in Catholicism, the Mass that commemorates Jesus' last meal and sacrifice and effects a communion between God and humanity. Catholics believe that Jesus is actually present in the transubstantiated Host during the Eucharist, through which he re-enacts his original sacrifice that saves humankind from God's punishment and each time offers the possibility of eternal salvation anew.

Over the centuries the Mass was the grounding rite of the Catholic Church, but by the nineteenth century belief in the Incarnation and the literal presence of Jesus during the Eucharist was "disappearing" from European consciousness.[12] Most characters in realist novels are not deeply religious, and many who are have some glaring deficiency: the fanaticism of Claude Frollo in Victor Hugo's *The Hunchback of Notre Dame* (1831), the cruelty of Robert Brocklehurst in *Jane Eyre*, the jealousy of Bradley

Headstone in *Our Mutual Friend*, or the remoteness of Abbé Bournisien in *Madame Bovary*. One is hard pressed to find a mid-century realist novel that begins with and centers on a serious religious matter and is grounded in religious faith, not skepticism.[13] Trollope's *Barchester Towers* (1857) is an exception with its beginning: "In the latter days of July in the year 185–, a most important question was for ten days hourly asked in the cathedral city of Barchester, and answered in every hour in various ways – Who was to be the new bishop?" The novel exposes the ambitions and hypocrisy of individual clergy but remains respectful of the institution of Christianity, as did most realist novels. It assumes unequivocally that the question the narrator poses is important and that someone ought to and will become the new bishop.

While realists were skeptical of religious zealotry and contemptuous of religious hypocrisy, they did not go as far as did Joyce, who ridiculed the most sacred and fundamental rite in Christendom by opening *Ulysses* with a mock Mass:

Stately, plump Buck Mulligan came from the stairhead, bearing a bowl of lather on which a mirror and a razor lay crossed. A yellow dressinggown, ungirdled, was sustained gently behind him on the mild morning air. He held the bowl aloft and intoned:
– Introibo ad altare Dei.
Halted, he peered down the dark winding stairs and called out coarsely:
– Come up, Kinch! Come up, you fearful jesuit!
Solemnly he came forward and mounted the round gunrest. He faced about and blessed gravely thrice the tower, the surrounding land and the awaking mountains. Then, catching sight of Stephen Dedalus, he bent towards him and made rapid crosses in the air, gurgling in his throat and shaking his head . . .
[Mulligan continues] – For this, O dearly beloved, is the genuine christine: body and soul and blood and ouns. Slow music, please. Shut your eyes, gents. One moment. A little trouble about those white corpuscles. Silence, all.

Joyce begins his parody with Buck Mulligan as the mock celebrant. *Stately* promises respect, but *plump* emphasizes sensuous indulgence, not priestly restraint. Mulligan is wearing a dressing gown instead of an alb and chasuble, and its yellow color is unsuitable for a priest because it suggests not holiness but hellish light, degradation, and deceit. Judas is often depicted wearing dingy yellow.[14] Being ungirdled leaves Mulligan's genitals open to the morning air, contradicting chaste priestly life style and dress. The gunrest of the Martello tower is the altar, suggesting war and not peace, and his shaving bowl is the chalice. The mirror represents the paten that would normally hold the Host. It is particularly meaningful to Stephen

Dedalus, who views it as "a symbol of Irish art," although Mulligan uses it prosaically to avoid cutting himself or missing a spot. The razor symbolizes slaughter, suggesting animal sacrifices from pagan cults and the priest as a butcher. Mulligan begins with the words that open the conventional Prayers at the Foot of the Altar, "*Introibo ad altare Dei*" (I will go to the altar of God). Stephen, a reluctant server, is supposed to respond by thanking God, who has gladdened the days of his youth, but he does not reply. During the Elevation, Mulligan refers to a blasphemous feminized Host "christine" that exalts the profane female body in place of the sacred "body and soul and blood and ouns [wounds]" of Jesus. Christine also foreshadows Molly on her chamberpot in the final episode, transmuting her body into emphatically untransubstantiated menstrual blood.[15] The chalice contains shaving lather (white corpuscles) instead of red wine, and the fate of those corpuscles belittles the holiest moment in the Mass, the transubstantiation of wine into blood, as merely "a little trouble."

In form and content, Joyce's beginning undermines the fundamental structuring principle in the Western world, anchored by an ultimate beginning in divine creation and then a grounding human event in the Fall, followed by the Incarnation of a divine Jesus that restarted human time redeemed from the punishments of sin by his sacrifice, subsequently reenacted in the Mass. Joyce subverts these ultimate originary moments by profaning the religious rite that marks a new beginning of Christian hope. That burlesque of a Mass is a warmup for Joyce's vengeance against a vengeful God with a hallucination of a full-blown Black Mass in "Circe" that takes place on the body of a naked and pregnant woman as an altar and is performed by a celebrant with two left feet back to front and a carrot stuck in his grey hairy buttocks, who begins with a prayer welcoming the devil and elevates a Host dripping with blood (*U*, 489). Thus does Joyce pick up his opening blasphemy hurled against the possibility of any ultimate or sacred beginning of human salvation. Deliverance will come from art, not from Jesus' sacrifice or divine Grace.

Modernists' beginning with immersion in the plenitude of experience undermined conventional originating moments for a meaningful life. Especially vulnerable to disruption were the family and religious narratives that grounded personal identity with a legitimate family lineage or with a chronology based on divine creation or the birth of God in a human form. Subversion of the religious narrative further subverted the authority of the national narrative in monarchies that derived sovereignty from God through the doctrine of the Divine Right of Kings. Absent those conventional ideas about a primordial family ancestor, divine creation at the beginning of time, the incarnation of God in man, and a divinely justified source of the right to rule, modernists looked to everyday existence for values and meaning. They denied that Jesus was the ultimate beginning of time. Acceptance of the "death of God" took away the expectation of such a beginning but expanded time experientially by grounding it in the consciousness of mortal humans. Modernists began novels *in medias res* or with anti-beginnings to capture as realistically as possible the actual circumstance of an existence that does not begin at some precise and knowable moment but rather comes into self-awareness as an endless search for origins in the erratically shifting stretches of the past.

ENDING: RESOUNDING IRRESOLUTION

One of the most appealing features of Christianity is its eschatological structure, specifically its vision of a meaningful end of time when Jesus will return bringing divine judgment and justification, guaranteed by his assertion that he is the end toward which all things move. However aimless or worthless a believer's life may seem to be, he or she can be reassured that existence has some ultimate purpose in the universe and promise of divine salvation. The endings of novels offer a scaled-down version of such resolution, comfort, and meaning. Although that general expectation of ultimate meaning is deeply imbedded in Western thought and literature, possibly a universal, as Frank Kermode and others have argued, it does have a history.[16]

Modernists criticized conclusive endings and created their own unresolved endings to capture the open-ended nature of life as without any ultimate meaning or purpose. In 1884 James chastised readers who insist on a "'happy ending,' on a distribution at the last of prizes, pensions, husbands, wives, babies, millions, appended paragraphs, and cheerful remarks." Novels should rather offer "the intensity of the impression," which his own endings worked to achieve.[17] Twenty years later Conrad congratulated James on his refusal to "satisfy the desire for finality, for which our hearts yearn," and appreciated the way James did not allow readers to rest and instead offered endings that captured "the sense of life still going on."[18] In 1925 Woolf celebrated the "inconclusive" stories of Anton Chekhov in contrast to "most Victorian fiction" in which "the tune is familiar and the end emphatic – lovers united, villains discomfited, intrigues exposed."[19] That same year the author-narrator of Gide's *The Counterfeiters* recorded that he writes without a clear sense of where he is heading, adding, "'might be continued' – these are the words with which I should like to finish my

Counterfeiters" (335). In "Journal of *The Counterfeiters*" (1927), Gide added that his novel "must not be neatly rounded off, but rather disperse, disintegrate" (*C*, 449). He carried out that dispersal by reintroducing in the final paragraph of the novel a minor character, Bernard's stepbrother Caloub, who had nothing to do with the novel's main action. Wyndham Lewis went so far as to introduce in the final two words of *Tarr* the new character Prism Dirkes as a lover for his protagonist. Her first name is an instrument for dispersing light, an apt vorticist image analogous to the dispersal of action that Gide sought to achieve. In 1927 Forster complained that "nearly all novels are feeble at the end," because the novelist has to "round things off, and usually the characters go dead while he is at work." He urged that novels be unplanned and "open out" in the end.[20] Two years later Ford joined the protest against "imbecile" endings that satisfy the "natural human desire for finality."[21] Modernist endings differ from realist endings formally in their degree of completion, timing, perspective, and structure.[22]

Realists invariably completed their novels, whereas some modernists left them pointedly incomplete. Richardson's narrator Miriam objects that if reading the ending spoils a book, there is something wrong with the book. She reads stories not to learn what happens in the end but "to find the author" (*P*, 1, 384). Because Richardson believed that the author was endlessly intriguing and ultimately unknowable, she left *Pilgrimage* unfinished. She tinkered with the final volume *March Moonlight* from 1937 to 1952, only to leave it unfinished at her death in 1957. Kafka left *The Trial* and *The Castle* incomplete. Musil was reluctant to complete *The Man Without Qualities*, and the final pages were published posthumously with the novel still unfinished. In it Ulrich develops a style of "living hypothetically" and elaborates a philosophy of "essayism" that is suited to his age of the provisional, the pragmatic, and the unsystematic in which "no self, no form, no principle, is safe, everything undergoing an invisible but ceaseless transformation" (*MQ*, 1, 269). Ulrich's essayism is not a half-baked expression of some insight but rather an imaginative exploration of life in an endlessly changing modern world with no pre-determined attributes to shape his character and no fixed moral values to govern his behavior.[23]

The second formal aspect of the ending, timing, is the interval between the end of the main action and the final words. Realists often used epilogues that sum up the fate of a number of characters years after the main action, whereas modernists more typically crafted scenic endings, an intense interaction between characters without any time lapse or authorial comment. The third aspect, perspective, is the vision of the narrator of the final events, which divides characteristically between realist overviews and modernist close-ups. The fourth aspect, overall structure, shifts from realist resolution to modernist irresolution, sometimes contrasted as closed and open forms. The difference between these four aspects of closure lines up consistently between realists and modernists, and so to avoid repetition I shall organize the historical evidence in this chapter according to the substance of the two master narratives that these endings most frequently engage.

In realist novels the personal and courtship narratives typically end with death or marriage. Modernists were especially troubled by such formulaic endings demanded by readers and delivered by popular writers. "If it was not for death and marriage," Forster commented, "I do not know how the average novelist would conclude."[24] That convention held particularly among realists. The last chapter of Trollope's *The Warden* (1855) begins, "Our tale is now done, and it only remains to us to collect the scattered threads of our little story, and to tie them into a seemly knot." The remainder of his epilogue, narrated with comprehensive knowledge and panoramic vision of everyone and everything "some years" after the main action, ties the composite knot with six deaths and a wedding. Eliot ends *Daniel Deronda* with a marriage as well as a death as Daniel and Mirah, recently wed, each hold a hand of their dying spiritual guide Ezra, who affirms with his last words, "Have I not breathed my soul into you? We shall live together."[25]

Personal narrative

The most historically marked ending of the personal narrative is death, which itself has a dynamic history across the years of my study. Victorians valorized death with custom and ritual: mourning costume and jewelry, black-edged paper and envelopes, elaborate plumes and other trappings of the Victorian funeral, and gravestones and pious epitaphs.[26] Into the twentieth century strict adherence to these conventions lessened, medical advances prolonged life, religion continued to lose its authority over death as well as life, and World War I undercut the romanticization of death. In realist novels deaths generally occur in the home, while in the twentieth century they move increasingly to hospitals. In *The Notebooks of Malte Laurids Brigge*, Malte complains about people dying in factory-like hospitals that treat death as a business. "A death of one's own" is as rare as "a life of one's own," as both life and death come ready-made.[27] That sense of "ownness" or authenticity is the conceptual ground of the most influential modernist philosopher of death, Martin Heidegger, who argued in *Being and Time* that authentic existence includes awareness of what it means "to be going to die" (*Sein zum Tode*). An authentic individual understands that death cannot be shared, because one faces it alone. It cannot be mediated, made easier, or rendered meaningful by anyone else, because it is uniquely one's own. It is not a stage to some higher existence, but an end of existence.

Victorian writers believed that death could and should be mediated respectfully by clergy and memorialized by conventions, also that death punishes the wicked, crowns a meaningful life, or serves as a point of departure for some transcendent existence in posterity if not the hereafter. While numerous realist villains succumb to poetic justice, such scenes do not typically end realist novels. One exception is the death of Nana in Zola's novel of that name. Not so much a villain as the vehicle of runaway sexual desire, she is in the end disfigured by syphilis – poetic justice for a courtesan who used her beauty to inflame men's sexual desire and lead them to ruin. Death at the end generally signifies fulfillment and hope as when Sydney Carton, in *A Tale of Two Cities*, sacrifices himself to save Charles Darnay and announces on the scaffold in the final lines of the novel, "It is a far, far better thing that I do, than I have ever done before; it is a far, far better rest that I go to than I have ever known." While Carton's noble sacrifice is a last-minute change of heart, Jean Valjean's death in *Les Misérables* culminates a meaningful life of hard work, generosity, and love. On his deathbed he tells his beloved adopted daughter Cosette and her husband Marius, "How sweet it is to die like this." He assures them that after he dies he will watch over them. In addition, God "watches us all from above." Valjean requests an unmarked gravestone, and in an epilogue a narrator explains that many years after Valjean's death, someone etched lines of verse on that stone.

> He sleeps. Although so much he was denied,
> He lives; and when his dear love left him, died.
> It happened of itself, in the calm way
> That in the evening night-time follows day.

Valjean dies as if falling into an eternal sleep according to a natural, gradual scenario like night following day. He is surrounded by loved ones, comforted that his death is meaningful, and confident that, watched over by God, he will continue to watch over and be remembered by Cosette and Marius.

For modernists death at the end is sudden, violent, absolute, godless, and absurd. In place of Hugo's epilogue that describes the afterlife of Valjean's gravestone and by implication the gentle sleep of his eternal soul, modernists craft intense and abrupt scenic moments such as Catherine's final exchange with Frederick in *A Farewell to Arms*. Her words are not a wise summing up or a hope that he will always remember her. She reassures him that he is "to have girls" but not to "do our things." Finally, she says, "I'm not a bit afraid. It's just a dirty trick." After she dies, Frederick does not sob and whisper his eternal love but reflects that his effort to say something to her corpse, disfigured by a botched Cesarean, "was like saying good-bye to a statue."

In place of overviews such as Trollope's in *The Warden*, modernists fashion close-ups such as the end of *The Trial* when Josef K.'s executioners hold him by the throat, stick a knife into his heart, and turn it twice. As he dies, he manages to comment on the indignity of his death, "like a dog!" Mann ends *The Magic Mountain* with Hans called to the trenches in 1914 as the narrator, surprisingly detached from his hero's fate, predicts a violent end: "Farewell, Hans . . . your chances are not good . . . we would not wager much that you will come out whole . . . to be honest, we are not really bothered about leaving the question open." In striking contrast to realist narrators' celebration of the hallowed ground of graveyards, the narrator in Raymond Chandler's *The Big Sleep* (1939) muses in the end, "What did it matter where you lay once you were dead? In a dirty sump or on a marble tower on top of a high hill? You were dead, you were sleeping the big sleep . . . not caring about the nastiness of how you died or where you fell." These modernist deaths end novels but not the instabilities introduced in the story: Josef K. never learns why he was "arrested" or gets "justice," Frederick senselessly loses his beloved Catherine and his stillborn child, Hans is epically caught up in the insanity of war, and Chandler's hard-boiled detective-narrator Philip Marlowe becomes "part of the nastiness."

The death of the protagonist at the end of *Lord Jim* is, like many modernist deaths, sudden, violent, and absurd. The narrator Marlow concludes that Jim sacrificed himself for honor, but his death, part suicide and part execution, brings despair to the Patusan community he worked to cultivate.[28] The novel dramatizes the difficulty of knowing anyone and the impossibility of ending a life story. Indeed, the novel is one long unresolved ending. Jim repeatedly disappears into the mist and into the obscurity of his otherness, and as a result, Marlow discovers, it is impossible to bring his story, or any life story, to a satisfactory end. "The last word is not said – probably shall never be said . . . I have given up expecting those last words, whose ring, if they could only be pronounced, would shake both heaven and earth" (*LJ*, 225). Marlow's last meeting with Jim is a close-up scene devoid of closure or understanding. In contrast to realist farewells of illumination and resolution, that between Jim and Marlow is opaque and inconclusive. As Marlow's boat sets off from the shore where Jim stands, Jim says, "Tell them . . .", and in expectation that Jim will have some final message for those back home, Marlow orders the rowers to stop. But after a while Jim's eyes look dumbly at Marlow, and he says "No – nothing" and motions the boat away. Marlow looks back at Jim's shrinking figure on the shore and ends his spoken narrative with "suddenly, I lost him" (335–36). The final paragraphs of the novel, just after Marlow reports on Jim's execution by Doramin, are in Marlow's written narration that twice refers to Jim as "inscrutable at heart." Jim sacrifices love and life for a dubious honor in death. As Marlow narrates, "He goes away from a living woman to celebrate his pitiless wedding with a shadowy ideal of conduct." Jim's execution is the antithesis of Sydney Carton's. Both men die for honor, but Jim leaves no posterity to celebrate it; rather he leaves his community without a leader and leaves his beloved Jewel feeling alone and betrayed, "leading a sort of soundless, inert life."

In other modernist novels main characters become mentally disordered. In the final scene of *The Sound and the Fury* on Easter Sunday, 1928, Luster is driving Benjy to the graveyard, site of the Compson family's ancient heritage. He sets out to circle the town square containing a statue of a Confederate soldier, symbol of the dead Confederacy. The ending is a momentary respite from Benjy's sudden fury when Luster drives the surrey an unaccustomed way round the square. Benjy begins bellowing, and brother Jason intervenes and turns the surrey around, restoring calm to Benjy's disordered mind: "serene again as cornice and façade flowed smoothly once more from left to right, post and tree, window and doorway and signboard each in its ordered place." There the novel ends amid the tempests of the Compson family, in the shadow of a monument to the debacle of the Southern Confederacy, on an Easter Sunday that does not bring resurrection or reconciliation. Order is restored for a moment in the mind of an "idiot" as a surrey reverses direction around the town square. Calm is achieved not by finding a way out of the morass of family or confederacy, but by driving in a circle signifying nothing.

Nightwood is a reverse *Bildungsroman*, because instead of the protagonist forging deeper relationships with people, she disengages; instead of her progressing toward illumination, she descends into darkness; and instead of evolving as a person, she devolves into bestiality, possibly insanity, culminating in the most bizarre ending in the modernist canon as she abandons her latest lover, leaves New York for the country, symbolically leaves the Catholic Church, and gives up language to remain in "fixed silence." She had been introduced as "beast turning human."[29] At the circus, a lioness attracted to her reached her paws through the bars, and her feline eyes flowed with tears. Robin was, Dr. O'Connor explained, "outside the 'human type' – a wild thing caught in a woman's skin, monstrously alone" (146). Her final effort to transcend that loneliness and relate with her animalistic spirit is with her former lover Nora's dog in a decaying chapel outside Nora's country home. As Nora sees Robin and the dog there, Robin goes down on all fours and begins dragging her knees. The novel ends with woman and dog struggling and failing to relate:

Then she began to bark also, crawling after him – barking in a fit of laughter, obscene and touching. The dog began to cry then, running with her, head-on with her head, as if to circumvent her; soft and slow his feet went padding. He ran this way and that, low down in his throat crying, and she grinning and crying with him; crying in shorter and shorter spaces, moving head to head, until she gave up, lying out, her hands beside her, her face turned and weeping; and the dog too gave up then, and lay down, his eyes bloodshot, his head flat along her knees.

In this final scene, the only light comes from two candles, the only sounds are a woman and a dog barking and crying, and the only contact is the dog's head on the woman's knees. Relatedness is limited to what can be exchanged between a human being and a dog. Clearly Barnes intended the affirmation of some primal relation that had been suppressed in modern society, but beyond this regress to animal origins, the meaning of the ending is unclear. Scholarly interpretation ranges widely to include "madness," Robin's preparation "for another sexual conquest," and "freedom from the prison of meaning."[30] For a novel that throughout resisted closed meanings and single interpretations, it is fitting that its ending should be open and unsettling.

Courtship narrative

Modernist criticism of conventional endings was particularly strong about conclusive happy endings between lovers. Substantively, modernists believed, again echoing Woolf, that life was not like that because courtships were carefully chaperoned, couples had little opportunity to get to know one another before marriage, honeymoons were often a nightmarish struggle between a sexually ignorant wife and a crudely apprenticed husband, and many marriages were motivated by money or social pressure. Modernists also objected for formal reasons, and instead of ending with the strong resolution of a promising marriage or a comprehensive epilogue about the blessings of a long marriage, they ended with unresolved scenic compositions and close-ups of ambivalent, conflicted, and indecisive couples facing an uncertain future.

Modernist resistance to concluding marriages reflects a striking fact about the history of marital love in literature, one that modernists did not note explicitly but that a survey of the literary record reveals – that no major love story before the twentieth century focused on love between a married couple. Love in literature was always pre- or extra-marital. Launcelot and Guinevere, Tristan and Isolde, and Paolo and Francesca loved outside of marriage. Dante scarcely ever talked to Beatrice and pined over her from afar, Petrarch's love for Laura was fueled by her unattainability, and Don Quixote's love for Dulcinea was a fantasy. Lovers Othello and Desdemona, Romeo and Juliet, and Antony and Cleopatra fail to realize marital happiness. Samuel Richardson's *Clarissa* traces a protracted refusal to marry, and the heroine of his *Pamela* marries her kidnapper half-way through, at which time the novel loses dramatic interest. In Rousseau's *The New Heloïse* (1761) and Goethe's *The Sorrows of Young Werther* (1774) a man yearns in vain for a married woman.

In realist novels, couples who are either already married at the beginning of the novel or marry in the course of it are typically unhappy. Thus, the marriages of Roger Chillingworth in Nathaniel Hawthorne's *The Scarlet Letter* (1850), M. Arnoux in *Sentimental Education*, Alexy Karenin in *Anna Karenina*, Léonce Pontellier in Kate Chopin's *The Awakening* (1899), Edgar Linton in *Wuthering Heights*, Edward Casaubon in *Middlemarch*, Henleigh Grandcourt in *Daniel Deronda*, Geert von Instetten in Theodore Fontane's *Effi Briest* (1894), and Jude Fawley in Thomas Hardy's *Jude the Obscure* (1895) are miserable.[31] These marriages are forged by miscommunication, sustained by insecurity, and weakened by self-deception and lies.

Other realist marriages promise happiness, but they begin at the end of novels and are more hope than actuality. However ironic Austen's beginning announcement of the "universally acknowledged" truth that a single rich man must want a wife, at the end of *Pride and Prejudice* Darcy gets Elizabeth with the seeming inexorability of Newton's laws of motion. Dickens capitulated to public pressure for a happy ending in *Great Expectations*: in place of the original ending that left Pip alone and Estella married to a country doctor, he wrote a revised one with Pip and Estella reconciled and, in the final line, walking into the morning mists hand in hand. Tolstoy ended *War and Peace* with the promise of marriage between Pierre and Natasha.

Realist epilogues offer resounding closure with marriages. The epilogue to *Bleak House*, written from a perspective of seven years after the main action, includes several of the objectionable items that James listed: Esther Summerson's appended paragraphs about her husband (a handsome and respected doctor), babies (her own and others'), and cheerful remarks (the ill wind from the East no longer blows). In the opening line of the last chapter of *Jane Eyre*, Jane proclaims triumphantly – "Reader, I married him" – and goes on to report on ten years of marital bliss. The epilogue of *Middlemarch*, written by the omniscient narrator thirty-five years after the end of the action, is primarily about the fate of several courtships: "Marriage," the narrator announces, "is still the beginning of the home epic ... which makes the advancing years a climax, and age the harvest of sweet memories in common." The epilogue concludes with an account of the marriage of Dorothea and Will, who were "bound to each other by a love stronger than any impulses which could have marred it."

An early pioneer of unresolved endings is Henry James. At the finale of *The Ambassadors* Maria Gostrey appeals to Strether with a thinly veiled proposal of marriage: "There's nothing, you know, I wouldn't do for you." He declines her offer by explaining that the only "logic" in his enterprise to persuade Chad to return to Massachusetts is "not, out of the whole affair, to have got anything for myself." So he cannot give in to his own love and accept Maria's poignant proposal. Paradoxically, his self-denial is what she cannot resist. Strether's declarative final line, "Then there we are!" ironically asserts the fact that Maria and Strether as well as the reader have no idea where they are. It anticipates the final line of *Mrs. Dalloway*, when Clarissa descends the staircase to join her party and the narrator records Peter's announcement of her presence to no one in particular – "'It is Clarissa,' he said" – and then concludes the novel, "For there she was." These endings affirm human existence simply being there, as the characters' existence precedes their essence, and that essence is uncertain.

While in the end James's Strether refuses marriage elusively, at the end of Henry James's *The Golden Bowl* (1904) Maggie and the Prince reaffirm their marriage ambivalently. The Italian Prince Amerigo marries the American Maggie Verver for her father's millions, while she is drawn to his aristocratic pedigree and manly charm. The Prince then has sex with his former lover, Charlotte Stant, who then marries Maggie's father Adam. The novel tracks Maggie's agonizingly slow realization of what Amerigo and Charlotte did and her struggle to come to terms with it and find a way to salvage both marriages. She must get the Prince to acknowledge his deceit without actually confessing and to experience the anxiety of being found out but not be paralyzed by her moral superiority, while she must take charge but still allow him to exercise his manly charm. She also has to salvage the marriage of her father and Charlotte, which she does in a final act of generosity by describing Charlotte to the Prince as "splendid." The last exchange between Maggie and the Prince in the final lines of the novel is a distinctly modernist, ambiguous Jamesian close-up.

"That's our help, you see," she added – to point further her moral.

It kept him before her therefore, taking in – or trying to – what she so wonderfully gave. He tried, too clearly, to please her – to meet her in her own way; but with the result only that, close to her, her face kept before him, his hands holding her shoulders, his whole act enclosing her, he presently echoed: "'See?' I see nothing but *you*." And the truth of it had with this force after a moment so strangely lighted his eyes that as for pity and dread of them she buried her own in his breast.

The Prince's words imply that Maggie's use of "our" is too generous to him, because she alone has the strength and moral authority to forgive Charlotte. He tries to take charge in his manly way by grabbing her shoulders and staring into her eyes, but the gesture does not work as did his former seizures of power but is rather a tempered show of respect. He does not enclose her so much as she overwhelms him. Her final act reflects the conflict of a woman who must take charge of her marriage but not take it over. She pities the Prince because she has made it impossible for him to do what he had previously done so effectively – to "charm her by his sovereign personal power into some collapse."[32] Without his old charm he is pitiful. She also dreads his "strangely lighted" eyes because she can never know precisely what is behind them, and her triumph is ambivalent. He may at any time reprise the power of his seductive gaze, and she may lose the power of moral superiority that came from her discovery of his adultery. The final image is a reminder that Maggie's new authority and responsibility are frightening, as she still seeks the protection of a strong man's breast and so buries her eyes in it.[33]

Less tortuous, but similarly open-ended, is the final exchange between the married couple in *Women in Love*. At the end of *The Rainbow* (1915) Ursula had rejected a marriage offer in order to experience the world on her own, and on the opening page of *Women in Love* she tells her sister that marriage is "more likely to be the end of experience." Still, she falls for Rupert but is put off by his reluctance to fuse with her in marriage. While courting her he repeatedly insists on "freedom together" and rejects the "dreadful bondage" of conventional marriage (*WL*, 199). He seeks rather "an eternal equilibrium in marriage" but not fusion with his beloved or the isolation of a couple from others (290). He tells Ursula, "I always imagine our being really happy with some few other people" (363). One description of their sex life is perhaps the novel's most historically significant moment: "She took hold of him and gathered her joy of him. And she enjoyed him fully. But they were never *quite* together, at the same moment, one was always a little left out" (435–36). Realists could not describe marital sex for a variety of reasons: public censorship, readers' sensibilities, aesthetic convention, or personal distaste. Had they described it, they would not likely have depicted the woman actively taking hold of the man and certainly would not likely have depicted a strongly bonded husband and wife failing to reach simultaneous orgasms. Rupert and Ursula explore sexual experiences in an adventurous and loving way but still keep something back and cannot achieve the highest intimacy and mutuality.

While failure to climax together is symptomatic of an incomplete sexual experience, refusing to fuse with a beloved in mind and body is, for Lawrence, a requirement for a fulfilling relationship. He explores the precarious balance between commitment and independence in the novel's unresolved ending. Ursula resents Rupert's resistance to total commitment and especially his wanting someone in addition to her, even if it is not another woman but his friend Gerald. Rupert does not want a secretive affair but an additional love that is open and expansive, as he explains in the final exchange:

> "To make it complete, really happy, I wanted eternal union with a man too: another kind of love," he said.
> "I don't believe it," she said. "It's an obstinacy, a theory, a perversity."
> "Well –" he said.
> "You can't have two kinds of love. Why should you!"
> "It seems as if I can't," he said. "Yet I wanted it."
> "You can't have it, because it's false, impossible," she said.
> "I don't believe that," he answered.

Lawrence resists ending his novel with loving fusion between Rupert and Ursula. Rupert cannot "make it complete" and concedes that his is perhaps a hopeless ideal when he replies, "Yet I wanted it." When Ursula piles on the disapproval and insists that such a goal is impossible as well as perverse, Rupert counters with the final line that he simply does not believe that. This understated reply is a protest against the constrictions of Victorian married life. The novel's final lack of resolution keeps open the future of love between Rupert and Ursula and how they will deal with the conflicting marital demands of fusion and autonomy, possession and freedom.

The most formally innovative and influential ending in the modernist canon is the last episode of *Ulysses*. Although Joyce conceived of it as eight "sentences," indicated by paragraph indentations alone, it is in fact a single literary *tour de force*, a 35-page unpunctuated interior monologue of Molly's swirling thoughts about myriad things but ultimately centering on her relationship with Leopold, as it keeps unresolved the fate of their marriage in her thoughts. She mixes diverse feelings about him, weaving and unweaving the fabric of their marriage after the manner of her fictional predecessor Penelope in her tapestry. Molly resents his many failed business schemes, and, because he has not had a steady well-paying job, she has had to skimp on food and clothing and repeatedly relocate. Their cramped space requires sleeping together in a narrow bed positioned head to foot. She resents his cold feet by her face, so close that she has no room, she exaggerates, "even to let a fart" (*U*, 628). They are physically close but emotionally distant and disoriented in this tragicomic arrangement. They have not had "complete carnal intercourse" since their son died over ten years earlier, and in the meantime he makes do sexually in other ways. He kisses, smells, and masturbates on her "bottom," and once she masturbated him with her foot (614). He is turned on by her "drawers" and once asked her to walk around in horse dung to excite him with her dirty boots. She dislikes his pursuit of other women – whores, servants, nurses, "or a nun maybe like the smutty photo he has" (608) – and worries about contracting venereal disease from him.[34] He makes her relate sexual fantasies about other men, and she accuses him of forcing her into adultery. She suspects that he had sex earlier in the day, as she reasons that "he came somewhere Im sure by his appetite" (608). He cannot even satisfy her by performing cunnilingus: "he does it all wrong too thinking only of his own pleasure his tongue is too flat" (635).

This vivid inventory of her husband's sexual deficiencies is unprecedented in the history of courtship literature, but its thoroughness also includes an interweaving of his unusual sexual qualities among other positive traits. Molly finds him admirable and loves him in a bemused, at times motherly way, intensified by many shared experiences, most importantly the death of their son. He is polite to old women and waiters, always raises his hat to people on the street, and is clean and wipes his feet on the mat. She recalls fondly the sound of him coming up the steps with the breakfast cups rattling and admires his knowledge of "a lot of mixed up things especially about the body and the inside" (612). She would like to "remember half of the things [he said] and write a book out of it the works of Master Poldy" (621). He wrote her "mad crazy" love letters, she recalls, "that had me always at myself 4 and 5 times a day" (634). He does not kiss as well as Lieutenant Gardner, and his penis is not as big as Boylan's, but, she concludes, "he's got more spunk" than Boylan, and then adds that she would "rather die 20 times over than marry another of their sex" (611, 613). Yet a few pages later her anger surfaces in an aggressive fantasy: "Ill put on my best shift and drawers let him have a good eyeful out of that to make his micky stand for him Ill let him know if thats what he wanted that his wife is fucked yes and damn well fucked too up to my neck nearly not by him 5 or 6 times" (641). From the previous context the reference to "his micky" seems to refer to Stephen's, about which Molly has been fantasizing, but the text suddenly refers to a jealous Leopold.

This final spurt of sexual hostility subsides into powerful memories of the intense sexual excitement she experienced sixteen years earlier on the day she got him to propose as they lay together among the rhododendrons on Howth head. Toward the end she reflects on his tenderness and empathy with women: "he said I was a flower of the mountain yes so we are flowers all a womans body yes that was one true thing he said in his life and the sun shines for you today yes that was why I liked him because I saw he understood or felt what a woman is" (643). Both Leopold and Molly not only empathize with the opposite sex but fantasize experiencing sex as the opposite sex.

Joyce spent the bulk of the novel presenting Leopold as a fully rounded and engaging person, but his and Molly's sex life, vitally important to both, was shattered by the death of Rudy and, given also Leopold's habitual sexism, may not be salvageable on the strength of her fond memory of a moment of passion and his few poetic words about her beauty. Molly and Leopold are sexually incompatible, clashing at every turn with different fantasies and sensibilities. The novel ends with an undertone of uncertainty as Molly interrupts her climactic recollection of Bloom's sensuous proposal kiss with the recollection of an earlier, innocent kiss from Lieutenant Mulvey under the Moorish wall in Gibraltar. She then returns to Bloom in thinking "well as well him as another," a far cry from the conventional notion of star-crossed lovers. A hopeful moment follows as Molly recalls her acceptance of Bloom's proposal with her famous final words, "yes I said yes I will Yes," but her monologue includes so many grievances against Bloom that one suspects she might change a future response to "no I won't No." In form and content the ending of *Ulysses* is open and unresolved in unprecedented ways by sustaining a continuous interior monologue that reworks the sexual experience and marital relations that were centerpieces of the traditional courtship narrative.

Modernists did not craft unresolved endings out of a perverse desire to withhold closure but because such endings opened up possibilities. Realist novels did not end with actual death and marriage as much as with the denial of death and the mythology of marriage. After their deaths, Sydney Carton is not going to go anywhere or do anything, and Jean Valjean is not going to sleep for eternity or watch over anyone. *The Mill on the Floss* ends with the epitaph on the shared tomb of Tom and Maggie Tulliver, found drowned "in close embrace," which reads *In their death they were not divided.* They may have been found dead and buried together, but the personification implied by togetherness is for living people, not dead bodies. Modernist deaths were sudden, violent, godless, and absurd because modernist writers believed that death occurs that way. They dramatized a philosophy, formalized by Heidegger, that a lucid understanding and forthright acceptance of the finitude of human existence enhances life more than self-deception about everlasting life in the hereafter.

Modernists would find it hard to believe Jane Eyre's report on ten years of marriage to Rochester – that they lived in "perfect concord" with her being "absolutely bone of his bone and flesh of his flesh" – suddenly transformed after a courtship in which she was subordinated to his patriarchal authority and deceived by his omissions and lies. Modernists generally resisted concluding with the prospect of long-sought weddings or epilogues about years of marital harmony. Instead they concluded with marital uneasiness, misunderstanding, conflict, betrayal, and uncertainty, as evident in the indelible frustration that separates Strether and Maria, the pity and dread in Maggie's final embrace with the Prince, Rupert's longing for another kind of love beyond what Ursula offers, and Molly's sustained reflection on her difficult relationship with Leopold. Lawrence and Joyce were unique in exploring marital sex with all the tensions and incompatibilities as well as the joys and fulfillment that it offers. The modernist marriage does not provide closure at the end but a resounding irresolution that opens new narrative threads. Novels cannot plausibly tie these up in the end if they are to do justice to life.

CHAPTER 6

Text

Narrative theory is based on the distinction between the events in the *story* and how they are rendered as a *text*. Narratological analysis is primarily about the tension between the two, which becomes increasingly explicit and creative among modernists. This chapter focuses on the modernists' innovations in the text's mechanics, language, and style. Their striking innovations in these areas transformed the language in which narratives were articulated and experienced. By inventing words, transforming syntax, exploring the strengths and weaknesses of language, and devising new styles, modernists forged new contexts for experience.

MECHANICS: COINED WORDS AND STYLIZED SENTENCES

Realists were acutely aware of the difficulty of finding the right words for experience, as Flaubert acknowledged in *Madame Bovary*: "Human speech is like a cracked kettle on which we tap crude rhythms for bears to dance to, while we long to make music that will melt the stars."[1] But even Flaubert did not seriously question the mechanics of letters, words, and sentences. Modernists experimented with these basic elements, including individual letters. In mini-dramas of that experimentation, Joyce had letters walk away, while Woolf had them blow away.

Joyce obliged readers to think about the conventional and arbitrary arrangement of letters that they always see locked in words by tracing throughout *Ulysses* the fate of five sandwich-board men each wearing a tall white hat bearing a single red letter: together the hats spell the name H. E. L. Y. 'S., for Wisdom Hely's, a stationery store where Bloom once worked. The fate of that five-piece walking sign suggests a breaking away from the conventional use of letters when the man carrying the letter Y lags behind to munch on a piece of bread, and moments later "apostrophe S" plods by (*U*, 127). Bloom's observation of that group allows him to reflect on his job as an advertising canvasser that will preoccupy him throughout the day as he contemplates the role of promotional language in stimulating capitalist enterprise.[2] In *Mrs. Dalloway* Woolf degraded the shape of letters in an advertisement made by a skywriting airplane. A group of people at the gates of Buckingham Palace look up and try to make sense out of the letters that "moved and melted and were rubbed out up in the sky" (20). Their varying success at reading the drifting letters and deciphering the text suggests how language is a collective interpretation of texts made from letters that are not permanently fixed in words and stable through time but rather malleable in their function and ultimately as impermanent as clouds. Such malleability is also evident in what modernists did with words.

The vocabulary of realists was made up of standard words that they arranged creatively. Flaubert struggled to find "*le mot juste*" but did not go so far as to invent words or think in terms of their lack of "wordness" as did Stein, who wrote: "You had to recognize words had lost their value in the nineteenth century . . . they had lost so much of their variety and I felt that I could not go on, that I had to capture the value of the individual words."[3] Other modernists invented new words. In *U. S. A.*, Dos Passos cut the authority of the Congress of the United States down to size by phrasing it as a mindless, habitual locution – "Congressoftheunitedstates." To expose the dishonesty of the propaganda that lured men to glory in World War I, symbolized by the Tomb of the Unknown Soldier, he coined words for the collection of body parts to fill the Tomb's coffin from the "puky dirtstench of the yearold dead."[4] A rich source of modernist neologisms is *Ulysses*, which includes the enigmatic adverbs *biscuitfully* and *underdarkneath*, expressive adjectives *snotgreen* and *scrotumtightening*, playful present participles *almosting* and *Sherlockholmesing*, and strings of letters (I hesitate to call them words) such as *eppripfftaph*, which combines the sound of a fart with *epitaph*, the word that Bloom is saying to himself as he releases it, and *Godblazegrukbrukarchkhrasht!*, the sound Boylan makes as he climaxes while having sex with Molly. Realists did not describe sexual experience at all, let alone render orgasmic outbursts with such inventions. In this same vein, Bloom expresses sexuality as "flood of warm jimjam lickitup secretness flowed to flow" (*U*, 226). These neologisms revolutionized the language of the novel even as they expanded the range of experiences that modernists attempted to capture.

A concise statement of modernist purpose in inventing words is an item in the opening manifesto of Eugene Jolas's journal *transition* in 1927: "The literary creator has the right to disintegrate the primal matter of words imposed on him by text-books and dictionaries." In 1929 Jolas elaborated the problems confronting writers and sketched requirements for a solution.

Contemporary literature exhibits "the same banal and journalistic fashion [of] worn-out verbal patterns" and the traditional conventions and institutions they uphold. He called for a "disintegration of words" and the invention of new ones to capture the functioning of the unconscious mind analyzed by Freud, the bizarre experiences explored by the surrealists, and the clashing and fusion of languages of big-city immigrants. Jolas was primarily concerned with defending the prodigious lexical inventions of Joyce's *Work in Progress*, subsequently published as *Finnegans Wake*, but he also hailed *Ulysses* for exploding "the antique logic of words."[5]

While some words were invented, others lost their conventional status and tone. Realist novels honored wartime sacrifice and romantic sensibilities in ways that became outmoded during World War I. Hemingway's narrator Frederic, an ambulance driver in *A Farewell to Arms*, reflects on the effusiveness of an Italian patriot who maintained that the disastrous summer campaign that destroyed his village "cannot have been done in vain." The war made Frederic "embarrassed by the words sacred, glorious, and sacrifice and the expression in vain." For him, every battle death was in vain. "Abstract words such as glory, honor, courage, or hallow were obscene" compared with the concrete names of villages and the real numbers of regiments decimated by the fighting.[6] In *A Room of One's Own* (1929) Woolf compares the romantic rhetoric before and after the war. The change was not in the words per se but in the murmur behind them which "changed the value of the words." She contrasts that new postwar tone with that of a Tennyson poem that includes the lines, "There has fallen a splendid tear / From the passion-flower at the gate. / She is coming, my dove, my dear."[7] The thought that people actually hummed such things before the war makes her laugh. She explains the change in the sense of words from the shock of war and wonders ironically, "Why, if [pre-war romantic sentiment] was an illusion, not praise the catastrophe, whatever it was, that destroyed illusion and put truth in its place? For truth . . ." (15). The ellipsis dots are Woolf's. She never returns to the subject, leaving open the value she attaches to the war having destroyed illusions that men and women expressed in pre-war language.

Modernists also transformed the sentence. The Hemingway sentence, the one true sentence, must be clear and direct with no scrollwork or ornamentation. It features spare punctuation, active verbs, and strong cadences. In James, the sentence, reflecting in all its twists and turns the movement of a character's thought about multiple motives for behavior, becomes long and complicated with lavish subordinate clauses and defers its meaning until the last word, which is unnervingly postponed because there is always a further subtlety to disclose. The Proustian sentence is longer and more lyrical, densely packed with similes whose elements unfold like the ribs of an accordion, with nested clauses within nested clauses from which a wandering, elegiac melody emerges, its multiple elaborations and hesitant qualifications resonating with some obscure yet poignant truth emerging from misty penumbras of sensation or remote caverns of memory. The Faulknerian sentence is longer yet, with cascades of stream-of-consciousness passages and convoluted subordination patterns, its clauses staging a drama of their own fraught with myriad tensions and complexities, tunneling deeper and deeper into the troubled psyches of his characters, into the vexed genealogies of families, and into the tragic history of the American South snaking through the story line like a wistaria vine through a wooden trellis.[8] Thomas Mann's sentences flow along smoothly, musically, yes, even lyrically, although the meditations they often convey are full of tensions and contradictions, tensions and contradictions the narrator tries to work through in a voice so earnest that, at a certain point, we begin to suspect that the earnestness itself is a form of irony, even as we know how much the ideas in play mattered to their august author. Stein's sentences use repetition with variation, always repeating and varying, repeating and always varying, often relying on playful euphonic resonance over conventional meanings and jarring combinations of textures, actions, and sounds. Some of her sentences are ungrammatical and thereby focus attention on the arbitrary conventions of usage and syntax that they violate. By running sentences off the rails she shows how much they are confined by rails.[9] Joyce's sentences are strikingly varied in length and structure. Fragments of thought and speech. Also stream-of-consciousness accumulations mirroring the movement of a mind in flux, unpunctuated and jammed with sensations sounds emotions memories judgments expectations and songs. Woolf said she would reinvent the sentence herself. What a challenge! What a plunge! For so it had always seemed to her when, blending the voice of an objective narrator with that of a character or the voices of two characters, she probed deep into their interpenetrating perceptions and thoughts and placed the reader within, between, or amidst their minds.

Aside from Hemingway's simpler sentence, these others made readers work harder to get through texts and think in new ways about new sorts of experience that sentences and other textual expressions might capture or create (or fail to capture or create). Thus did modernists innovate with letters, words, and sentences the conventional ways that language shapes experience.

LANGUAGE: ILLUMINATING OPACITY

Romantic poets celebrated the creative function of language, following Kant's theory of the creative role of the mind in constituting knowledge. That thinking, however, primarily influenced philosophers and poets, not realist novelists. They told stories through trustworthy narrators, who might question their own opinions and literary skills but not the adequacy of language itself to communicate. The growing awareness of the active role of language in generating experience came to be known as "the linguistic turn."[10] This movement originated with Bertrand Russell, G. E. Moore, and Ludwig Wittgenstein, who came to see philosophy not as a direct study of thought and reality but as an analysis of how thought and reality are constituted by language. Historians trace this turn back to Wittgenstein's claim in 1922 that "all philosophy is a 'critique of language.'"[11] That critique in modernist writers included a variety of ways language can succeed or fail in carrying out its communicative functions.[12]

An early critique of language is a letter published by Hugo von Hofmannsthal in a Berlin newspaper in 1902. Purportedly authored by a fictional Lord Chandos and sent to that master of reason and clear prose, Francis Bacon, dated August 1603, the letter recounts a crisis when Chandos lost the ability to think or write coherently. Before his crisis he assumed that the world was aligned with his own unified self that was capable of understanding accounts of the world in conventional language and of using language to express his relation to it. Then suddenly he "lost completely the ability to think or to speak of anything coherently." Words crumbled in his mouth like moldy fungi. Character analysis with terms such as *thrifty* or *pitiful* seemed mendacious and hollow. As he reports, "Single words floated round me; they congealed into eyes which stared at me and into which I was forced to stare back – whirlpools which gave me vertigo and, reeling incessantly, led into the void." He had powerful experiences "so exalted and moving that words seemed too poor to describe it." He concludes by renouncing conventional language and proclaiming that he will write no more books and that this letter to Bacon will be his last.[13]

In *The Counterfeiters* Gide suggests that the language of the novel is counterfeit and that like money, even gold, it has no absolute backing, no guaranteed frame of reference. He wrote the novel during the postwar period of financial instability but set it in the months just before the war when gold-backed money was still in use. Unlike those who longed for the sureties of the gold standard, which was fatally weakened during the war, Gide insists that the gold standard was a grand illusion, a prime symbol of all arbitrary systems of value. His novel relates the representational function of money to that of language and uses counterfeiting as a metaphor for the unreliable representational function of all signifiers (or coinages) including gold, paper money, paternity, nation, religion, love, and even literature. In his novel, characters pretend to be worth more than they are, ranging from an unfatherly father to the novelist Edouard who repeatedly subverts belief in language as a reliable tool.[14]

A daring modernist rendering of the limits of language is the stylistically compromised "Eumaeus" episode in *Ulysses*. Its action corresponds to the moment in *The Odyssey* when Odysseus, after a twenty-year absence, is recognized by his son Telemachus. Joyce transposes that thrilling moment into the desultory meeting between Stephen, lacking a loving and dependable father, and Bloom, missing his dead son and harboring fantasies of becoming a substitute father to Stephen. Joyce renders their potentially climactic meeting with tired clichés, flabby sentences, and meandering digressions. His language is deflated by bureaucratese ("embark on a policy"), dead metaphors ("made a bee line"), popular melodrama ("balderdash"), clichés ("He knows which side his bread is buttered on"), redundancy ("Whereas the simple fact of the case was it was simply a case of"), and three clichés in a row – "in one fell swoop at a moment's notice, your money or your life" (*U*, 504). Joyce boldly challenges his readers to stay interested through this boring episode near the end of his demanding novel. To clarify how language could be used artfully he abuses it mercilessly with this compendium of bad writing.

Other modernists comment on specific problems with language in expressing love, defining family life, and achieving justice. Language fails a number of couples. Proust's Marcel expresses feelings for Albertine that she is incapable of understanding because of their different education and principles; and so, Marcel explains, "we cannot tell whether our words have aroused in her anything that resembles their meaning" (1, 942). Stein's Jeff tells Melanctha: "I certainly do wonder, Miss Melanctha, if we know at all really what each other means by what we are always saying."[15] Richard Dalloway is unable to word his love for Clarissa, and so he says it with flowers (*MD*, 116). Mrs. Ramsay's final act in *To the Lighthouse* is not telling Mr. Ramsay that she loves him, although Woolf reassures readers that he knew anyway. Hans Castorp feels unable to express his love for Clavdia in German and must resort to his shaky French. These failures to communicate, however, are not distinctively modernist. They are personal failures of nerve, honesty, or knowledge, not failures of language itself, and they occur widely in the realist novel, for example, between Heathcliff and Cathy, Jane and Rochester, even

Emma Bovary and her lovers. In *Anna Karenina* Levin proposes marriage to Kitty in code by writing on a table the first letters of each word of what he wants to say and relying on her to decipher it (Pt. 4, Ch. 14).

More distinctively modernist are critiques of language itself. In *Women in Love* Rupert tells Ursula: "The point about love . . . is that we hate the word because we have vulgarized it. It ought to be . . . tabooed from utterance, for many years, till we get a new, better idea" (*WL*, 130). Rupert agonizes about the exhausted language of love that threatens to vitiate his passion for Ursula and so resists uttering the ultimate cliché "I love you." He eventually says it to her, but grudgingly. In *As I Lay Dying*, Faulkner captures the moribund state of everyday language by having his one dead narrator, among fourteen others, comment on its deficiencies. Addie Bundren dismisses the word *love* as "just a shape to fill a lack," adding, that "when the right time came, you wouldn't need a word for that." After her first child was born, she reports, "I learned that words are no good; that words don't ever fit even what they are trying to say at . . . [and] motherhood was invented by someone who had to have a word for it because the ones that had the children didn't care whether there was a word for it or not." Addie strains with language, ironically, to convey its inability to capture her experience (*AD*, 171–75).

Language also obfuscates justice in the courts, an institutional center-piece of the liberal narrative. Lord Jim realized that speech was useless when he addressed the court that would decide his fate, because there were no words for what he wanted to say. As he explains to Marlow: "If I had opened my lips just then I would have simply howled like an animal" (124). The language of Josef K.'s legal difficulty appears first as the pornographic text of the law books he discovers, then as the legal gibberish in the scraps of law relayed to him by his lawyer and Tintorelli, and finally as the text that the man in the Parable of the Law cannot access during a lifetime of futile waiting. Legal language also works against Musil's Moosbrugger during his crime and before the court. Unaccustomed to conventional metaphors, he breaks language into elements or puts it together improperly and is repeat-edly confused by it. The night he stabbed the prostitute, her solicitous words attached themselves to his fractured ego, and he felt compelled to cut away the source of her words with a knife in a desperate act of self-definition, mutilating her in the process. His literalism sets off fear of him by others and panic and rage in himself. Psychiatric and court jargon are another source of confusion and torment, leading to his conviction and execution. Although Moosbrugger is deranged, Musil's reconstruction of the way he uses language and the way legal jargon uses him dramatize how justice is derailed by conventions of word usage and syntax.[16]

While modernists were acutely aware of the limits of language, they coupled such insight with broad recognition of its creative and generative power. The last section of *Swann's Way*, subtitled "Place Names: The Place" explores the magic of names as when Marcel records the effect on him of the name Gilberte, whom he loved at first sight. While playing in a garden near the Champs-Elysées with his family's maid Françoise, he heard a girl say to another girl playing battledore and shuttlecock, "Good-bye Gilberte, I'm going home now; don't forget we're coming to you this evening, after dinner." Marcel's account of the impact of hearing Gilberte's name warrants lengthy quotation because it captures Proust's way of exploring seemingly simple experiences in exceptional depth and illustrates the long Proustian sentence.

The name Gilberte passed close by me, evoking all the more forcefully the girl whom it labelled in that it did not merely refer to her, as one speaks of someone in his absence, but was directly addressed to her; it passed thus close by me, in action so to speak, with a force that increased with the curve of its trajectory and the proximity of its target; – carrying in its wake, I could feel, the knowledge, the impressions concerning her to whom it was addressed that belonged not to me but to the friend who called it out, everything that, as she uttered the words, she recalled, or at least possessed in her memory, of their daily intimacy, of the visits that they paid to each other, of that unknown existence which was all the more inaccessible, all the more painful to me from being, conversely so familiar, so tractable to this happy girl who let it brush past me without my being able to penetrate it, who flung it on the air with a light-hearted cry; – wafting through the air the exquisite emanation which it had distilled, by touching them with the utmost precision, from certain invisible points in Mlle Swann's life, from the evening to come, just as it would be, after dinner, at her home; – forming, on its celestial passage through the midst of the children and their nursemaids, a little cloud, delicately coloured, resembling one of those clouds that, billowing over a Poussin landscape, reflect minutely, like a cloud in the opera teeming with chariots and horses, some apparition of the life of the gods; – casting, finally, on that ragged grass, at the spot where it was at one and the same time a scrap of withered lawn and a moment in the afternoon of the fair battledore player (who continued to launch and retrieve her shuttlecock until a governess with a blue feather in her hat had called her away) a marvellous little band of light, the colour of heliotrope, impalpable as a reflection and superimposed like a carpet on which I could not help but drag my lingering, nostalgic and desecrating feet, while Françoise shouted: "Come on, button up your coat and let's clear off home!" and I remarked for the first time how common her speech was, and that she had, alas, no blue feather in her hat. (*RP*, 1, 428–29)

This sentence reveals the power of a single word, a young girl's name, to transform time and space. It conjures up the life of Gilberte that Marcel does not know as well as the intimacies present and past that he longs to share as the other girl does. It uses five long participial phrases to elaborate how the word transforms Marcel's ambient space by *evoking* Gilberte's proximity, *carrying* impressions of her, *wafting* her emanations through the air, *forming* a setting suitable for gods, and *casting* a marvelous heliotrope light over everything.[17] The word reverberates in time, reworking Marcel's past life and present feelings as it resonates throughout this sentence, which Proust extends like a promise of future love, as though he could not bear to end it.

Modernists also show the power of language to serve capitalism with advertising. By the last quarter of the nineteenth century capitalism was in a crisis of saturated markets and over-production from improved factory and managerial techniques. One set of responses was on the demand side: to increase the number of goods people believed they must have and the urgency of those perceived needs and to identify specific brands as preferable to others, a set of attitudes that Marx referred to as *the fetishism of commodities*. To achieve those ends, businesses sought to transform advertising from a source of information about goods, as it functioned in earlier years, to a source of imperatives about how to live. Thus advertisers had to exploit the power of language.

An early moment in this transformation is dramatized in James's *The Ambassadors*, where the commercial world dependent on advertising becomes one focus of the final action.[18] The firm in need of advertising is a "big brave bouncing business" that "may well be on the way to become a monopoly," as Strether explains to Maria. The business is owned by Mrs. Newsome, who is engaged to Strether. She has commissioned him as an ambassador to go to Paris and rescue her son Chad from his Parisian life, and especially from the clutches of Madame de Vionnet, and bring him back to Woollett, Massachusetts to produce advertising for the family business. Paradoxically, the firm's prosperity, Strether tells Maria, is based on a "trivial ridiculous object of the commonest domestic use" that is wanting in "dignity," because it is "vulgar."[19] Strether never says what the product is. Its secret and vulgar nature suggests the devious and undignified advertising needed to sell it.

The novel is structured around sudden revelations about people that parallel formally the function of advertising to reveal products. At pivotal moments Strether realizes that he is old and has not lived, that Chad and Madame de Vionnet are lovers, that he himself loves her, and that his ambassadorial mission is ill-conceived. He renounces Mrs. Newsome's money and all that Woollett represents and urges Chad to remain in Paris and not go into advertising, but the original promotional mission prevails.

Chad has had his own revelation, as he explains to Strether. He will leave Madame de Vionnet and Paris and return to work in the family business, because "advertising scientifically worked" is the "great new force." "It's an art . . . in the hands, naturally, of a master" (*A*, 504–05). Thus, the ambassador on behalf of advertising renounces its worth, while the novice seeks to become its master, as contrapuntally they make their respective ways into and out of the world of the arts that James revered. In the end Chad sets off to forge not the conscience of his race but unconscionable texts to gin up demand for a vulgar product.

While James was scandalized about the way advertising used language, Joyce was ambivalent. He was intrigued by the plethora of signs that filled magazines, newspapers, and cities. He was profoundly interested in the way advertising creates a language in which life styles and social customs are shaped.[20] Early on in *A Portrait of the Artist as a Young Man* he criticizes through Stephen's reflections how "every mean shop legend bound his mind like the words of a spell and his soul shrivelled up sighing with age as he walked on in a lane among heaps of dead language" (*PA*, 178). But in *Ulysses* Joyce opens to the imaginative possibilities of advertising. He refers to over a hundred ads, makes advertising the profession of his protagonist, and integrates its techniques into his own writing with fragmentation, parody, collage, and puns in the production of a novel that ironically violates every tenet of advertising wisdom.[21]

Bloom's job as an ad canvasser requires that he travel the city, think about how to help shops make a profit, and negotiate between their owners and newspaper editors who daily mold consumer tastes. Among many ads he sees, one sets off throughout the day a series of memories and fantasies that engage his identity as a Jew and an Irishman as well as his sexual identity and relationship with Molly. While waiting in a butcher's shop to buy a pork kidney, he takes a page from a pile of cut sheets used to wrap meat and reads an article in it about a model farm in Palestine, illustrated by a picture of the farm with grazing cattle.[22] While walking home he reads an accompanying ad on the same page.

Agendath Netaim: planters' company. To purchase waste sandy tracts from Turkish government and plant with eucalyptus trees. Excellent for shade, fuel and construction. Orange groves and immense melonfields north of Jaffa. You pay eight marks and they plant a dunam of land for you with olives, oranges, almonds or citrons. Olives cheaper: oranges need artificial irrigation. Every year you get a sending of the crop. Your name entered for life as owner in the book of the union. Can pay ten down and the balance in yearly instalments. Bleibtreustrasse 34, Berlin, W. 15.

Nothing doing. Still an idea behind it. (*U*, 49)

This ad derives from an actual ad Joyce may have seen sometime after 1909. Agendath Netaim in Hebrew (actually *Agudat Neta 'im*) means Plantation Company and was modeled after the Palestine Land Development Company with offices in Berlin. The actual promotional literature for that company makes no reference to melons, which are Joyce's addition, as that fruit is repeatedly related in Bloom's mind to Molly's buttocks. The other promised crops trigger Bloom's subsequent thoughts about women, fertility, and sterility. The reference to a life ownership "in the book of the union" suggests his own unstable marital union. The Company's address on Bleibtreustrasse (Stay True Street) is another reminder of infidelity in Bloom's marriage. The final contrasting thoughts – "Nothing doing. Still an idea behind it" – capture his ambivalence about Zionism and Judaism, underscored by the fact that he has just purchased from a Zionist butcher a pork kidney that is forbidden by Jewish law.

Joyce shows the power of the ad to have an abiding influence by exploring Bloom's subsequent associations to it. The olives remind him of Molly spitting out olive pits. The citrons conjure up the feel and taste of the fruit as well as an old neighbor named Citron, and happier days with Molly rocking in his basket chair. As a cloud darkens the sky, Bloom's thoughts darken, and he envisions ancient Palestine, "a dead sea in a dead land . . . grey sunken cunt of the world" (50). Chilled by these thoughts, he puts the ad in his pocket and rushes home to Molly. Throughout the day he recalls "Agendath" eleven more times, sometimes in relation to his identity as a Jewish outsider or Irish colonial, but mostly in connection with fertility and sterility and centering on Molly. Around lunchtime, while looking into a shop window, he contemplates gifts for her: "silkwebs, silver, rich fruits spicy from Jaffa. Agendath Netaim. Wealth of the world" (138). In early evening, after masturbating while gazing up Gerty's skirt, he launches into an inventory of sexual experiences and fantasies that includes a reference to the ad: "O sweety all your little girlwhite up I saw dirty bracegirdle made me do love sticky we two naughty . . . years of dreams return tail end Agendath swoony lovey showed me her next year in drawers return next in her next her next" (312). His mind wanders from the memory of his recent erotic gazing, to dreams of harvesting oranges and melons from a barren wasteland, and finally to the hope that perhaps next year he may return, not to Jerusalem, but to Molly's drawers.[23] The ad finally goes up in smoke when Bloom, after returning home and finding it in his pocket, uses it to light the incense he burns symbolically to remove Boylan's presence from his home.

The magical power of advertising preoccupies Bloom to his last moments before falling asleep when he theorizes about "the infinite possibilities hitherto unexploited of the modern art of advertisement," which include "maximum visibility," "maximum legibility," and "magnetising efficacy to arrest involuntary attention, to interest, to convince, to decide" – precisely the effects that the Agendath Netaim ad had on him. The first listed of his final meditations is of "one sole unique advertisement to cause passers to stop in wonder, a poster novelty, with all extraneous accretions excluded, reduced to its simplest and most efficient terms not exceeding the span of casual vision and congruous with the velocity of modern life" (592). Joyce understood the techniques of effective advertising but violated each of them. *Ulysses* was designed to keep professors busy deciphering it but also, and for that reason, insured that the masses would pass it by. It is overloaded with extraneous accretions, far exceeds the attention span of a normal reader, and is not even in accord with the velocity of modern life, because it moves with many velocities, some painstakingly slow. Still, in the long run, Joyce did make the Western world stop in wonder by crafting the poster child, if not the poster novelty, of this most formally innovative modernist novel.

The major shift in the goal of advertising in the early twentieth century was from selling things to selling signs in the form of brand names.[24] By the 1920s major cities were fields of signs clamoring for attention from an increasingly selective commercial audience. Times Square became a gallery of signs. Between 1917 and 1924 its most prominent ad was for Wrigley's Chewing Gum, a block-long sign using 5,000 lamps and 15,000 multi-colored bulbs. An estimated 12,228 electric advertising signs lit up New York City in 1925, when Dos Passos published *Manhattan Transfer*.[25] In that novel, signs direct traffic and encourage people to buy products as well as reshape their self-image. Dos Passos uses advertising strategies of fragmentation and collage to capture Manhattan and illustrate the power of advertising to exploit customers and secure the hegemony of an economic and political elite. His alter ego in the novel, the journalist Jimmy Herf, burns with resentment against capitalist injustice and has lost faith in language exploited by commercial use. As he complains: "I know that every sentence, every word, every picayune punctuation that appears in the public press is perused and revised and deleted in the interests of advertisers and bond-holders. The foundation of national life is poisoned at the source."[26] By the time of *U. S. A.* in the 1930s, Dos Passos made J. Ward Moorhouse a villain whose ad firm launches a publicity campaign to promote American patriotism for "The Big Money," the title of the final volume of his trilogy.

One ironic contrast in the history of language in the modernist period is that at a time when novelists were struggling with the limits of language, the advertising industry was booming and learning how to exploit language to sell goods. James, Joyce, and Dos Passos were acutely sensitive to the growing power of advertising and its numbing effect on literary art. James was resolutely hostile in interpreting Chad's decision to become an ad man. Joyce was more ambivalent, fascinated by the advertising industry's promotional skills but disinclined to use them to promote his inaccessible and un-commercial novel. Dos Passos parodied newspaper and cinematic journalism in *Manhattan Transfer*, and pilloried it in *U. S. A.* for being used to sell useless goods and fire up chauvinism.

STYLE: FEMININE, ABSTRACT, SURREAL, COLLAGIST

Among many new styles in the arts of the period, four had a distinctive impact on the novel. Richardson and Woolf devised a female style to render female ways of seeing and writing about the world that they believed had been neglected by the dominant "masculine style." Abstraction subverted the recognition of objects and the authority of ruling institutions by replacing icons of authority with abstract forms, evident in the writings of Stein, Lewis, Gide, and Woolf. Surrealism created a "surreality" of unconscious mental processes and defamiliarized objects in the novels of Breton and Aragon. Collage subverted the coherent source of materials that gave unity to works of art and authority to their dominant motifs, substituting an artistic eclecticism as in the urban novels of Joyce and Döblin.

Female style

After 1890 love relationships were shaped by depolarized gender roles from new findings in genetics, endocrinology, embryology, feminist theory, and psychoanalysis.[27] Novelists innovated stylistically to capture these changes as the New Woman made her way in society as well as in literature and the arts. They identified male and female literary styles and developed the latter to capture women's new roles.

A number of nineteenth-century female novelists, far from proclaiming a distinctive female style, used male pseudonyms – George Sand, Currer Bell, Ellis Bell, and George Eliot – to be taken seriously. Richardson and Woolf openly proclaimed a distinctive female, feminine, or woman's style. This variety of adjectives indicates the complexity of their task. *Female* suggests universal characteristics deriving from sexual physiology, *feminine* suggests culturally varying gendered characteristics, while *woman's* ambiguously suggests both. Richardson sought to create "a feminine equivalent of the current masculine realism."[28] Woolf identified a woman's sentence and sequence of sentences to capture new gender roles and love relationships. These authors also identified gender characteristics, present in all women, that their styles were intended to capture. They distanced themselves from feminist campaigning for political and economic rights but were energized by contemporary feminism to try rendering the experience of women working to make their way in a man's world.

Richardson became pregnant by H. G. Wells and had a miscarriage in 1907. She took his novels as a model of the "masculine realism" against which she undertook in 1913 to create a feminine style. She recalled, "Monstrously, when I began, I felt only that all masculine novels to date … were somehow irrelevant, & the feminine ones far too much influenced by masculine traditions, too much set upon exploiting the sex-motif as hitherto seen depicted by men."[29] The end product of that undertaking was *Pilgrimage*.

For Richardson, women cannot be represented by men "because by every word they use men and women mean different things" (*P*, 1, 4, 93). Feminine consciousness is receptive, in contrast to masculine assertiveness, and is capable of processing things simultaneously instead of one at a time. Women live more fully in the present; men strive to become something else. Her feminine style includes a weak plot that skips over her pregnancy and miscarriage but devotes five pages to hair care (1, 60–65). Her space includes the interior of Miriam's consciousness navigating a man's world in a way that is "all contradictory, up and down, backwards and forwards, all true" (11, 306). Although Richardson rejects the idea that she uses stream of consciousness – a "lamentably ill-chosen metaphor," as she puts it – she does work to capture how Miriam's mind processes multiple layers of consciousness simultaneously.[30] She also slows the pace as against men's novels: "Bang, bang, bang, on they go, these men's books, like an L. C. C. Tram" (111, 239). She resists strong closure, which in the masculine novel usually involves a woman's marriage or death. Her narrative is structured instead around repeated self-discovery and artistic self-cultivation as indicated by her title, *Pilgrimage*.

Her feminine style has a distinctive word use and syntax. It also has spare punctuation to force readers to slow down and create their own pacing. She uses ellipsis dots generously, anticipating Woolf's call for "breaking" the masculine sentence, as in the account of Miriam's humiliation when a man accosts her: "that afternoon at Hyde Park Corner … just when everything flashed out after the rain … the sudden words close to her ear … my beauty … my sweet … you sweet girl … the puffy old face" (11, 96–97).

According to Woolf, Richardson developed "the psychological sentence of the feminine gender. It is of a more elastic fibre than the old, capable of stretching to the extreme, of suspending the frailest particles, of enveloping the vaguest shapes . . . It is a woman's sentence, but only in the sense that it is used to describe a woman's mind."[31] Woolf's final caveat emphasizes content over style; and if her sentence is feminine only because it renders a woman's mind, it is not a feminine *sentence*.[32]

The difficulty of identifying a literary style as feminine is also evident in Woolf's claims. In *A Room of One's Own* (1929) she proposes a distinctive woman's sentence to break the hegemony of "a man's sentence" that is "unsuited for a woman's use."[33] But she offers no specific example of a woman's sentence from any actual author. Instead, she imagines a novel by an imaginary author, Mary Carmichael, who uses a distinctly female style: "First [Carmichael] broke the sentence; now she has broken the sequence" (81). But Woolf omits any example of a broken sentence or sequence from Carmichael. Instead, she continues to elaborate the mind set in which the female sentence ought to be created in order to avoid the linear structure of the man's sentence and exhibit a female structure that is expansive and incandescent. Her ultimate goal, however, is not to produce female sentences; rather, the most accomplished writers capture men and women alike with an androgynous mind capable of crafting a man-womanly or woman-manly syntax (77, 98). Woolf's most consequential call, however, as it resonated in feminist movements in Europe and the United States, was not for androgynous sentences, but for women's sentences. The feminist challenges of Richardson and Woolf reshaped the form and content of late modernist writing even if they did not produce sentences or sequences that could be identified as unambiguously female or male.

Abstraction

Abstraction was the most revolutionary stylistic development of the modernist period. No fully abstract novel emerged, but the artistic style influenced writers nevertheless. Abstraction was an explicit rejection of realism's goal of depicting identifiable objects in the real world. Although it was most fully developed in the plastic arts, a few poets did briefly use it. Stein and Lewis flirted with it, while Gide and Woolf addressed it through characters concerned with its possibilities. Finally, in art it drew from and aligned with anarchism and secularism, as Broch noted in essays distributed throughout *The Sleepwalkers*.[34]

From the time of ancient cave drawings to cubism, a goal of pictorial art was to capture recognizable objects. Then, from 1909 to 1914, artists in Germany, Italy, Holland, Russia, Austria-Hungary, and England went abstract, influenced by a variety of challenges to conventional ways of experiencing the world. Biologists looking through microscopes found abstract forms in microorganisms, leaves, and crystals. Psychologists studied the impact of colors on the mind, which suggested the possibility of compositions with color alone independent of identifiable objects. Modern dance freed the body from the melodramatic narratives of classical ballet and instead produced an abstract movement dictated by sensuous impulses. Fauvists liberated painting from actual colors, and cubists violated visual perspective and anatomically correct forms. While the motives for this movement differed, abstract artists shared the goals of rejecting the subject matter of the material world and the formal technique of mimesis and sought instead to express pure spirit with abstract forms. Abstractionists also accorded with the anarchist objective of liberating the long-suppressed human spirit from oppression by familial, national, capitalist, and religious institutions.[35]

In 1861 the realist painter Gustave Courbet wrote to a group of artists: "Painting is essentially a *concrete* art and consists only in the representation of *real* and *existing* things. It is an entirely physical language that uses for words all visible objects; an *abstract* object, not visible, nonexistent, is not of the domain of painting."[36] Fifty years later Kandinsky filled that domain with abstract objects. In his manifesto, *On the Spiritual in Art* (1911), he identified this development as part of a broad cultural rejection of materialistic representation as he bemoaned the "soulless content of modern life" with its atheism, positivism, and naturalist art.[37] He proposed an art that would enrich by communicating directly from the inner spirit of the artist to the spectator unmediated by narrative themes or associations with recognizable objects.

In his art, to address a public accustomed to familiar narratives, he began with imagery from the Book of Revelation such as angels and serpents.[38] His titles also conjured up familiar biblical narrative: *Deluge*, *Resurrection*, and *Apocalypse*. But soon the images became abstract, and the paintings were given non-representational titles such as *Composition*, *Improvisation*, or *Impression*.

Mann's *Death in Venice* opens with a warning about 1911, "a year that for months glowed threateningly over our continent." In that year Germany sent a gunboat to Agadir to protect German interests in Morocco, creating a crisis that almost plunged Europe into an apocalyptic war. Kandinsky's barely representational paintings from that same year are composed with abstracted apocalyptic imagery including guns and boats, which he also related to his personal sense of doom as well as hope.[39] At the upper left of *Composition IV* (1911, see Cover Illustration) two horsed riders battle with sabers, and below them two lines of guns clash in a world of lost souls. The theme of battle is also indicated by the fortress atop the blue mountain in the middle. In contrast, the right side has a reclining couple symbolizing love and two standing saints symbolizing hope.[40] In the lower-left corner two boats with oars row to salvation suggested by a rainbow. In the center foreground three ghostly Cossacks wearing red hats and holding two spears confront viewers visually as the painting confronts them formally. As Kandinsky explained, the color is balanced between the cool blue in the center and the warm reds and yellows on the right side. The bent, entangled lines of the battling horses in the upper left contrast with the parallel lines of the harmonious figures on the right. Summarizing how these formal aspects of colors and lines suggest the substantive content of a battle he added: "The juxtaposition of this bright-sweet-cold tone with angular movement (battle) is the principal contrast in the picture."[41] Thus, colors and lines clash but also resolve as he hoped modern politics and culture would do, with himself as St. George, as depicted in other images, doing battle with the dragon of materialism, by which he meant representational art as well as a chaotic and vulgar modern world. *Composition IV* is a farewell salute to representation in art with horses, riders, boats with oars, saints, reclining lovers, and Cossacks taking, as it were, a final bow, before passing into a new kind of art altogether, into unrecognizable, pure artistic forms. Later in 1911, with *Composition V*, Kandinsky became fully abstract in that the painting's imagery cannot be identified without comparison with other works and at first glance looks like just oddly shaped colors and black lines.

Kandinsky's abstraction was the centerpiece of a broad artistic shift. In 1909 the Italian futurists dissolved objects in depictions of modern technology that by 1913 became images of speeding cars and finally "abstract speed" with no object identifiable in the composition or referenced in the title.[42] Also in 1909 the Dutch painter Piet Mondrian began depicting trees that by 1912 became geometricized forms. His rhetoric of purity through abstraction was echoed by the Russian painter Kasimir Malevich, who in 1913 developed an abstract style he called suprematism. In a manifesto of 1915, Malevich announced its historical role. Suprematists rejected art that depicts recognizable things and figures. They had been inspired by futurist renderings of machines and movement but eventually rejected that art, because even when it represented "abstract speed," its inspiration derived from and remained attached to the speeding car that produced the speed. Non-objective suprematism began with the inner processes of the mind.[43] It cleared from art the accidental objects and narratives of a chaotic world of moribund nations, commercialized religions, and manufactured products. Malevich characterized his painting of a black square within a white border, titled *The Black Square*, as "the icon of our times."[44] He first exhibited it in 1915, hung across the upper corner of a room, the spot in Russian Orthodox homes where religious icons, sometimes of Christ, are placed, looking down into the room.[45] By representing holy icons of the Christian religion as a black square, Malevich proclaimed that art need not reference any real object but only itself as shapes of color celebrating a restoration of life. God could not be more dead iconographically than as a black square. In 1927 Malevich explained the historical context of his suprematist goals: "Art no longer cares to serve the state and religion . . . it wants to have nothing further to do with the object, as such, and believes that it can exist in and for itself, without 'things.'"[46]

On the eve of World War I, the leading British painter Wyndham Lewis attempted to apply his abstract vorticist style to a literary work. In the first issue of the vorticist journal *Blast* in July 1914, he published *Enemy of the Stars*, an account of the production of a play with two main characters. A sketch accompanying the text shows one of the characters as an abstracted, mechanized form with a featureless head that looks like the arc of a circle from a piece of machinery. In the text Lewis violates rules of semantics and syntax as verbs are omitted in strings of phrases linked ungrammatically in clusters of images or literary vortices: "Throats iron eternities, drinking heavy radiance, limbs towers of blatant light, the stars poised, immensely distant, with their metal sides, pantheistic machines."[47]

During the war Lewis was in an artillery unit and saw quasi-abstracted material forms such as shell-craters, skeletons, and blasted tree-stumps that recalled pre-war formal abstraction.[48] But those images were so full of reality that a return to pre-war abstraction was impossible, as he explained. "My literary contemporaries I looked upon as . . . not keeping pace with the visual revolution. A kind of play, 'The Enemy of the Stars' . . . was my attempt to show them the way. It became evident to me at once, however, when I started to write a novel, that words and syntax were not susceptible of transformation into abstract terms, to which process the visual arts lent themselves quite readily. The coming of war and the writing – at top-speed – of a full-length novel ('Tarr') was the turning point. Writing – literature – dragged me out of the abstract cul-de-sac . . . The war was a sleep . . . Upon waking I found an altered world: and I had changed, too, very much. The geometrics which had interested me so exclusively before, I now felt were bleak and empty."[49] The overpowering experience of the war killed Lewis's inclination to produce abstract literature as well as art.

Other writers also tried to write if not abstract, at least abstracted, literary texts. In 1914 Stein published *Tender Buttons*, which used identifiable words grouped in intelligible phrases that jarred conventional syntax but were not abstract. In later years she explained her rejection of abstraction while working on *Tender Buttons*: "I took individual words and thought about them until I got their weight and volume complete and put them next to another word, and at this same time I found out very soon that there is no such thing as putting them together without sense ... I made innumerable efforts to make words write without sense and found it impossible."[50] If Gertrude Stein found abstract writing impossible, it is.[51]

The overpowering narrative of the war made weak plots and literary abstraction seem out of touch as well as irreverent. But one group of writers used abstraction to be as irreverent as possible. Their poetry was part of a movement whose name itself is a pair of meaningless syllables – dada. In a Zurich cabaret on July 14, 1916, the dadaist poet Hugo Ball read his first poem of abstract nonsense: "*gadgi beri bimba glandridi laula lono cadori*," and so forth. Ball violated rational semantics and syntax to rescue language from its subservience to the insanity that led to a senseless war. As he explained in his diary: "The human figure is progressively disappearing from pictorial art, and no object is present except in fragmentary form. This is one more proof that the human countenance has become ugly and outworn, and that the things which surround us have become objects of revulsion. The next step is for poetry to discard language as painting has discarded objects, and for similar reasons."[52] During one reading, as his audience became anxious, he began to chant the syllables "like a recitative, in liturgical style." Even this high moment of literary abstraction was delivered with a cadence that evoked Catholic ritual. Ball eventually gave up nonsense poetry, and dadaists went on to produce unorthodox but not abstract texts. Poetry could not entirely discard words that always evoke some meaning, and abstract sounds could not sustain interest, even for dada enthusiasts.

Neither Gide nor Woolf wrote an abstract novel, but they were influenced by abstract art and created characters who contemplate its aesthetic potential. Abstract art avoids the clichés associated with conventional themes and familiar objects, but literature can never entirely dispense with words or replace recognizable subject matter. In *The Counterfeiters*, when offered a chance to found a new literary journal, the misanthropic student Strouvilhou proposes to get rid of "those promissary notes which go by the name of *words*." Literature, he explains, has failed to keep up with the abstractionist impulse. "In painting today, just see how the '*motif*,' as it used to be called, has fallen into discredit. *A fine subject!* It makes one laugh. Painters don't even dare venture on a portrait unless they can be sure of avoiding every trace of resemblance . . . I don't ask for more than two years before a future poet will think himself dishonored if anyone can understand a word of what he says" (*C*, 332–33). Gide conveys the radical abstractionist impulse of the pre-war years that tempted writers but never could become a viable literary style. Gide subsequently discredits Strouvilhou by having him bully and eventually plot to murder a timid student.

Woolf invokes the abstractionist position in *To the Lighthouse*. Her diary records how the second section, "Time Passes," was "the most difficult abstract piece of writing" she undertook because she had "to give an empty house, no people's characters, the passage of time, all eyeless & featureless with nothing to cling to."[53] The section is not abstract, but its effort to capture passing time and featureless characters is abstractionist. Woolf also explores abstraction with Lily's painting. Lily's inspirations emanate from abstractionist impulses – to capture the instinct that attracts bees to sweetness, to become one with her art like water poured into a jar. An early composition draws the attention of Lily's friend Mr. Bankes, who asks what "the triangular purple shape" signifies. She explains that it is "Mrs. Ramsay reading to [her son] James," but, the narrator adds, "she had made no attempt at likeness." She introduced the shape only because she felt the need of a dark area to offset a bright one. Bankes tries to see the purple triangle as a "reduction" of mother and child, but, Lily explains, "the picture was not of them," at least not in the conventional sense (*TL*, 51–53). When she resumes painting ten years later to recapture her feelings about Mrs. Ramsay reading to James, she understands the abstract impulse of her art: "Beautiful pictures. Beautiful phrases. But what she wished to get hold of was that very jar on the nerves, the thing itself before it has been made anything" (193).[54] Lily has witnessed love, marriage, motherhood, war, and death. She aspires to capture not likenesses of these experiences but something abstracted from them like the homing instinct of bees. The final account of Lily's painting is of pure abstraction: "There it was – her picture. Yes, with all its greens and blues, its lines running up and across, its attempt at something" (208). Lily's final gesture, drawing a line in the center of her canvas, is an abstract rendering of a tree.[55]

In the ten "Disintegration of Values" essays of *The Sleepwalkers*, Broch relates abstract style on a grand scale to the secular and anarchist tendencies of the modern age. Each age is defined by its style, these essays contend, and the dominant style of the contemporary age is abstraction. That style Broch links to the destruction of World War I, the historical context of the last part of the novel set in 1918. As he explains: "An epoch which is completely under the dominion of death and hell must live in a style that can no longer give birth to ornament."[56] The defining ornament of the Medieval Church, the cross, was replaced by an abstract art that signifies the emptiness of the modern world, swirling out of control in a plurality of debased values. The current slogans "war is war" and "business is business" embody "the values and non-values of our age," which are embodied in secularism and anarchism and graphically represented in abstract art (446).

Surrealism

To get millions of men to kill millions of other men, authorities had to dehumanize the enemy with propaganda. For that purpose painters produced blood-stirring war posters, while writers crafted emotionally charged texts. Those writers included Anatole France, Paul Claudel, and Charles Péguy in France; Thomas Mann, Max Reinhardt, and Max Weber in Germany; Thomas Hardy, Arthur Conan Doyle, Ford Madox Ford, and Arnold Bennett in England. In response, dadaists recoiled from an art debased by service to war and declared war on art itself. The dadaist moment, roughly 1916 to 1924, is the one time in the modernist period when the artistic master narrative came under assault, although dadaist iconoclasm was directed primarily at those artists who failed to be creative and were complicitous in the war. That brief subversion of the artistic narrative in dadaism was the springboard for surrealism, which sought to transform life with a transformative art.

Surrealism was conceived and defined by the French writer André Breton. The term refers to a superior reality, a sur-reality, inaccessible by reason and logic, which he sought to capture in life, art, and literature. In 1917 he was posted to the psychiatric center of Saint-Dizier that treated shell-shocked soldiers. Of that experience he recalled: "I was able to try out experimentally on the patients the processes of [psychoanalytic] investigation, make a recording for the purpose of interpretation of dreams, of dissociations of involuntary thought."[57]

Freud contributed to surrealism his method of revealing the unexamined nature of reality, most pointedly for Breton the nightmarish reality of the war years. Freud devised a way to access repressed impulses with a psychoanalytic theory that could also be used to interpret how nations, corporations, and churches – like dreams, jokes, and neurotic symptoms – are contingencies of history, constructs by people who nevertheless cling to their fictions as divinely sanctioned institutions, as that which is meant to be. Freud rejected not only the notion that whatever is, is right, but also the notion that anyone can know what is. For him, all mental events are surreal, that is, shaped by unconscious mental processes into patterns of living whose ultimate meaning remains uninterpreted and whose ultimate sources remain unknown. His sentences and arguments are not surreal, but the unconscious memories and impulses interpreted in his works are precisely the sort that Breton sought to capture in his writings.

Breton was influenced by Freud's analysis of the unconscious mechanisms of dream work including symbolism, displacement, and projection. He was also impressed by Freud's interpretation of the meaning of slips of the tongue and jokes. Central to Breton's surrealism is Freud's theory of the dialectical unity of opposites – that the unconscious mind produces only positive thoughts and images, but with negations underlying them. That is, one cannot dream a negative, the non-existence of something, only a positive content elaborated by disruptive imagery such as accompanying anxiety (from being chased by a bear) or impediments (legs that do not move properly). Freud sought to cure mental illness by interpreting and removing neurotic symptoms, while Breton sought to expand mental life by disclosing repressed memories and impulses. To that end he adapted Freud's technique of free association to his own automatic writing, a surrealist exercise to produce texts supposedly without censorship or rewriting. In 1919 he and Philippe Soupault began sessions of automatic writing of phrases that occurred to them in self-induced hypnotic trances, which they purported to transcribe in that state free from the distortions of memory or conscious reasoning. They published these sessions in 1920 as *Magnetic Fields*, later tagged by Breton as the first surrealist text. Breton's definition of surrealism focused on this activity: "SURREALISM, *n.* Psychic automatism in its pure state, by which one proposes to express – verbally, by means of the written word, or in any other manner – the actual functioning of thought."[58]

In 1924 Breton published *Manifesto of Surrealism*, which defined surreality as a resolution of dream and reality and the ultimate joy and goal of his life.[59] Surrealism cultivates the everyday marvelous that opens the mind to experience in contrast to the religious miraculous that constricts experience by sacred dogma. It opposes bourgeois family life that crucifies love, religious morality that degrades sex, and the eight-hour work day that alienates labor. The *Manifesto* also indicts realist literature. "The realist attitude," he argues, "is made up of mediocrity, hate, and dull conceit. It is this attitude which today gives birth to these ridiculous books, these insulting plays. It constantly feeds on and derives strength from the newspapers and stultifies both science and art by assiduously flattering the lowest of tastes." He targets novels that give too many explanations of behavior and descriptions of events with "images taken from some stock catalogue," as he found in Dostoevsky's description of Raskolnikov's room in *Crime and Punishment.*[60]

As an alternative to stultifying realist novels, he wrote three surrealist novels about the marvelous, beginning with his memoir-novel *Nadja* in 1928.[61] In it Breton crafted his meeting with a Parisian woman in 1926 into a story about a mentally disturbed woman of the streets. His first-person narration asks "Who am I?", and his encounters with Nadja contribute to an answer. He seeks to break through apparent reality to surreality by relinquishing rational planning and strict chronology, and being open to chance, sensitive to unexpected juxtapositions of seemingly unrelated objects in ways that surpass rational understanding. He meets her by chance when she is going nowhere, wanders with her through Paris without a goal, and opens himself to a relationship with her built on whimsey as her mind becomes progressively disorganized. She feels as though she had participated in a scene from Breton's surreal text, *Soluble Fish* (1924), which she had read – "a scene," Breton concedes, "whose precise meaning I have never been able to determine and whose characters are alien, their agitation as enigmatic as possible."[62] Nadja seems to live in the surreal world that Breton senses at the base of dreams. Her life is a surreal itinerary of marvelous moments that lead Breton back to himself through an appreciation of convulsive beauty and mad love.

The political implications of surrealism are explicit in the title of Breton's journal, *La Révolution surréaliste.* In 1924 he was impressed with Russian communism and anticipated a broader revolutionizing of consciousness through surrealism. By the time he wrote *Nadja* in 1927, however, he was pulling away from involvement with the French Communist Party because of its iron discipline and the limited conception of art in socialist realism. His *Second Manifesto of Surrealism* of 1930 made explicit his dissatisfaction with communism and underscored the primacy of language. Surrealist writers subvert language with neologisms and distortion in a world that violates conventional logic. Surrealism seeks to revolutionize how people live by disrupting the conventional categories of experience as they view a face with breasts for eyes and read about a man cut in two by a window.[63]

Collage

The first modernist collage was Picasso's *Still Life with Chair Caning* of 1912, produced by pasting onto a still-life painting a piece of oilcloth designed to look like caning. Fifty years later Picasso noted the historical implications of collage in estranging objects from their conventional roles in order to capture an increasingly estranged world: "If a piece of a newspaper can become a bottle, that gives us something to think about in connection with both newspapers and bottles . . . And this strangeness was what we wanted to make people think about because we were quite aware that our world was becoming very strange."[64] Collage quickly spread across Europe and America before World War I, constituting what at least one art historian called "the single most revolutionary formal innovation in artistic representation to occur in our century."[65]

Realist artists developed a uniform style; preserved dichotomies of figure and ground, real and fake, art and world; viewed objects in that world as familiar and discrete; used conventional artistic materials to create those objects; rendered that world on a flat surface that was supposed to create the impression of a transparent window on three-dimensional reality; and generated meaning with easily readable renderings of perspective, scale, and solidity. Collage reworked these stylistic features.

The mixed styles that Picasso introduced with cubism were expanded in collage into mixed artistic materials that included paint, photographs, prints, newspapers, and mass-produced objects such as fabrics. These objects retained their non-artistic meaning as they acquired another meaning in the work, conflating art and world by suggesting the creative significance of everyday objects and the worldly significance of art. By moving ordinary objects into unfamiliar contexts, collage defamiliarized them, mirroring a world that was increasingly unrecognizable. Collage blurred the discreteness of objects and subverted their singular functions, as bits of newspaper pasted to the picture surface became new surfaces on which the artist could paint numbers and musical instruments. The original function of the newspaper was thus both subverted and retained, as it became a surface to paint and a text to read. The distinction between fake and real also blurred. Instead of the oilcloth's commercial function to fool observers into thinking that a table top was real caning, the oilcloth drew attention to its actual nature and to the surface on which it was pasted. Collage blocked the realist function of that surface as a transparent window onto reality; instead it became an opaque base for objects built out from the picture surface. Collage confounded realist perspective, played havoc with realist scale, and confused realist solidity as single artistic materials such as a newspaper could be opaque and transparent at different places on the same picture surface.

Literary collage is a metaphorical pasting of disparate sources or even, with Döblin, a literal pasting of newspaper clippings onto a manuscript.[66]

Some modernist novels approximate the heterogeneity of artistic collage with a variety of literary and graphic sources from the commercial world. *Ulysses* is a collage of multiple sources including literary references, newspaper articles, ads, songs, jokes, posters, prayers, handbills, and Bloom's budget. An inventory of the contents of Bloom's drawer is a collage of miscellaneous items: his daughter's copybook and drawings, two fading photographs, a butt of sealing wax, a box of pen nibs, a bazaar ticket, a cameo brooch, and so forth (*U*, 592). The narrator also interpolates texts written in different styles.

Döblin began writing *Berlin Alexanderplatz* in 1927, the year Walter Ruttman's montage film *Berlin − Symphony of the Metropolis* premiered and *Ulysses* appeared in German translation. Döblin elaborated cinematic montage into a collagist literary style with jarring juxtapositions of sources from Berlin life − newspaper articles, notices from advertising kiosks, restaurant menus, police reports, encyclopedia articles, and telephone directories. He was directly influenced by Joyce because after reading *Ulysses* he added the strongly collagist sections 1 and 2 of Book 2 that begin with reproductions of the insignia of ten Berlin public agencies. These are followed by notices of diverse texts and activities on the Rosenthaler Platz − a weather report and a tram schedule followed by shopwindow ads for fruit brandies and a rejuvenation treatment for elephants.[67] Then, apropos of nothing, Döblin lists seventeen sub-agencies of an electric company; bits of conversation by anonymous train passengers; a newspaper report of two lovers' suicide; and, finally, narratives of two women shopping for a truss, a man on his way to exchange a defective iron, and the life history of a fourteen-year-old boy until his death at age fifty-two, including his obituary. Collagist techniques capture how these impressions and circumstances impact an individual chaotically, not how they can be interpreted by a single authorial consciousness. These items do not enrich Biberkopf. They pull in myriad directions that lead away from him and for that reason suggest the disjointed nature of modern urban life.

The artistic revolution signified by collage disrupted narrative unity, institutional authority, and historical continuity. Personal breakdowns, family crises, urban uprisings, political revolutions, financial panic, and the death of God are collagist narrative disruptions with anarchistic underpinnings. The dominant subversive episode, World War I, was a prolonged collage of chaos and destruction. The aftermath of the battles of Fleury, a French town that was taken and retaken sixteen times, looked like a horrific collage with bits of objects and buildings strewn about the landscape − a city in ruins where objects lost their identity and figure-ground distinctions collapsed in a composition with no single author. The revolutionary stylistic changes of collage conjured up a world in which the conventions for ordering the space, time, and material reality of the master narratives no longer predominated. While collage was fundamentally creative and life-affirming and was conceived, as Picasso noted, to bring attention to the actual nature of artistic materials and everyday objects, its defamiliarizing function also had deconstructive implications. If "unartistic" objects can be pasted on to the artistic surface, conventional notions of the unity of art no longer hold. The appearance of capriciousness and disarray in collage had broad historical implications, especially during the war and after, when a highly disorganized and destroyed world, as Picasso noted, "was becoming very strange."

CHAPTER 7

Narrator

In the realist period, novelists such as Eliot and Thackeray created third-person narrators who assumed command by telling their story with broad vision, a singular authoritative voice, and seemingly unlimited knowledge. Other realists, such as Emily Brontë (*Wuthering Heights*), Dickens (*Bleak House*), and Wilkie Collins (*The Moonstone*, 1868), used multiple narrators with different points of view. Their uses of multiple narrators, however, were different from modernists'. Realist multiple narrators introduced variety while preserving the same kind of interpretive stability created by single, authoritative third-person narrators. In *The Moonstone*, for example, argues D. A. Miller, the multiple narrators' "different points of view, degrees of information, [and] tendencies of suspicion are never allowed to tamper with" the text's production of "basic interpretive securities about character and language." The novel is "always speaking a master-voice that corrects, overrides, subordinates, or sublates all other voices."¹ In contrast, modernists reworked narratorial power with marked ways of restricting and presenting their stories. They devised new ways of seeing or, more precisely, focalizing stories that ranged from James's strictly limited singular focalization to varieties of multiple focalization. These innovative modes of focalization did destabilize the "basic interpretive securities" that realists had worked so hard to stabilize. Modernists also developed a range of voices to tell the many ways their narrators knew, or did not know, what their characters were doing and why. Thus, the polyvision and polyphony of modernist narrators aligned with their multiple ways of knowing. These changes were symptoms of a creative reworking of the narrator's function, reflecting a new understanding of what can and cannot be seen, articulated, and known about human behavior and how best to dramatize it.

VISION: SINGULAR, SERIAL, PARALLEL, EMBEDDED

The vision of the realist narrator extended seemingly at will into the mind of every character and out of it to encompass events across vast stretches of time and space. In *Middlemarch*, for example, Eliot's third-person narrator can see into the mind of all her characters and gives the impression that she offers a reliable picture of the entire world of Middlemarch and could narrate any event that occurred in it, even where characters are alone or when events occur simultaneously in different places. Modernist narrators characteristically rejected such wide-ranging vision monopolized by a single third-person narrator and instead devised a variety of restricted and multiple ways of viewing characters and events through singular, serial, parallel, and embedded focalizations.

Henry James adhered rigorously to a singular focalization with his third-person narrator who limits the narratorial outlook to the experience of a single character in such a way as "to get into the skin of the creature" and tell the story through that character's consciousness alone.[2] The significance of that technique is evident from its first precise identification in one of the most important insights in the history of narrative theory – Genette's distinction in 1972 between vision and voice. As Genette explained, leading critics confused the vision or point of view of characters experiencing a story with the voice of the narrator telling it.[3] For example, in 1961 Wayne Booth argued that in *The Ambassadors* "Strether in large part 'narrates' his own story, even though he is always referred to in the third person."[4] The quotation marks around *narrates* reveal Booth's uneasiness, because Strether is not a narrator. His experience is the exclusive focus of the story's action, but that story is told by a third-person narrator. Genette summarized the reigning confusion and clarified his important distinction: "most of the theoretical works on this subject," he wrote, suffer from "a confusion between the question *who is the character whose point of view orients the narrative perspective?* and the very different question of *who is the narrator?* – or, more simply, the question *who sees?* and the question *who speaks?*"[5] But that distinction is too schematic, he added, because the first term of that distinction is not merely a question of who sees, and everything a character experiences is not visual. Some experiences come from hearing, smell, touch, or taste as well as thoughts, memories, or emotions; and so Genette proposed referring to the experience as *focalization* rather than *vision*.[6] That it took seventy years for someone to identify accurately James's technique suggests how unprepared scholars were to understand it over those years and how innovative it was.

James's control of the narrator's focalization replicates how characters themselves are locked in their consciousness and access the world with strict limits and biases. But by remaining within a single mind, a narrator can explore exceptionally detailed aspects of it. James's first systematic use of that technique is in *What Maisie Knew* (1897) where the narrator focalizes the story through the "small expanding consciousness" of Maisie from age six to twelve.[7] The novel dramatizes what Maisie knew and how she acquired that knowledge in addition to what she did not know, was not allowed to know, did not want to know, and understood but could not express. Her knowledge might be unprecedented, the narrator claims, in that she understood "much more than any little girl, however patient, had perhaps ever understood before" (39). Her knowledge includes precocious amorous fantasies stimulated by exposure to her mother's numerous lovers, which enable her to match-make her two step-parents.

James subverts the family narrative substantively with this story of divorced parents mistreating their daughter in what one critic characterizes as an "antifamily."[8] Divorce was rare in nineteenth-century society and novels, but James explores with a vengeance the impact of a divorce on Maisie. By a court order she was shuttled between her mother and father at six-month intervals, during which times "they had wanted her not for any good they could do her, but for the harm they could, with her unconscious aid, do each other" (36). Each impressed on Maisie the sins of the other and thereby increased her suffering, as the "evil" they thought of each other "they poured into her little gravely-gazing soul" (42). The novel depicts new modes of child abuse – not by a cruel aunt (*Jane Eyre*), a violent stepfather (*David Copperfield*), or a conniving villain (*Oliver Twist*), but by the child's own cruel, violent, and conniving parents along with their second spouses.

James innovates formally by seeing exclusively through Maisie's consciousness. Here and throughout James conflates vision and knowledge. In the Preface, James explains that he rejected first-person narration because it did not allow him to explore experiences that Maisie did not grasp or lacked the language to express, as in the following report: "She [Maisie's stepmother] talked mainly to her other neighbor, and that left Maisie leisure to note the manner in which eyes were riveted and nudges exchanged as well as to lose herself in the meanings that, dimly as yet and disconnectedly, but with a vividness that fed apprehension, she could begin to read into her stepmother's independent move" (225). Children do not think about or describe their experiences with such language. James notes that his strict limitation to Maisie enables the narrator to capture "the child's confused and obscure notion" of her parents' behavior but express it with his own intricate language (27). James's formal technique is well suited to capture the substance of Maisie's oppressive family situation, because it confines the reader inside her mind, recreating the limited knowledge she has of her predicament and the limited power she has to free herself from it.

Singular focalization intensifies concentration and enriches the immediacy of narrated experience. As James explains in the Preface to his next singular focalization novel, *The Ambassadors*: "the business of my tale and the march of my action, not to say the precious moral of everything, is just my demonstration of this process of vision."[9] Learning to see or, more broadly, to grasp the entirety of experience is the heart of the story, from Strether's initial blindness about love and life to his final groping toward insight into how blind he had been all along. As he tells Maria Gostrey in the end, "I do what I didn't before – I *see* her [his fiancée, Mrs. Newsome, and the world her business represents]" (510). By remaining within Strether's consciousness as he struggles to understand, the narrator creates in the reader a growing sense of what Strether fails to see, developments all around him of which he remains ignorant. Singular focalization thus carries the freight of Strether's original narrow-mindedness that kept him from understanding the value of Chad's love for Madame de Vionnet, the significance of his ambassadorial mission to serve the commercial world, and the wider possibilities of life, as he realizes in the novel's pivotal moment of insight – the need to "live all you can" (215).

In *The Golden Bowl* James alternates the singular focalization between the experiences of a married couple – in the first half of the novel exclusively Amerigo's, and in the second half Maggie's. With that modification the technique is still suited to capture the novel's content that is primarily the breakdown of a flawed marriage. The first half's focalization constructs the narrow vision of Amerigo's financial reason for marrying Maggie, his limited grasp of the possibilities of marriage, and his short-sighted abuse of Maggie's trust shown by his affair with his former mistress Charlotte after she has become the wife of Maggie's father. The second half follows Maggie's homing in on Amerigo's and Charlotte's betrayals. When Maggie observes Amerigo's reaction to seeing Fannie Assingham break the golden bowl, Maggie realizes his adultery, and that exchange of glances and understanding passes through her. James explores how each imagines what the other might see and say but does not, as in the following convoluted account of the couple's tortuous evasiveness: "'Yes, look, look,' she seemed to see him hear her say even while her sounded words were other – 'Look, look both at the truth that still survives in that smashed evidence and at the even more remarkable appearance that I'm not such a fool as you supposed me.'"[10] After that confrontation, Amerigo slowly relinquishes control to Maggie. In the last scene, he redefines their relationship by turning over his vision and understanding to Maggie's, for the moment at least, as he concedes, "'See?' I see nothing but *you*.'"

While singular focalization narrowed and sharpened vision, other innovative focalizations expanded and varied it. These aligned with other efforts
in the period to see and interpret from different points of view to expand
understanding and aesthetic possibilities. Einstein posited a plurality of
spaces produced by their observation from moving reference systems.
Geometers envisioned non-Euclidean geometries, Émile Durkheim identified a plurality of spaces determined by different social systems, Otto
Spengler elaborated different conceptions of space in different historical
cultures, and Jakob von Uexküll explored the different space-worlds of
animals as well as humans – surrounding world, inner world, and counter-
world. Cubists superposed multiple perspectives on the same object in still
lifes and portraits, cinema created multiple views of the same event with
quick-cut editing, while collage, as I have noted, used multiple materials
that implied different spatial contexts for those materials and multiple
meanings.[11] Nietzsche and Ortega each formulated philosophies of "perspectivism" distinctive to their age. Nietzsche capped that philosophy with
an outburst against Platonic idealism and Kantian rationalism: "Let us be on
guard against the dangerous old conceptual fiction that posited a 'pure, will-
less, painless, timeless knowing subject'; let us guard against the snares of
such contradictory concepts as 'pure reason,' 'absolute spirituality,' 'knowledge in itself,' . . . there is *only* a perspective seeing, *only* a perspective
'knowing' . . . the *more* eyes, different eyes, we can use to observe one
thing, the more complete will be our 'concept' of this thing, our
'objectivity' . . . To eliminate the will [would be] to *castrate* the intellect."[12]
In accord with the pluralistic and perspectivist spirit of the age, modernist
narrators devised serial, parallel, and embedded focalizations.

With serial focalization, narrators told their story through several characters who related different parts of it. In *Lord Jim* the frame narrator
introduces the first-person narrator Marlow who relates to a group of
listeners Jim's story that comes from numerous characters who recall fragments of Jim's character and fate – the first engineer of the *Patna*, the
French Lieutenant, Captain Brierly, Chester, Engström, Stein, Jewel,
Cornelius, Gentleman Brown, Doramin, Tamb'Itam, and Jim himself.
This medley of observers still offers only an incomplete and distorted
view of Jim. As Marlow concedes: "It is impossible to see him clearly –
especially as it is through the eyes of others that we take our last look at him"
(*LJ*, 339). In *Nostromo* Conrad uses serial focalization by a third-person
narrator, again focalized through dozens of characters but without their
concentrating on one person as in *Lord Jim* and without a main internal
first-person narrator to articulate and organize them, such as Marlow. In

these novels serial focalization captures the elusive aspects of characters and the expansive aspects of events spread over the globe characteristic of imperialism and capitalism.

Woolf's serial focalization in *Mrs. Dalloway* mixes the vision of the narrator and numerous focalizing characters, primarily Clarissa, but also Peter Walsh, Richard Dalloway, Septimus Smith, Lucrezia Smith, and at times a collective group of anonymous others. This technique makes possible the narration of variable perspectives on characters and events but also conflates perspectives as characters' thoughts and emotions interlace with those of the narrator. Woolf exploits this technique in the hallucinations of Septimus, who confuses persons and things that are, or are not, before his eyes, recreating the trench warfare that ultimately drives him insane. Readers see as he sees faces laughing at him and fingers pointing at him, a dog turning into a man and flowers growing through his flesh. In his final moments before committing suicide, he sees himself through the dying eyes of his wartime buddy Evans, through the insensitive eyes of his patronizing physician Bradshaw, through the effusive eyes of his long-suffering wife Lucrezia, and through the shocked eyes of an old man going down the stairs who sees him just before he jumps out of a window. Behind these eyes are those of the narrator and of Woolf, who suffered grievously from the death of her brother Thoby. Woolf uses serial focalization to recreate the patchwork world of postwar London in 1923 as a psychological combat zone of multiple focalizations pathologically confused in Septimus's war-torn mind.

In another modernist technique, parallel focalization, multiple narrators relate the same entire story. Faulkner develops this technique in *The Sound and the Fury* with first-person narratives by the Compson brothers Benjy, Quentin, and Jason, and a third-person narrative that centers on the experiences of the Compson family servant Dilsey Gibson. In *Absalom, Absalom!* Faulkner uses four major character-narrators – Rosa Coldfield, Mr. Compson, Quentin Compson, and Shreve McCannon – who are introduced by a third-person frame narrator and relate information in dialogues with one another. In both novels this formal clashing of perspectives structures the substantive clashing of family members: in *The Sound and the Fury*, the decline of the Compson family through promiscuity, desertion, and suicide; and in *Absalom, Absalom!*, the ruin of the Sutpen dynasty through hubris, incest, and murder.

A final narrative technique, embedded focalization, is evident in Gide's novel about writing a novel with focalizations *mis en abyme*, literally "put in the abyss."[13] Like heraldic shields with a smaller image of the entire shield in their center (or abyss, as it is called), Gide put in the center of his novel a novelist writing the novel in which he appears. Gide's focalizations are embedded as follows: he wrote *The Journals of André Gide*, which recount how he wrote his novel *The Counterfeiters* about many characters including Edouard, who is writing a novel to be titled *The Counterfeiters*, to which Gide appended an essay, "Journal of *The Counterfeiters*," two years after the novel appeared. There he wrote: "I see this journal in which I am writing the very history of the novel poured into the book in its entirety and forming its principal interest."[14] It elaborates Edouard's theory of the novel, as does his journal within the novel that also describes his writing. The novel's third-person narrator also recounts Edouard's theory of the novel that he relates to friends (*C*, 181–94).

Realists invented many diverse characters with different outlooks but presented them through an external third-person narrator who seemed to have unlimited range of vision in a population that found comfort in the family, took pride in nation and empire, retained some belief in divine providence, and aspired to, even though it never achieved, common values. In contrast, modernists sought with multiple modes of focalization to capture characters who are orphaned or illegitimate and do not belong in families (Lafcadio, Bernard), venture beyond national frontiers (Kurtz, Aschenbach), aggressively reject religion (Stephen Dedalus, Meursault), break major social codes by killing (Huguenau, Joe Christmas), and trans-value their values (Ulrich, Roquentin). Singular focalization served the modernist interest in interior experience that Woolf proposed in "Modern Fiction": to trace the pattern "which each sight or incident scores upon the consciousness."[15] Serial, parallel, and embedded focalization served the cultural pluralism and multi-perspectivism of the age with authors and their characters re-evaluating the received institutions, especially those of marriage, family, nation, and religion. These modes of modernist polyvision are the counterpart of modernist polyphony.

VOICE: NONHUMAN, SHIFTING, MULTIPLE, HETEROGLOSSIA

Voice is the literary instrument that narrators use to tell stories. Modernists innovate that function with nonhuman entities, shifting narrators, multiple narrators, and multiple voices or polyphony. In contrast to realist narrators who are generally human, some modernist narrators range beyond the human. In *A Passage to India* the Marabar Caves turn every sound made in them into an echo that undermines Mrs. Moore's hold on life as it murmurs

"Pathos, piety, courage – they exist, but are identical, and so is filth. Everything exists, nothing has value." The Caves' sound effaces rational thought but is articulate enough to persuade Mrs. Moore that "poor little talkative Christianity, and . . . its divine words from 'Let there be light' to 'It is finished' only amounted to 'boum.'"[16] In *Absalom, Absalom!* Shreve's account of what happened the night Rosa Coldfield drove Quentin to the Sutpen mansion fades into an account of what he speculates that the dust cloud stirred up by their buggy might have warned: "*Come on if you like. But I will get there first; accumulating ahead of you . . . and there will be nothing for you to do but to return and so I would advise you not to go, to turn back now and let what is, be*" (*AA*, 143). That supposed audible dust cloud symbolizes the murkiness that surrounds the buggy ride as well as the destiny of the Sutpen family. The narratorial voices of inanimate objects in the "Time Passes" section of *To the Lighthouse* sketch transformations of a house and family over destructive years spanning World War I: air drafts question how long a flap of wallpaper will hang before falling and whether the torn letters in a wastepaper basket are allies or enemies; gold letters on marble pages "describe death in battle," and "the voice of the beauty of the world" sings to everyone in the house but especially to Lily, who awakens energized to resume her painting (*TL*, 142). Modernists shift narrative voices as third-person narrators become first-person narrators, characters become narrators, and character-narrators fuse with other characters. Until the last three pages of the third volume of *Pilgrimage* the narrator recounts the life of Miriam in the third person. Then, following a break in the text that marks the suicide of Miriam's mother, the narrative voice switches back and forth between third and first person as if searching for a voice to articulate her loss.

Miriam clasped her hands together. She could not feel them. Perhaps she had dreamed that the old woman had come in and said that [the suicide had occurred]. Everything was dream; the world. I shall not have any life. I can never have any life; all my days . . . There was a tray of plates of fish and fruit on the table. She looked at it, heaving with sickness and looking at it. I am hungry. Sitting down near it she tried to pull the tray. It would not move. I must eat the food. Go on eating food, till the end of my life. (*P*, 1, 489–90)

These voice shifts from outside her mind to inside occur three times in succession to capture Miriam's frantic state, literally out of her mind with grief. In *As I Lay Dying* Faulkner switches the voice in Darl's final narration between third and first person and concludes with the second-person plural voice of Darl's family to capture the bewildering experience of his being sent to a mental institution.

Darl has gone to Jackson. They put him on the train, laughing, down the long car laughing, the heads turning like the heads of owls when he passed. "What are you laughing at?" I said . . .

Two men put him on the train . . . "Is it the pistols you're laughing at?" I said . . .

They pulled the seat together so Darl could sit by the window to laugh . . . they are riding on the state's money which is incest. A nickel has a woman on one side and a buffalo on the other; two faces and no back. I don't know what that is. Darl had a little spy-glass he got in France at the war. In it it had a woman and a pig with two backs and no face. I know what that is. "Is that why you are laughing, Darl?" . . .

Darl is our brother, our brother Darl. Our brother Darl in a cage in Jackson where, his grimed hands lying in the quiet interstices, looking out he foams.

These shifting clamorous voices come from Darl's deranged mind, the men taking him to the asylum, and his family (*AD*, 253–54).

Modernists shift narrative voice in other ways as characters become narrators and vice versa. At the end of Part Two of *The Sleepwalkers*, narrated in the third person, Edouard von Bertrand commits suicide. In Part Three he re-emerges, transformed into Bertrand Müller, a first-person narrator of chapters about a Salvation Army girl, which explore his immersion in unreason and fathom his existence in a state of sleepwalking between knowledge and ignorance.[17] In other chapters Müller authors ten essays on the "Disintegration of Values" that expound the philosophy governing the entire novel. Broch calls this technique "narrator as idea," based on his interpretation of Einstein's theory of relativity (confused with an even bigger problem in quantum theory) in which the observer's subjectivity must be part of any description of physical phenomena.[18] Broch's contribution to the modernist novel is this subversion of objective narration with a dead character emerging as a new narrative voice.

As sleepwalkers hover between knowing and not knowing, counterfeiters hover between genuine and fake. The major narrative voice of *The Counterfeiters*, the novelist Edouard, appears in several guises between objectivity and subjectivity. All of Gide's embedded focalizations that I identified in the previous section have their distinctive voices that alternate between third and first person, past and present tense, and among Edouard's various personas as a character in Gide's novel, a character in his own novel, and a journal writer. Multiple focalizations and voices make this the "cubist novel" par excellence, defracting and deflecting points of view, ventriloquizing and disguising voices, to capture the kaleidoscopic nature of love and the counterfeit nature of family life, religion, and even art.[19]

Faulkner shifts narrative voices in *Absalom, Absalom!* between character-narrators and characters, interlacing stories from the 1830s to the 1860s as they are pieced together beginning in 1909 in Jefferson, Mississippi, through multiple accounts, as, for example, Sutpen told Grandfather Compson who told his son Mr. Compson who told his son Quentin. By the time the story gets to Quentin it is not clear whose voice is being heard or whose version is reliable. In Chapter 6, set in January, 1910 in the Harvard dorm room shared by Quentin and Shreve, the narrative voice becomes fourth-hand as Quentin tells Shreve what he has learned. Their two voices mix when Shreve recalls what Quentin had told him previously, and they piece together and ultimately invent incidents and elaborate interpretations.

The conflation of their narrative voices peaks in Chapter 8 when they combine with one another and merge with their characters in competing to rework the story of Henry's murder of Charles. "It was Shreve speaking, though . . . it might have been either of them and was in a sense both . . . [with] the two of them creating between them, out of the rag-tag and bob-ends of old tales and talking, people who perhaps had never existed at all anywhere" (*AA*, 243). Their fusion with one another extends to identification with Charles and Henry, making at first four characters and then two: "Now it was not two but four of them riding the two horses through the dark over the frozen December ruts of that Christmas eve: four of them and then just two – Charles-Shreve and Quentin-Henry" (267). Faulkner adds a final shift in voice as Shreve and Quentin each become both Henry and Bon. "It was not even four now but compounded still further, since now both of them were Henry Sutpen and both of them were Bon, compounded each of both" (280). Faulkner shifts narrative voices to capture the confused history of the disintegrating Sutpen family dynasty by having his character-narrators fuse with one another and with their characters in a polyphonic free-for-all.

Realist narrators are primarily third-person objective voices that use the refined language of accomplished writers. First-person narrators, like the housekeeper Nelly Dean in *Wuthering Heights* or young Pip in *Great Expectations*, use diction more cultivated than their class, education, or age would warrant. Realists rarely turn narration over to lower-class, poorly educated, emotionally distraught, or mentally deranged narrators.[20] Modernists multiply narrative voices to capture individuals' changing needs, aspirations, and even delusions arising from changing family stress, gender roles, courtship conventions, political activity, urban dynamism, and war trauma. Their polyphony is expressed through multiple characters in Faulkner, multiple styles and voices in Broch, and multiple parodies and stylistic imitations in Joyce.

Separate voices come from fifteen poorly educated rural characters, most of them members of the discordant Bundren family, who narrate most of the fifty-nine chapters of *As I Lay Dying*. Darl opens the novel with a sober account of events and continues with eighteen more of the remaining chapters until his mind unravels. The youngest child, mentally retarded Vardaman, has nine narratives that reveal him processing the trauma of his mother's death with a delusion that she is a fish like the one he caught earlier in the day and cut up and watched die; as he explains: "I can feel where the fish was in the dust. It is cut up into pieces of not-fish now, not-blood on my hands and overalls" (*AD*, 53). Vardaman continues with his limited command of language: "It was not her because it was laying right yonder in the dirt. And now it's all chopped up. I chopped it up. It's laying in the kitchen in the bleeding pan, waiting to be cooked and et" (66). In strong rural dialect Cash Bundren disapproves of his brother Darl being branded insane: "Sometimes I aint so sho who's got ere a right to say when a man is crazy and when he aint. Sometimes I think it aint none of us pure crazy and aint none of us pure sane until the balance of us talks him that-a-way" (233). The novel captures polyphony in rural Mississippi with the authority of first-person narratives.[21]

Broch credits his polyphony in *The Sleepwalkers* to Joyce: "The essential thing in Joyce is that which I (at a suitable distance) have also strived for, and to a certain extent achieved, namely *architectonic polyphony*."[22] Broch's reading of *Ulysses* led to revisions of Part Three of the novel, "The Realist 1918," that includes multiple narrative voices. Chapter 30 includes verbatim items from a legal contract for transferring ownership of the Kur-Trier Herald newspaper from Esch to Huguenau. Chapter 33 is an article in that newspaper of June 1, 1918, authored by Major Joachim von Pasenow, which celebrates the virtues of the family, Christianity, German militarism, and the white race. The article is broken with lines of ellipsis dots to suggest that it is a set of newspaper cuttings. Chapter 59 is a drama similar to the "Circe" episode in *Ulysses*. The next chapter, a victory celebration for the Battle of Tannenberg, is a montage of different characters, written like a movie screenplay. Chapter 65 lists epigrams that sum up various characters' struggles with the disintegration of values from the hyper-rationality of war-making.

The foremost compendium of multiple narrative voices is *Ulysses*. In "Cyclops" the first-person narrator's account of events in Barney Kiernan's bar culminates in a confrontation between a tolerant and open-minded Bloom and a xenophobic and closed-minded "Citizen," Joyce's correspondence to the one-eyed cyclops in *The Odyssey*. Joyce mirrors formally Bloom's openness to different life styles by inserting into the narrator's account thirty-three literary parodies of theosophy, sentimental fiction, newspaper feature stories, minutes of the proceedings of the House of Commons, Irish myth, biblical prose, and many other voices.[23] The parodies elaborate the incident in the story they interrupt. Thus, an angry exchange in the bar over the cruelty of British imperialism is interrupted by a parody of the Apostles' Creed that mocks British rule:

They believe in rod, the scourger almighty, creator of hell upon earth, and in Jacky Tar, the son of a gun, who was conceived of unholy boast, born of the fighting navy, suffered under rump and dozen, was scarified, flayed and curried, yelled like bloody hell, the third day he arose again from the bed, steered into haven, sitteth on his beamend till further orders whence he shall come to drudge for a living and be paid. (*U*, 270)

The polyvocality of the "Oxen of the Sun" episode of *Ulysses* is a sequence of adulterated imitations of styles from Anglo-Saxon to modern slang, an episode self-described as an "allincluding most farraginous chronicle" (345). The plot line is a meeting of Bloom with Stephen and his increasingly drunken friends in a maternity hospital where a woman in labor already for three days is about to give birth. She delivers while the men joke about myriad aspects of courtship including erections, masturbation, sex, rape, adultery, sterility, contraception, artificial insemination, midwifery, abortion, Cesarian section, and birth defects. Joyce's imitation of Dickensian sentiment captures the moment after delivery when Mina looks for her baby and her husband under the protective eye of divine providence.

Reverently look at her as she reclines there with the motherlight in her eyes, that longing hunger for baby fingers (a pretty sight it is to see), in the first bloom of her new motherhood, breathing a silent prayer of thanksgiving to One above, the Universal Husband. And as her loving eyes behold her babe she wishes only one blessing more, to have her dear Doady there with her to share her joy, to lay in his arms that mite of God's clay, the fruit of their lawful embraces . . . And Doady, knock the ashes from your pipe . . . You too have fought the good fight and played loyally your man's part. Sir, to you my hand. Well done, thou good and faithful servant! (343–44)

While voices from different authors creep into such sections, these passages are largely distinct voices patterned after selections that Joyce found in contemporary literary anthologies and that he identified in a letter to Frank Budgen in March of 1920.[24] The multiple voices that interrupt the first-person narrator in "Cyclops" and the third-person narrator in "Oxen of the Sun" have a recognizable style that Joyce parodied and imitated. In other episodes Joyce mixed voices to achieve an even more historically innovative kind of polyvocality.

In 1934–35, when Soviet authorities purged deviations of thought and speech and insisted on a monophonic recitation of the Stalinist party line, the Russian critic Mikhail Bakhtin wrote "Discourse in the Novel," which developed a theory of the polyphonic aspect of literary utterances, a feature also translated as *heteroglossia*. He held that utterances are a composite of "social dialects, characteristic group behavior, professional jargons, generic languages, languages of generations and age groups, tendentious languages, languages of the authorities, of various circles and of passing fashions, languages that serve the specific sociopolitical purposes of the day."[25] Although all languages are heteroglossic, they admit of degree, and the state-enforced Russian language during the Stalinist regime was at a low point for diversity.

Bakhtin argued that heteroglossia is evident throughout the history of literature; but it is exceptionally rich in the nineteenth-century novel, as in the following passage, one of eight he analyzed from Dickens's *Little Dorrit* (1857). It celebrates Mr. Merdle, who runs an investment bubble that eventually ruins his investors.

That illustrious man and great national ornament, Mr. Merdle, continued his shining course. It began to be widely understood that one who had done society the admirable service *of making so much money out of it*, could not be suffered to remain a commoner. A baronetcy was spoken of with confidence, a peerage was frequently mentioned. (Bk. 2, Ch. 24)

The satirical praise in the first sentence indicated by *illustrious*, *great*, and *shining* emerges into the main narrative voice from other sources of ceremonious discourse. The start of the second sentence that celebrates the "admirable" Merdle is tinged with the voice of public opinion, but the italicized words, Bakhtin contends, are the author's. This and the other quoted passages are heteroglossic as they draw on languages of ceremonial hypocrisy, banal gossip, and high epic. These languages "infect" other characters as well as the narrator so that the novel is "dotted with quotation marks that serve to separate out little islands of scattered direct speech and purely authorial speech, washed by heteroglot waves from all sides."[26] This explanation is ambiguous because "dotted" and "islands" suggest discrete voices, while "washed by . . . waves" suggests merging ones. The emphasis on merging is more prevalent in modernist novels.

Heteroglossia in Dickens is framed by stable irony joining author, narrator, and reader with a shared moral sense centered in confidence that in the end justice will prevail, that Merdle's crimes will be punished. The main narrative voice is inflected by other voices but remains the source of a stable moral philosophy and world view that anchor the narrative.[27] In contrast, modernists develop an "absolute heteroglossia" as the sensibilities of different professions, classes, and regions do not merely interrupt the main narrative voice, as do the parodies in "Cyclops" or the adulterated imitations in "Oxen of the Sun," but permeate that authoritative voice as if from within, erupting sometimes in the middle of a sentence.[28] Modernist heteroglossia is similar to what Hugh Kenner calls the "Uncle Charles Principle," which is, he speculates, "apparently something new in fiction, the normally neutral narrative vocabulary pervaded by a little cloud of idioms which a character might use if he were managing the narrative."[29] Kenner offers another metaphor for this technique as a narrator influenced by the gravitational field of the nearest person.

A modernist heteroglossia is evident in the "Nausicaa" episode of *Ulysses*, which Kenner also uses to illustrate the Uncle Charles Principle. Joyce indicated the varied heteroglossia of that episode when he wrote to Frank Budgen in 1920: "*Nausikaa* is written in a namby-pamby jammy marmalady drawersy (alto là! [over the top, literally, up there]) style with effects of incense, mariolatry, masturbation, stewed cockles, painter's palette, chit-chat, circumlocutions."[30] That is, it is made up of maudlin, sugary, erotic, inflated, ceremonial, religious, gustatory, artistic, conversational, and roundabout idioms. The plot allows the narrator to use these voices to capture Gerty MacDowell's richly textured experience, which is suggested formally by having her the focus of four loci of action – where she sits and three other places. While she sits on a rock at Sandymount Strand with two friends and three young children, Bloom looks at her from behind a low wall. Several hundred yards away a men's temperance retreat celebrates a benediction service at a church, and down the beach a fireworks display begins. The men in the church are inspired by worshiping at the shrine of the Blessed Virgin while Bloom is aroused by looking up Gerty's skirt as she leans back and holds her knee up with her hands to help him along by exposing her underwear until he climaxes simultaneously with the bursting of a Roman candle up in the sky over the beach. In the midst of a description of Bloom's arousal, the narrative voice is pervaded by voices of religious ecstasy, sexual euphemism, and fashion ads.

And she saw a long Roman candle going up over the trees, up, up, and, in the *tense* hush, they were all *breathless with excitement* as it went *higher and higher* and she had to lean back more and more to look up after it, high, high, almost out of sight, and her face was suffused with a *divine*, an *entrancing* blush from straining back and he could see *her other things* too, *nainsook knickers, the fabric that caresses the skin,* better than those other *pettiwidth*, the green, four and eleven, on account of being white and she let him and she saw that he saw. (300, emphasis added)

Key words and phrases in this passage are double-voiced by Bloom and Gerty, and underlying these are other voices that shape Gerty's world. *Tense, breathless with excitement*, and *higher and higher* refer to Bloom's arousal, Gerty's embarrassed thrill, and the excited crowd watching the fireworks. *Divine* and *entrancing* suggest Bloom's idolatry, Gerty's emotions, and the religious service. *Her other things* refers to the object of Bloom's desire, conjures up Gerty's self-exposure, and is elaborated with brand names *nainsook* and *pettiwidth* along with advertising copy, *the fabric that caresses the skin*. A fuller listing of heteroglossia in "Nausicaa" includes numerous other voices:

1. Girl talk: "cosy chat," "darling little fellows."
2. Cliché: "good as gold," "nose was out of joint."
3. Proverbs: "Boys will be boys," "every little Irishman's house is his castle."
4. Romance fiction: "the story of a haunting sorrow was written on his face," Gerty was "as fair a specimen of winsome Irish girlhood as one could wish to see."
5. Fashion magazine: "It was Madame Vera Verity, directress of the Woman Beautiful page of the Princess Novelette, who had first advised her to try eyebrowleine."
6. Advertising: Gerty wore a "neat blouse of electric blue selftinted by dolly dyes [brand name] (because it was expected in the *Lady's Pictorial* that electric blue would be worn)."
7. Religion: "Through the open window of the church the fragrant incense was wafted and with it the fragrant names of her who was conceived without stain of original sin."
8. Popular song: "from the days beyond recall," "the last glimpse of Erin."
9. Sexual euphemism: "matters feminine," "that thing" [menstruation], "something not very nice" [masturbation], "the other thing" [coitus].
10. French and Latin words and phrases: "The slight *contretemps* claimed her attention," "*Ora pro nobis*."
11. Shakespeare: "many a time and oft," "more sinned against than sinning."
12. Poetry: "the love that might have been," "a man among men."
13. *The Odyssey*: "the gentleman in black . . . intercepted the ball." Odysseus is awakened by a shout from girls playing ball. (281–300)

These and other identifiable voices packed into "Nausicaa" are not what Gerty says or even thinks but voices that define the fantasy world in which she lives from sources that shape her ambient world. They make up a language that she wishes she could speak but cannot, because she does not know it, and even if she knew a word such as *contretemps* and used it, her girlfriends would tease her mercilessly. The voices are processed by the popular magazines she reads that constitute an objective heteroglossia as they mix beauty hints, fashion ideas, and romance fiction with ads for clothing, cosmetics, and health aids. They establish what Bakhtin calls a "character zone" that permeates the entire episode, even before she is introduced. This heteroglossia, he explained, is "diffused throughout the authorial speech that surrounds the characters, creating highly particularized *character zones*. These zones are formed from the fragments of character speech, from various forms for hidden transmission of someone else's word, from scattered words and sayings belonging to someone else's speech, from those invasions into authorial speech of others' expressive indicators (ellipsis, questions, exclamations)."[31] Gerty's character zone reverberates with many voices that she has read in magazines and absorbed without realizing it or more remote voices that influence the narrative voices of what she reads and hears. They jangle around in her ambient world as they are mixed up on magazine pages and in the exchange of ideas and fantasies with friends who trigger her jealousy, remorse, guilt, and desire. In this heteroglossia, secular romance runs into religious discourse, itself reduced to misunderstood Latin words and phrases in her own colloquial idiom infused with sexual euphemism.

Some voices interrupt others sequentially. "Had her father only avoided the clutches of the demon drink, by taking the pledge [temperance society] or those powders the drink habit cured in Pearson's Weekly [advertising], she might now be rolling in her carriage, second to none [romance fiction]" (290). In some passages voices drown out other voices as if on an auditory palimpsest: "With all the heart of her she longs to be his only, his affianced bride for riches for poor, in sickness in health, till death us two part, from this to this day forward" (289). Here the narrator's voice includes the voice of popular romance within which is a mangled version of the wedding vows behind which sounds the voice of a cleric administering them.

The passage that transitions from Gerty's focalization to Bloom's after he has climaxed alternates between the two characters or even renders their experiences simultaneously.

Leopold Bloom (for it is he) stands silent, with bowed head before those young guileless eyes. What a brute he had been! At it again? A fair unsullied soul had called to him and, wretch that he was, how had he answered? An utter cad he had been! He of all men! But there was an infinite store of mercy in those eyes, for him too a word of pardon even though he had erred and sinned and wandered. Should a girl tell. No, a thousand times no. That was their secret. (300)

With "it is he" we are out of Gerty's focalization, but the "bowed head," "guileless eyes," and "what a brute" are still in the stylized voice of her romance novels. "At it again?" is Bloom's self-pitying question referring to the masturbation that has replaced coitus with Molly and recalls countless low moments in his flawed marriage. "A fair unsullied soul ... wretch ... [and] An utter cad" are more of the elevated voice that suffuses Gerty's fantasy world but here seems also to belong to Bloom. "He of all men!" registers Gerty's vicarious post-orgasmic disappointment and tinge of remorse over his masturbation even though she knew about it all along and helped him do it. "Infinite store of mercy in those eyes" seems to refer to Bloom's eyes, on which Gerty had commented when she saw him earlier, but as the sentence concludes we realize that the voice reports his view of her eyes that offer "a word of pardon" in the language of her sentimental fiction. "Erred and sinned and wandered" is a shared moralistic religious voice that expresses their shared guilt. "Should a girl tell?" is something either could wonder. "No, a thousand times no" comes close to Gerty's colloquial style, whereupon each is reassured that "That," their remote erotic interaction, is a shared secret.

The distinguishing features of such modernist heteroglossia are the large variety and number of voices in play, the frequency and density of their occurrence, their contamination of surrounding voices, and the lack of any single authoritative voice.[32] Unlike Dickens's sequence of voices framed by the narrator's confident moral philosophy, understanding of his characters, and belief in divine providence, Joyce's absolute heteroglossia of conflicting voices takes over the entire narrative throughout a text that has no framing voice and is not anchored by any clear moral philosophy or divine gaze. In contrast to Dickens, whose heteroglossia clearly identifies sins of the villain Merdle, Joyce has no villain. The source of responsibility for what is most importantly wrong – Gerty's domination by commercial values – is a generalized public ethos forged by publishers of the magazines and novels that shape her values. This high point of modernist polyphony evinces the multi-faceted nature of a society in transition and captures a potent reworking of the master narratives that attempted to hold that society together with such single authoritative voices as a paterfamilias, mayor, judge, corporate head, president, king, or god.

KNOWLEDGE: CREATIVE UNCERTAINTY

The philosophy of the enlightenment was grounded on Newton's physics and Locke's sensationist psychology. The French *philosophes* derived systems of thought from these thinkers, confident that they could explain experience rationally from universal principles à la Newton working with empirical evidence of their senses. That optimism pervaded nineteenth-century positivism, which applied scientific method to the study of human experience. Realists wrote in such a thought world, and their work was secured by enlightenment confidence in the possibility of knowing. Their readers wanted narrators to tell stories with the certainty of scientific knowledge if not God-like omniscience. The term is sometimes used figuratively to refer to third-person realist narrators in contrast to the more limited knowledge of first-person modernist narrators.[33] While realist narrators were of course not omniscient, they seemed to narrate from the perspective of society as a whole with vast resources of knowledge.[34] Modernist narrators had more limited knowledge which functioned as a limiting condition, an enduring state, a basis for insight, or a stimulus for imagination.

Ignorance is progressive in Kafka, whose narrator in *The Trial* begins puzzled and winds up bewildered by the many obstacles to understanding encountered by his protagonist, Josef K. A shared confusion between narrator and protagonist is evident from the opening sentence. "Someone must have slandered Josef K., for one morning, without having done anything truly wrong, he was arrested." The narrator appears not to know who slandered Josef, what was wrong about what Josef did, what law he broke, or even what sort of arrest is involved. While the narrator speaks as an objective observer who presumably understands more than his protagonist, the close alignment between the two involves him in Josef's increasing mystification. Toward the end, pondering the parable of the law, Josef realizes that truth about life is for him alone to fathom, but over the years he has become progressively less able to grasp it. The narrator draws no insight from Josef's inability to understand and shares his protagonist's mounting confusion as the knife plunges into Josef's heart.

Limited knowledge is an enduring state for narrators in Bely and Woolf. Realist narrators acknowledged their inability to understand the mysteries of the mind but at least knew what their characters did and said. By contrast, modernist narrators may not know the most obvious things. Bely's narrator in *Petersburg* is ignorant not merely of his characters' psyches or the meaning of their words but also of their overt actions and what they said. "The past few nights," he reports, "Nikolai Apollonovich has been out Lord knows where."[35] The narrator is equally ignorant about Nikolai's father: "what it was they [he and Anna Petrovna] talked about there, over tea, in the hotel room, forever remained an impenetrable mystery" (272). The crucial feature of this modernist narrator is his inability to know the simplest things, a seeming deficiency that Bely elaborates into an engaging narratorial candor based on accepting the limits of knowledge. Similarly, Woolf captures Jacob's conspicuous absenteeism with a narrator who at times does not know where Jacob is or what he is doing or saying. Describing Jacob in his college room with friends, the narrator wonders, "Was it an argument? A bet on the boat races? Was it nothing of the sort? What was shaped by the arms and bodies moving in the twilight room?" (*JR*, 44). The narrator looks through a window at Jacob but cannot see him clearly. Jacob speaks, but she cannot hear him. What she does know is biased by class, age, and personal interest. "Even the exact words get the wrong accent," and so "life is a procession of shadows" (72–73). The ignorance of Woolf's narrator is no conventional recognition of the complexity of the human spirit. She cannot always track Jacob's movements or hear what he says, let alone fathom its meaning. Bely's and Woolf's renditions of the impenetrable opacity and otherness of people transform creatively what writers could expect to achieve in reconstructing the personal narrative.

Other modernist narrators highlight how their limited knowledge spurs self-discovery. The more these narrators learn, the more they realize how much more there is to know and how little they understand what they think they know. But such understanding is its own kind of knowing. That dialectic of not knowing and knowing is the core dynamic of character-narrators in Conrad and Ford.

Heart of Darkness inventories Marlow's uncertainties. The object of his journey, Kurtz, is an enigma. Going up the Congo River, Marlow is cut off from everything he had known and is unclear about what he sees, which he repeatedly describes as impenetrable or inscrutable. But darkness in the Congo elicits new ways of knowing. His discoveries of how little he knows about himself ground further insight. The most one can learn from life, Marlow realizes, is "knowledge of yourself," which for him happens during encounters with Kurtz. While navigating through darkness Marlow learns more about the complexity of the self, the voraciousness of capitalism, and the irrationality of imperialism, although Kurtz remains a mystery. In *Lord Jim*, Marlow reports a similar dialectic of ignorance and knowing. First encounters with Jim leave Marlow skeptical that he will ever understand a man who remains opaque to himself and others. Frustration from trying to understand Jim leads Marlow to consider that everyone is "incomprehensible, wavering, and misty," and he remains unsure how to evaluate Jim – whether he is admirable or foolish, and lives up to a worthy ideal or falls short (*LJ*, 180). Eventually Marlow finds illumination in the mystery of Kurtz. As he notes: "the less I understood the more I was bound to him in

the name of that doubt which is the inseparable part of our knowledge"
(*HD*, 221).

Conrad's friend and sometimes co-author, Ford, created in *The Good
Soldier* the narrator John Dowell, who is even more pessimistic than
Marlow about knowing anyone and expressing it. In 1935, Ford explained
what he and Conrad had attempted. "The novel must be put into the
mouth of a narrator – who must be limited by probability as to what he can
know of the affair that he is adumbrating." Such a narrator "may indulge in
any prejudices or wrong-headedness."[36] Thus Ford intentionally deprives
Dowell of the ability to know characters and events and judge them
accurately, making him what critics have called an unreliable narrator.
Limited in what he knows, he underreports or misreports what happened,
and his judgments are wrong-headed as to what things mean.[37] He lacks
information to understand and evaluate his marriage, and cannot reliably
interpret or evaluate his friend Edward Ashburnham. Early on Dowell
confesses, "I know nothing – nothing in the world – of the hearts of
men."[38] But to learn that one does not know is the beginning of insight.
Although Dowell remains blind to Edward's true character, he does learn
that for nine years Edward's wife pimped for him and that he himself was a
cuckold. The self-knowledge that emerges from his story of self-deception
rests on a merciless confession of ignorance.

In contrast to the enlightenment idea that the deeper one probes the
greater one's knowledge, in *Absalom, Absalom!* Faulkner dramatizes how the
deeper his character-narrators probe, the greater their mystification. Their
ignorance is a spur to invention, however, as when Quentin narrates to
Shreve his spotty knowledge, acquired from Rosa Coldfield, of Judith
Sutpen's confused awareness of what happened between her father
Thomas and Wash's granddaughter Millie, whom Thomas had impreg-
nated and insulted when she failed to give him a son: "When [Thomas] left
the house before day that morning Judith thought he was going to the
stable, who knew what and how much about her father and Wash's granddaughter nobody knew, how much she could not have helped but know
from what Clytie [Sutpen's illegitimate daughter] must have known (may
have or may not have told her, whether or no)" (*AA*, 228). Quentin's
narration is a tissue of such speculation within speculation, gaps within
gaps. Nobody knows how much Judith knew about Thomas and Wash's
granddaughter, what Judith might have learned from Clytie, or what Clytie
knew. The novel is like a detective story in reverse that increases reader
interest as motives become increasingly unknowable. While realist plots
come into focus as they move toward resolution, Faulkner's plot gets

murkier as it proceeds toward increasing confounding with no final illumination. Faulkner's narrators are stopped by their ignorance of why people act as they do, even of what they do, and wind up with ever-deeper mysteries, which they attempt to solve by creative speculation and invention. Their limitation of knowledge undercuts the reliability of their interpretations. But where Ford has Dowell get some things right and other things wrong, Faulkner puts Quentin's and Shreve's entire narration under a question mark.

Gide crafts a similar dialectic of creative imagination and ignorance. In *The Counterfeiters* Edouard does not know what the characters in his novel are doing: he is "curious to know" what Antoine told his friend the cook, he "should have liked to know" what Olivier thought at Laura's wedding, he "cannot tell" why Bernard leaves Sarah without a kiss, and he "was not expecting" Boris's suicide (*C*, 24, 98, 307, 394). These surprising admissions blatantly reverse the posture of narratorial omniscience of Balzac or Zola. Edouard's ignorance is compensated by a faculty, he explains, "which enabled me to feel other people's emotions as if they were my own, compelled me, as it were, to enter into Olivier's feelings – those that I imagined him to be experiencing." Not knowing what Olivier went through at a sterile Protestant wedding makes it possible for Edouard to feel the experience intensely by actively imagining it. "I felt as if, like him, I were seeing for the first time the bare walls, the abstract and chilly light which fell upon the congregation . . . [and] the whole spirit of this angular and colorless architecture" (98). Not knowing what his characters are doing, he is forced to invent it. Ignorance generates a new mode of creative knowing. Of course realist authors imagined all sorts of things for their characters but not as urgently as does Edouard, who cannot experience anything fully unless he imagines it. By refusing the kinds of knowing that were readily available to realist narrators, modernist narrators posed new questions about what it means to know anything.[39]

Two literary critics identify skepticism at the heart of modernism. Brian McHale proposes that the dominant concept of modernism is epistemological uncertainty. That dominance hinges on questions such as "What is there to be known?; Who knows it?; How do they know it, and with what degree of certainty?; How is knowledge transmitted from one knower to another, and with what degree of reliability?" and so on. By restricting what their narrators knew, modernists dramatized these questions, enriched the process of thinking about them, and underscored the urgency of answering them. McHale elaborates how such a restriction works in Faulkner: "*Absalom* foregrounds such epistemological themes as the accessibility and circulation of knowledge, the different structuring imposed on the 'same' knowledge by different minds, and the problem of 'unknowability' or the limits of knowledge." In Chapter 8 of the novel, he adds, when Quentin and Shreve stop sorting out what they know and start inventing, the novel "dramatizes the shift of dominant from problems of knowing to problems of modes of being – from an epistemological dominant to an *ontological one*."[40] Such moments evince a new kind of knowing and of being that emanates from narrators' imaginations. McHale's emphasis on "intractable epistemological uncertainty," however, is overly negative for a period bursting with positive ideas and creative achievement. Modernists questioned the under-examined conviction of their realist predecessors who wrote as though they knew precisely what their characters did and said. Nonetheless, epistemological skepticism is not the dominant focus of the modernist novel. Rather, modernists clarified and magnified the possibilities of knowing by side-stepping scientific standards of certitude and expanding their sources to include speculation and imagination.

Philip Weinstein's study of modernism also centers on epistemological skepticism, as indicated by its title: *Unknowing: The Work of Modernist Fiction*. He focuses on the way modernist authors create characters who resist the realist scenario of a subject making his or her way in the world by acquiring knowledge. Rather, Kafka's Josef K., Proust's Marcel, and Faulkner's Joe Christmas whom Weinstein cites as examples, find themselves in uncanny worlds that they cannot know and that are threatening, alienating, or dangerous. Their progress in those worlds is not a gradual acquisition of knowledge but a scenario of increasing estrangement from the world. The positive yield of unknowing is what Weinstein calls "acknowledging." He leaves the narrator largely out of his analysis and concludes with an account of the reader enriched by reading modernist fiction and thereby working through unknowing to acknowledgment of the world. "If we would know, we must endure – spend some time in – the darkness of unknowing, must relinquish our canniness in order actually to see ourselves in the field of space and time and others."[41]

McHale and Weinstein center their definitions of modernism on the nature and process of coming to know. Both see the epistemological confidence of realists as a naiveté that modernists developed a literature to surmount. While their focal terms – epistemological uncertainty and unknowing – are negative, their elaborations imply an affirmation of the subtle and probing view of the world created by modernists. Modernist narrators worked on behalf of that affirmative project by creating multiple ways of focalizing stories, multiple voices to tell them, and multiple means of knowing what it was they knew or did not know about their characters and their world. Indeed, some of their most original and powerful moments were candidly acknowledging what they could not see, hear, or know. Their innovative polyvision, polyphony, and multiple ways of knowing and not-knowing meshed with the increasingly pluralistic world in which conventional confidence in a narrator's focalization, voice, and knowing unraveled and reformed. The essentially pluralistic and perspectival nature of modernist narration reflects the central philosophical problem of the age, the want of a single basis for meaning. While that problem was fatal for religion, it also destabilized all the other conventional certitudes except for artistry that embraced pluralism and uncertainty.

Conclusion

This concluding chapter shifts toward the content side of the form-content distinction. It focuses on and is organized according to the subversion and reworking of the master narratives in the modernist period. To this development can be added two specific theses about substantive history: that the modernist world witnessed the breakdown of a shared sense of meaning, and that the dominant value distinctions used to interpret the meaning of individual lives shifted gradually from moral in the realist period to more aesthetic and existential in the modernist period.

Subversion, breakdown, and crisis in meaning are leitmotifs of the age. Woolf identified its prevailing sound as "breaking and falling, crashing and destruction." Grammar was violated, syntax disintegrated; and Joyce's *Ulysses* was the "calculated indecency of a desperate man who feels that in order to breathe he must break the windows."[1] Woolf found the crashing "vigorous and stimulating," while others found it disorienting, as subversion of master narratives left them without guidelines, especially for personal identity, courtship conventions, family relationships, national ethos, and religious faith. Some longed for the past, while others, including most artists, welcomed iconoclasm and even alienation, or at least productive solitude, as a precondition for meaningful life and art. While subversion attracted greater literary attention, a measure of reworking made up the positive content of modernist novels.

In realist novels personal narratives take shape around choices of behavior based on shared moral values that give life meaning. Individuals may differ about their choices but not about the authority of those values. In *Crime and Punishment* Raskolnikov chooses to violate them when he murders the pawnbroker and is momentarily intoxicated with the idea that he is superior to their authority, but he never questions their role in defining his crime. In *Heart of Darkness*, by contrast, Kurtz appears to have gone beyond the pale morally into a life that cannot be interpreted by values that he acknowledges as valid and in which the concept of crime loses meaning. Marlow concludes that Kurtz was a remarkable man but cannot say why, and Kurtz's final cry, "The horror! The horror!" explains nothing. Marlow speculates that it "was an affirmation, a moral victory," but that victory is amoral in that he was beyond all codes of behavior (*HD*, 70). Conrad, writes David Daiches, was "the first important modern novelist in English ... [whose] finest novels and stories are all concerned, directly or obliquely, with situations to which public codes – *any* public codes – are inapplicable, situations which yield a dark and disturbing insight which cannot be related to any of the beliefs or rules which make human societies possible."[2] Kurtz is followed by Michel in *The Immoralist* and by Aschenbach in *Death in Venice*, who are willing to risk lives in the pursuit of erotic pleasures that subvert and rework the ethical code of the personal narrative and the gender roles and heterosexual pairings of the courtship narrative.

These characters' journeys beyond geographical borders and beyond the pale of conventional morality enact a dangerous misinterpretation of Nietzsche's philosophy. Nietzsche urged his followers to go beyond good and evil – not to do evil, but to re-evaluate the moral distinction for evaluating existence and instead substitute an aesthetic and ultimately an existential one. That is, he wanted to evaluate life beyond the judgment of whether it is good or evil, especially when that judgment is framed by a slave morality that started with the Jews and culminated in Christianity. Instead life ought to be evaluated in terms of creativity and ultimately of authenticity and meaning. These criteria distinguish the way to greatness, to the overman. Kurtz, Michel, and Aschenbach simply do evil when they imperil the lives of others. Many modernists including Kafka, Hesse, Mann, Gide, Lawrence, and Joyce followed the intended spirit of Nietzsche's philosophy as their transcendence led to more creative and authentic lives, not morally upstanding ones.[3]

Modernists reposition characters with respect to aesthetic and existential values by substituting imaginative exploration such as Ulrich's "essayism" in *The Man Without Qualities*. In this life style he sees "the moral norm no longer as a set of rigid commandments but rather as a mobile equilibrium that at every moment requires continual efforts at renewal." He explores experience from many sides. "Moral events take place in a field of energy [and] ... what is seemingly solid ... becomes a porous pretext for many possible meanings" (*MQ*, 1, 270–72). Ulrich's proposal for an endlessly reworked personal life aligns with Nietzsche's philosophy of perspectivism and with the polyvision, polyphony, and multiple ways of knowing of modernist narrators.

That shift of values beyond good and evil is also evident in stories of courtship. James captures the persistence of traditional moral evaluations of love relationships in *The Ambassadors* when Strether misinterprets what Little Bilham means by calling the relationship between Chad and Madame de Vionnet a "virtuous attachment" (187). Strether assumes that Bilham means sexually innocent, whereas he means, rather, erotically as well as aesthetically and existentially fulfilling. Strether spends most of the novel refusing to see that the virtue of Chad's relationship with Madame de Vionnet has nothing to do with morality but rather has to do with the couple's sensuous gratification as well as artistic sensibilities and creative life style.

The shift in interpreting love relationships can be seen across the years of this study in the difference between a realist and a modernist novel about love. In *The Mill on the Floss* (1860) Maggie must choose between Stephen, whom she loves, and Philip, to whom she is committed by a promise elicited out of pity. She explains her decision to leave Stephen in terms of the public code, which she fully internalizes. It requires that promises be kept, especially when they contradict personal inclinations. If there is a conflict between duty and love, love must be sacrificed. The fate of many other realist characters turns on their being honest or honorable, personally consistent or socially responsible, qualities consecrated by a utilitarian ethic to maximize the greatest good or a categorical imperative to do one's duty in accord with public codes. Far different are the myriad rationalizations and fantasies that stream through Molly Bloom's mind after she indulges her sexual desire and betrays Bloom during her tryst with Boylan, shouting profanities as she recalls the pleasure of one of her "5 or 6" orgasms, inconceivable behavior for a heroine sixty years earlier. Eliot affirms her heroine's devotion to a shared public code, while Joyce affirms his heroine's undisciplined commitment to a personal code far beyond good and evil.

Modernist characters' most radical challenges to received courtship norms are unconventional sexual activities, which subvert and rework gender identities and sex roles: homoerotic in Rupert Birkin and Gerald Crich (Lawrence) and Gustav von Aschenbach (Mann); homosexual in Baron de Charlus and Robert de Saint-Loup (Proust); lesbian in Robin Vote (Barnes) and Alice B. Toklas (Stein); transvestite in Dr. Matthew-Mighty-grain-of-salt-Dante-O'Connor (Barnes); bisexual in Michel (Gide) and Miriam Henderson (Richardson); and transsexual in Orlando (Woolf). The attachment of Proust's narrator Marcel to Albertine is heterosexual but was inspired by Proust's homosexual love for his chauffeur Alfred Agostinelli; so was Bernard's love for Olivier in *The Counterfeiters* inspired by Gide's love for Marc Allégret, and Fielding's friendship with Aziz in *A Passage to India* based on Forster's love for Syed Masood.[4]

Modernists subvert many aspects of the family narrative. In *Misalliance* (1910) George Bernard Shaw urges that "No man should know his own child. No child should know its own father. Let the family be rooted out of civilization!" In *Women in Love* Gudrun comments that she gets "no feeling whatever from the thought of bearing children." Other works show family degeneration with sickly children in Thomas Mann's *Buddenbrooks* (1901) and *Nightwood*, and childless unions in D. H. Lawrence's *Lady Chatterley's Lover* (1928) and John Galsworthy's *The Forsyte Saga* (1906–21). Cuckolded husbands play key roles in *Parade's End* and *Ulysses*, while child suicides occur in Hardy's *Jude the Obscure* and Hesse's *Beneath the Wheel* (1906). In *The Sound and the Fury* and *Absalom, Absalom!* families deteriorate against a backdrop of the discredited Southern plantation society. In *As I Lay Dying* the declining Bundren family comes to a macabre end as the recently widowed father celebrates the burial of his wife's rotting corpse by purchasing a set of false teeth to secure a new wife with "hardlooking pop eyes" whom he introduces to his dispirited children "kind of hangdog and proud." Throughout the modernist period, family narratives continue to hold lives together but without the celebrated status they enjoyed in the nineteenth century as a "haven in a heartless world."[5] After James, Gide, Freud, and Faulkner, the family would be rather a potential hotbed of child abuse, counterfeit values, Oedipal tensions, and haunting memories.

New transportation and communication technologies accelerated the movement of people out of small towns and into increasingly dynamic urban centers. Modernists recreated cities with multiple social and commercial opportunities as well as diverse languages and cultures. Even novels about urban dislocation and alienation such as *Manhattan Transfer*, *Berlin Alexanderplatz*, and *Paris Peasant* evoked an undercurrent of stimulation and opportunity. Dislocation differently viewed was relocation and rejuvenation. Alienation also meant anonymity and freedom from stultifying gossip. Geometric street grids also created impressive vistas and more efficient transportation opportunities. The crush of signs intensified crude commercialism but also literary inventiveness, at least for Bloom. Traffic was loud and obstructive, but the new ways to travel brought new ways to socialize and make money. The new telephones, wireless, radio broadcasts, daily newspapers, cinema, and views from airplanes and skyscrapers created new auditory and visual experiences of simultaneity. The big city was a composite of new technologies and stimulating possibilities.

Throughout the nineteenth century the national narrative provided a sense of meaning from hallowed origins to a future of continuing progress and glory. While early in the century nationalism challenged local, traditional privileges, especially in Central Europe, by the end of the century it had become conservative, racist, and imperialistic. Earlier grounding of nationalism in liberal ideas about the rule of law and individual rights gave way to veneration of racial heritage and cultural purity. This transformation created a "crisis of liberal nationalism" as when chauvinistic English nationalists argued that the Irish and the Indians were incapable of self-government, and French nationalists deemed Jews unworthy of French citizenship.[6] Aggressive nationalism intensified in the countries of the alliances that led to World War I, although the war itself destroyed nations: it toppled four monarchies, fomented social unrest and civil war, displaced millions of refugees, and led to a redrawing of frontiers at the Peace of Paris that violated the nationalist aspirations of populations even as it purported to institutionalize the self-determination of peoples from Woodrow Wilson's Fourteen Points.

The vexed fate of the national narrative is writ large in the history of the Austro-Hungarian Empire, a patchwork of subject nationalities seeking independence from the Dual Monarchy. Its capital, Vienna, is the setting for *The Man Without Qualities*, which centers on a campaign during 1913 for an upcoming celebration of the 30th anniversary of the reign of the German Kaiser and the 70th anniversary of the reign of Franz Josef to be commemorated together in 1918, the year when, as Musil's readers in the 1930s knew all too well, the two empires collapsed. This coordinated celebration was supposed to show "that the Austro-Hungarian Monarchy stands together, grouped firm as a rock around its Sovereign" (*MQ*, 180). To double the irony, Musil has the planning committee create a symbol of the monarch's unifying role as an "Emperor of Peace" (189). Musil subverts nationalist values with this intended celebration of national glory in what turned out to be a time of national disgrace.

Other novels challenge the rationale of post–World War I reconstruction. In *Parade's End* Ford envisions a postwar world of nationalism without militarism. During the war Tietjens found a plan for disbanding a battalion. "The band would play *Land of Hope and Glory*, and then the adjutant would say: *There will be no more parades . . .* For there won't . . . No more Hope, no more Glory, no more parades for you and me any more. Nor for the country . . . nor for the world, I dare say . . . None . . . Gone . . . Napoo finny! No . . . more . . . parades!"[7] *Napoo finny* is British war slang for the French *Il n'y en a plus, fini*. Ford lavishes contempt on military parades symbolizing the pageantry necessary to get men to hurl themselves into senseless combat for four years. The title of Ford's tetralogy, *Parade's End*, and the title of one of its volumes, *No More Parades*, underscore his determination to efface the militarist component from nationalist sentiment.

Woolf detested the politicians who fumbled into the war, the bureaucrats who financed it, and the officers who waged it, but she still acknowledged, at least for her protagonist Clarissa Dalloway and a group of Londoners, the deep need to restore national wholeness in the postwar period, symbolized by monarchs back on their thrones. On a morning walk in 1923, Clarissa has the reassuring thought that "it was over, thank Heaven – over. It was June. The King and Queen were at the Palace" (*MD*, 5). Moments later a motor car backfires and people turn to see in the car's window what they expect to be "a face of the very greatest importance." Woolf renders their collective expectations in the context of a reworked national narrative: "Nobody knew whose face had been seen. Was it the Prince of Wales's, the Queen's, the Prime Minister's? . . . In all the hat shops and tailors' shops strangers looked at each other and thought of the dead; of the flag; of Empire" (14, 18). Nobody knew whose face had been seen but all hoped that whoever it was in the car could restore the national unity symbolized by the flag and the national prestige embodied in the Empire. A hunger for wholeness and prosperity rekindled in the postwar years as the living struggled to come to terms with the massive deaths and injuries, while the jumbled territorial settlements of the Peace of Paris left Europe a mass of clashing nations that worked frantically to reconstitute the coherence of their national histories.

Of all the master narratives, the imperial was the most morally charged. Salutary ventures such as scientific exploration and missionary activity were operative, and railroad construction and disease eradication did occur, but these features pale compared with the primary goals of land grab and investment, widespread cultural disruption and economic exploitation, and the dehumanizing realities of racism, slave labor, and killing. Critical judgments against the morality of imperialism were sharpest about the Belgian Congo, where millions were slaughtered in pursuit of ivory and rubber. Conrad had a less critical view of English imperialism; in *Heart of Darkness* Marlow notes that in English colonies "some real work is done," but the novel still indicts the imperial powers (*HD*, 10).

While *Heart of Darkness* impugned the imperial narrative, twenty-five years later Forster's *A Passage to India* began to rework it. The significance of that change can be seen by tracking British imperial attitudes following the Indian Mutiny of 1857, when Indian soldiers and civilians reacted to decades of British assaults on Indian lives, property, and religion with armed revolts culminating in a massacre in Cawnpore, where the dead British women and children were dumped into a well. The British retaliated by looting and killing residents and executing rebels without trial, and British views of Indians became racist and hateful. In 1865 the historian Sir George Trevelyan characterized the Mutiny as an "atrocious act ... in a cause" that was "detestable to God and man."[8] Such epithets skewed British rhetoric until the end of the century – with generous and humanitarian Christians on one side and bloodthirsty and superstitious Hindus and Muslims on the other. At least fifty novels about the Mutiny appeared by 1900, dramatizing polarities of good versus evil, civilization versus barbarism.[9] A number of developments prepared for Forster's reworking of such rhetoric. The Montagu Declaration of 1917 provided India with self-governing institutions that eventuated in Dominion status. The Amritsar Massacre of 1919 realigned the moral compass of Anglo-Indian relations after Indian soldiers, commanded by the British General Dyer, fired on a group of Indian men, women, and children, killing nearly 400 and wounding over 1,200. British imperialism reached a new low of moral bankruptcy when the commanding officer explained to a court of inquiry that his men stopped shooting only when they ran out of ammunition, and they left without attending to the wounded. While British officials did not condone Dyer's actions, they did condone sending Ghandi to prison for civil disobedience in 1922, the same year Forster began writing the final version of his novel.

After Adela withdraws her accusation that Aziz raped her and the case is dismissed, the remainder of the novel tracks the reconstruction of Anglo-Indian society and by implication the larger history of the imperial narrative. It had been defined by the British with a view of Indians as incapable of having their own legal institutions, racially backward, morally and religiously deficient, and inalterably alien, making friendship between Indians and the English impossible. The novel undercuts each of these characteristics. The bigoted Mr. Turton smarts with indignation that the court must allow Indians full legal rights and longs for the good old days "when an Englishman could do as he pleased, with no questions asked." In a more compromising spirit, after some initial blustering, Aziz decides not to press for damages against Adela following the recantation of her accusation. The justice that had been denied to Indians for so long worked well as an Indian judge managed the trial under explosive circumstances. Bigoted British views of Indian racial inferiority are exposed as the consequence of ignorance and fear, while the Indians exhibit patience and understanding toward the British. The supposed immorality of Indians appears absurd against the way Adela's confused charge is amplified by conscious lies and efforts to circumvent justice in order to secure Aziz's conviction. British religious intolerance gives way to religious understanding on both sides, especially in Mrs. Moore, who becomes enamored of the Hindu religion that preaches goodness and peace and herself is transformed by Indians into a Hindu goddess.

Affirming the possibility of friendship between Indians and the English is the novel's main theme. Its introductory chapters sketch the failure to unite East and West, dramatized by the hypocritical "Bridge Parties" given by the exclusive English Club that forbids Indians to be members and in private talk foments national and racial antipathy. But friendships do grow between Mrs. Moore and Professor Godbole and between Fielding and Aziz. Fielding is Easternized, while Aziz is Westernized, as the novel works to lessen the radical otherness of the two cultures and make connection possible. The ending precludes friendship because of fear and misunderstanding on both sides but offers hope to replace opposition when Aziz says to Fielding: "yes, we shall drive every blasted Englishman into the sea, and then . . . you and I shall be friends."

The capitalist narrative was reworked by a variety of developments captured in novels. The gold standard collapsed shortly after World War I and exposed the artificiality of monetary standards along with other supposedly universal values. Gide depicts that new instability in *The Counterfeiters*, which questions the authenticity of all signifiers or coinages, be they gold, paper money, paternity, the state, religion, or even the novel itself. All are counterfeit.[10] Increasing prosperity was interrupted by the depression of 1873–93 and again in the 1930s, featured in the final volume of Dos Passos's trilogy *U. S. A.* with the telling title *The Big Money*.[11] Technological improvements and rationalized production magnified the productive capacity of human labor; but those developments could also dehumanize people such as Gerald Crich, the "god of the machine" in *Women in Love*, who runs a coal mine with state-of-the-art equipment but brutalizes his workers, family, lovers, and, in the process, himself.

Greed motivates many realist characters. Balzac's Vautrin in *Old Goriot* plots a murder to get 200,000 francs to buy a farm. Conflict over the inheritance of a family farm leads to rape and murder in Zola's *Earth* (1887). Dickens is full of profit-obsessed villains: Uriah Heep, Mr. Quilp, Ebenezer Scrooge, and Mr. Merdle ruin lives, while Jonas Chuzzlewit kills for an inheritance. Modernists show more nuance in rendering greed. In Theodore Dreiser's *An American Tragedy* (1925) Clyde Griffiths plots a murder to secure financial and social advancement, but his tragedy, and America's, derives not so much from greed as from the illusion of fulfillment in an upper-class world of fancy cars and country clubs. While the novel is stylistically conventional naturalism, Dreiser uses interior monologue for over a hundred pages to capture Clyde's growing conflict as he prepares for the murder. Conrad explores the power of greed in *Nostromo*, about the exploitation of a silver mine in an imaginary South American country where everyone is dazzled and corrupted by the shiny metal. The notion that capitalism secured the stability of nations was challenged by the rise of revolutionary socialism and by a successful communist revolution in Russia that reconstituted the political economy of that country and threatened to spread to Western Europe and America. Bely's *Petersburg* addresses the situation in Russia on the eve of the Revolution of 1905 against a background of assassinations, mutinies, and uprisings as revolutionary crowds move through Petersburg protesting political tyranny and capitalist exploitation.

The main literary assaults on the liberal narrative are legal proceedings against accused men that result in unjust death sentences. Lord Jim is found guilty because he cannot provide the court with reliable facts, answer its questions, or explain why he jumped from the *Patna*. The court's revocation of his sailor's certificate is tantamount to a death sentence, which is carried out years later under different circumstances in Patusan. The notion that courts protect individual rights is reversed in *The Trial*. The court is attracted to guilt which its own activities generate, and once it brings charges, it can never be swayed. None of the three possible outcomes can resolve Josef K.'s case: actual acquittals never occur, apparent acquittals drop charges for the moment but can reinstate them at any time, and protractions reduce the likelihood of conviction but keep the defendant in protracted contact with the court. Musil's Moosbrugger is incapable of understanding his trial or defending himself against a court that sees his conviction and execution as necessary social hygiene. Camus dramatizes the impossibility of assigning cause and hence legitimate criminal responsibility in *The Stranger* when Meursault shouts out to the judge that he killed the Arab because of the sun. Yet another death sentence in a comically flawed court is handed out in the "Circe" episode of *Ulysses*, albeit one hallucinated and not carried out. Bloom's trial begins with flagrant impropriety as the clerk of the court invites him to plead his case "with a bogus statement" (*U*, 376). Accusers arise to articulate charges projected out of Bloom's own guilty conscience and malign him with sexual and scatological improprieties, not capital offenses. Still he is sentenced to be hanged and is saved not by the triumph of justice but by Bloom's coming out of a hallucination. His trial and capital sentence introduce some rare levity into modernist dramatization of the courts, but like the other more serious trials, his also subverts by mocking the possibility of achieving justice so central to the liberal agenda.

Realist renderings of religion are grounded in shared values. *Les Misérables*, Hugo explains, "treats the advance from evil to good, from injustice to justice, from falsity to truth, from darkness to daylight, from blind appetite to conscience, from decay to life, from bestiality to duty, from Hell to Heaven, from limbo to God."[12] Excessive even by nineteenth-century standards, these polarities bracket the values of the realists' world of lives progressing toward goodness, justice, and godliness. Hugo's statement is a world away from that of the modernist novel in which the values that establish meaning become increasingly uncertain. In *Middlemarch* Eliot comes closer to acknowledging this uncertainty and the cultural fragmentation underlying it. The Prelude evokes the figure of Saint Theresa as a model of a life based on religious values. Unlike Theresa, whose reforming of a religious order was meaningful in her time as "a constant unfolding far-resonant action," in Dorothea's day such acts are impossible. Like many "later-born Theresas," Dorothea finds that her efforts are "dispersed among hindrances, instead of centering in some long-recognizable deed." She lives in a world of "no coherent social faith and order." This awareness places her between realism and modernism. While unable to reform the world order, she lives according to a widely shared ethos of sympathy and selflessness.

Modernists lined up to subvert religion and especially its churches and the narrative that defined its historical role. Nietzsche saw at the heart of Christianity a revenge of the weak against the strong, the lame against those who can dance, of the sin-ridden against those who can say *yes* to life including the body. Historians separated fact from fiction in the life of Jesus, logical positivists dismissed the content of religion as cognitively insignificant if not meaningless, and theologians increasingly interpreted religion as myth or symbol. Durkheim analyzed religion's varied social origins, William James identified its psychological varieties, Bertrand Russell rejected its public institutions, Sartre characterized its faith as bad faith, and Freud likened it to an obsessive-compulsive neurosis centering on the projection of a childhood belief in a wise and powerful father into an adult illusion of an omniscient and omnipotent God.

Novelists characterized religion as dogmatic, vengeful, fraudulent, inhibitory, and potentially violent. Musil's Ulrich, in *The Man Without Qualities*, rails against the prefabricated dogma that shaped him before he had any say in the meaning of his existence, a sentiment that hits him full force while standing outside a church (*MQ*, 1, 136). In *Mrs. Dalloway* the suitably named Doris Kilman epitomizes a vengeful religious fanatic: "Whenever the hot and painful feelings boiled within her, this hatred of Mrs. Dalloway, this grudge against the world, she thought of God" (*MD*, 124). Although her resentment stems from personal circumstances, its religious manifestation will tolerate no deviation from its exacting demands. Gide emphasizes the fraudulence of the church. In *Lafcadio's Adventures*, it is a world of gullible and vacillating believers, fake icons, fake clerics, a fake conspiracy about a fake Pope, and by implication a fake God. Gide's hostile atheism is further evident in his comment that "Dostoevsky's heroes inherit the Kingdom of God only by the denial of mind and will and the surrender of personality."[13] *The Counterfeiters* targets a commercially preoccupied church whose mission is suggested by the name of the man posing as Bernard's father, Judge Profitendieu (profit in God).

The inhibitory effect of Christianity's emphasis on sin makes some believers turn against sexual desire and become unable to love a flesh-and-blood human being. In Gide's *Strait is the Gate* (1909), Alissa believes that any physical contact, even just looking at Jerome, is a profanation. He tries in vain to follow Christ's teaching that "strait is the gate, and narrow is the way, which leadeth unto life," but that course cannot accommodate the twists and turns of sensuous life or open wide enough to let two lovers pass through together. Christian piety spoils sex in the first two generations of Brangwens in *The Rainbow*. Third-generation Ursula proposes exorcizing the imagery of "Jesus with holes in his hands and feet" by exchanging passionate caresses in a church. In *Lady Chatterley's Lover* Lawrence protests how Jesus separated people from the body by teaching that "happiness lay in abstracting oneself from life." In *Light in August* several sexually repressed religious fanatics show how the violent component of Christianity cursed the South. When one, Johanna, goes through the menopause, her obsession shifts from sexual desire to religious fervor, and she emerges as a female reincarnation of the manipulating religious fanatic McEachern, who raised Joe Christmas and deformed his sexuality. As she attempts to coerce Christmas's religiosity, he cuts her throat and nearly decapitates her. He in turn is beaten by the demented religious fanatic Doc Hines and then fatally shot and castrated by Percy Grimm, who claims that God justified his act.

Modernists did not break away from religion lightly. Nietzsche's spokesman Zarathustra burns with rage over the dehumanizing import of Judaism and Christianity, yet he mimics the itinerant life style and preachy rhetoric of biblical prophets. Although Lawrence railed against Christian asceticism, he repeatedly drew on Biblical imagery to refashion a religion of the flesh as well as the spirit, an image of Jesus resurrected and not crucified, and a God of the earth and not of heaven.[14] In contrast to the pointed degradation of Christianity in *Light in August*, Faulkner created a humanized Christianity in *The Sound and the Fury*, with the Reverend Shegog's sermon on Easter

Sunday signifying resurrection and hope. While Joyce rebelled against Catholicism, his work remained preoccupied with it.[15]

Roger Martin du Gard dramatized modernists' conflict over religion in *Jean Barois* (1913). Its titular character struggles to pull away from his early, small-town Catholicism and pious wife. In Paris he starts a free-thinking journal, opposes the Catholic Church during the Dreyfus Affair, and gives public lectures defending reason and science against religious dogma and blind faith. As an ailing old man, however, he returns to his wife and the Church and receives Extreme Unction before dying. Afterwards the local priest discovers his will, written years earlier at the height of his determination to reject religious dogma. In the final scene his wife reads the will and then burns it. Jean's lifetime struggle against traditional faith is symbolized by a plaster cast of Michelangelo's sculpture of a slave "struggling to free his aching limbs and rebellious shoulders from their stony thrall." It remains with Jean throughout his life as a reminder of his unsuccessful efforts to get beyond the shackles of traditional faith.[16] Similar struggles and ambivalences are evident in other anti-religious art and literature of the period, as several scholars have noted.[17]

One reworking of religious faith was not ambivalent – its transformation into art. The *locus classicus* of this transformation in the modernist canon is Joyce's *A Portrait of the Artist as a Young Man*, which tracks Stephen's renunciation of family and nation but especially religion in order to become an artist. He admits to doubts about the Eucharist and the divinity of Jesus and refuses to perform his Easter duty as his mother wished. As he declares, "I will not serve that in which I no longer believe, whether it call itself my home, my fatherland, or my church" (*PA*, 247). He seeks to free himself from his Catholic faith and find a meaning in life through art. So he proposes to go into exile, like Joyce himself, to distance himself from all the institutional nets that hold him back and, as the epigraph to the novel puts it, "work upon unknown arts."

Stephen's is the prototypical modernist scenario of the artist in exile from the values that have lost the ability to give life meaning. For each of the modernists' fictional avatars, art is a beacon guiding their rough passage toward an inspiring but elusive goal. These characters dramatize the creative process with the following variants:

- corrupted artists: Kurtz in *Heart of Darkness*, Gustav von Aschenbach in *Death in Venice*, Herr Loerke in *Women in Love*, Otto Kreisler in *Tarr*;
- unrealized artists: Edna Pontellier in *The Awakening*, Lambert Strether in *The Ambassadors*, Mrs. Gould and Martin Decoud in *Nostromo*, Leopold Bloom in *Ulysses*, Dr. O'Connor in *Nightwood*, Antoine Roquentin in *Nausea*;

- artists-in-the-making: Malte Laurids Brigge in *The Notebooks of Malte Laurids Brigge*, Paul Morel in *Sons and Lovers*, Miriam Henderson in *Pilgrimage*, Stephen Dedalus in *A Portrait of the Artist as a Young Man*, Frederick Tarr in *Tarr*, Edouard in *The Counterfeiters*, André Breton in *Nadja*, Harry Haller in *Steppenwolf*, Bertrand Müller in *The Sleepwalkers*, Jack in the "Camera Eye" sections of *U. S. A.*;
- fulfilled artists: Marcel in *Remembrance of Things Past*, Julius de Baraglioul in *Lafcadio's Adventures*, Mark Rampion in *Point Counter Point*, Lily Briscoe in *To the Lighthouse*.

This list shows the celebrated role of the artistic narrative in the modernist period. The historical significance of these novels is underscored by the fact that most of the characters in them are autobiographical.[18] In addition, Mann based Aschenbach on the Austrian composer Gustav Mahler as well as himself, Joyce based Bloom partly on the Italian novelist Ettore Schmitz (Italo Svevo), and Huxley based Mark Rampion on D. H. Lawrence. More than any other modernist characters, these various artists illuminated and warmed the universe that Nietzsche's Madman, following the death of God, found so dark and cold. They surpassed the small-mindedness of Nietzsche's "last man," achieved authenticity in the face of a herd mentality, and, most importantly, created in ways that redeemed and glorified human existence.

The profusion of artist protagonists in the modernist canon, often embodying the personal itinerary of their authors, challenges the suitability of the many negative terms used to characterize modernism listed in my introduction, such as irrationality, bewilderment, disenchantment, despair, and crisis. These descriptive terms focus subtle arguments, many of them extended to developments in science and philosophy as well as non-literary arts, but their featured roles in books do not do justice to the spirit of creation and discovery among writers and artists as well as the new ways of thinking and understanding put forward by philosophers and scientists. Gide was not irrational, Faulkner was not bewildered, Stein was not disenchanted, Proust was not despairing, and Joyce was not in crisis, nor can such characteristics and attitudes define Bergson, Einstein, Freud, or Picasso. Even Nietzsche, for all his biting criticism of contemporary life and values, concludes *Zarathustra* (Part Three) with a full-throated celebration of "the laughter of creative lightning" and the refrain, repeated seven times, "*For I love you, O eternity!*"

The subtitle to *Twilight of the Idols* expresses Nietzsche's desire to "philosophize with a hammer." He intended that image to signify the destructive blows of his iconoclasm, but his hammer also had creative significance. Elsewhere he indicated that it was a piano tuner's hammer (he himself played the piano and composed), suggesting that he wanted to tune his means of expression, while in other places it was a sculptor's mallet, suggesting that he wanted to craft beautiful forms out of shapeless matter. Woolf had four mental breakdowns, but writing helped her overcome her sense of helplessness, as she countered the hypocrisy of bourgeois society and the mindless brutality of militarism until she saw that, properly viewed, "the whole world is a work of art."[9] *Kafkaesque* came to signify the alienation and anxiety of the modern age, but for Kafka personally, writing was a restorative act because he believed that by capturing the terrifying aspects of the age, his work would help meliorate it. Joyce was alienated from his family, country, and church but was at home in the literary world that he influenced in revolutionary ways. *Ulysses* is a compendium of modernist innovation about an exceptional everyman who finds treasures in Dublin's outsiders and misfits and thoroughly enjoys his bodily appetites and processes. "In my book," Joyce recorded with pride, "the body lives and moves through space and is the home to a fully human personality."[20] Proust was cut off from society by snobbery and illness as well as by his commitment to writing, but for over 3,000 pages his great novel sustains an investigation into why involuntary memories gave him such joy and how to capture their magic enduringly in literary art. Creativity inspired Nietzsche, healed Woolf, reassured Kafka, invigorated Joyce, and restored Proust. Modernist writers were alienated from conventional society but at home in the house of fiction with its million windows through which they devised new ways to show black and white, big and small, coarse and fine.[21] They took unmistakable satisfaction from creative innovation, and their sustained output attests to an abiding conviction that they were forging new ways of interpreting the world.

Appendix: novels discussed in this book

Aragon, Louis. *Paris Peasant*. 1926. Translated by Simon Watson Taylor.
Boston: Exact Change, 1994.

Balzac, Honoré de. *Old Goriot*. 1834. Translated by Marion Ayton Crawford.
Harmondsworth: Penguin, 1951.

Barbusse, Henri. *Under Fire*. 1917. Translated by Robin Buss.
Harmondsworth: Penguin, 2003.

Barnes, Djuna. *Nightwood*. 1936. New York: New Directions, 1961.

Bely, Andrei, *Petersburg*. 1913–16. Translated by Robert A. Maguire and
John E. Malmstad. Bloomington: Indiana University Press, 1978.

Bennett, Arnold. *Anna of the Five Towns*. 1902. Ware, Hertfordshire:
Wordsworth, 1994.

Breton, André. *Nadja*. 1928. Translated by Richard Howard. New York:
Grove, 1960.

Broch, Hermann. *The Sleepwalkers*. 1931–32. Translated by Willa and
Edwin Muir. San Francisco: North Point Press, 1985.

Brontë, Charlotte. *Jane Eyre*. 1847. Harmondsworth: Penguin, 2006.

Camus, Albert. *The Stranger*. 1942. Translated by Matthew Ward. New York:
Vintage, 1988.

Chandler, Raymond. *The Big Sleep*. New York: Knopf, 1939.

Chopin, Kate. *The Awakening*. 1899. New York: Modern Library, 2000.

Conrad, Joseph. *Heart of Darkness*. 1902. 4th edn. Harmondsworth:
Norton, 2006.

Lord Jim. 1899–1900. Oxford: Oxford University Press, 1983.

Nostromo. 1904. Oxford: Oxford University Press, 1984.

The Nigger of the "Narcissus." 1897. New York: Norton, 1979.

Under Western Eyes. 1911. Harmondsworth: Penguin, 1989.

Dickens, Charles. *A Tale of Two Cities*. 1859. Harmondsworth: Penguin,
1970.

Bleak House. 1853. Harmondsworth: Penguin, 1996.

David Copperfield. 1850. Harmondsworth: Penguin, 1977.

Great Expectations. 1861. Harmondsworth: Penguin, 1979.

Little Dorrit. 1857. Harmondsworth: Penguin, 1967.

Martin Chuzzlewit. 1844. Harmondsworth: Penguin, 1995.

Oliver Twist. 1838. Harmondsworth: Penguin, 1985.

Our Mutual Friend. 1864–66. Oxford: Oxford University Press, 1998.

Döblin, Alfred. *Berlin Alexanderplatz: The Story of Franz Biberkopf.* 1929. Translated by Eugene Jolas. Harmondsworth: Penguin, 1978.

Dos Passos, John. *Manhattan Transfer.* 1925. Boston: Houghton Mifflin, 1953.

U. S. A. 1930, 1932, 1936. New York: Library of America, 1996.

Dostoevsky, Fyodor. *Crime and Punishment.* 1866. Translated by Jessie Coulson. New York: Norton, 1989.

The Karamazov Brothers. 1880. Translated by Ignat Avsey. Oxford: Oxford University Press, 1994.

Dreiser, Theodore. *An American Tragedy.* 1925. New York: Signet, 1981.

The "Genius." 1915. New York: World, 1946.

Dumas, Alexandre. *The Count of Monte Cristo.* 1844–45. Translated by Robin Buss. Harmondsworth: Penguin, 1966.

Eliot, George. *Adam Bede.* 1859. Harmondsworth: Penguin, 1985.

Daniel Deronda. 1876. Harmondsworth: Penguin, 1986.

Middlemarch. 1872. New York: Norton, 1977.

The Mill on the Floss. 1860. New York: Penguin, 1979.

Faulkner, William. *Absalom, Absalom!* 1936. New York: Vintage, 1990.

As I Lay Dying. 1930. New York: Vintage, 1990.

Light in August. 1932. New York: Vintage, 1987.

The Sound and the Fury. 1929. New York: Vintage, 1990.

Fitzgerald, F. Scott. *The Great Gatsby.* New York: Scribner's, 1925.

Flaubert, Gustave. *Madame Bovary.* 1857. Translated by Francis Steegmuller. New York: Vintage, 1957.

Ford, Ford Madox. *Parade's End.* 1924, 1925, 1926. New York: Knopf, 1992.

The Good Soldier. 1915. New York: Norton, 1995.

Forster, E. M. *A Passage to India.* 1924. New York: Harcourt, 1984.

Howards End. 1910. New York: Norton, 1988.

Gide, André. *Lafcadio's Adventures.* 1914. Translated by Dorothy Bussy. New York: Vintage, 1953.

The Counterfeiters. 1925. Translated by Dorothy Bussy. New York: Vintage, 1973.

The Immoralist. 1902. Translated by Richard Howard. New York: Vintage, 1970.

The Journals of André Gide. 4 vols. Translated by Justin O'Brien. New York: Knopf, 1947, 1948, 1949, 1951.

Hardy, Thomas. *Tess of the D'Urbervilles.* 1891. Harmondsworth: Penguin, 1985.

The Return of the Native. 1878. Oxford: Oxford University Press, 1990.

Hemingway, Ernest. *A Farewell to Arms.* New York: Scribner's, 1929.

In Our Time. New York: Scribner's, 1925.

The Sun Also Rises. New York: Scribner's, 1926.

Hesse, Hermann. *Steppenwolf.* 1927. Translated by Joseph Mileck and Horst Frenz. New York: Holt, 1963.

Narcissus and Goldmund. 1930. Translated by Ursule Molinaro. New York: Farrar, Straus and Giroux, 1989.

Hugo, Victor. *Les Misérables.* 1862. Translated by Norman Denny. Harmondsworth: Penguin, 1976.

Notre-Dame of Paris. 1831. Translated by John Sturrock. Harmondsworth: Penguin, 1978.

Hurston, Zora Neale. *Their Eyes Were Watching God.* 1937. New York: Perennial, 1990.

Huxley, Aldous. *Eyeless in Gaza.* 1936. New York: Carroll & Graf, 1995.

James, Henry. *The Ambassadors.* 1903. Harmondsworth: Penguin, 2003.

The Golden Bowl. 1904. New York: Penguin, 1966.

The Portrait of a Lady. 1881. New York: Penguin, 1963.

What Maisie Knew. 1897. Harmondsworth: Penguin, 1985.

Joyce, James. *A Portrait of the Artist as a Young Man.* 1916. New York: Viking, 1956.

Ulysses. 1922. New York: Vintage, 1986.

Kafka, Franz. *The Castle.* 1926. Translated by Mark Harman. New York: Schocken, 1998.

The Metamorphosis. 1915. Translated by Stanley Corngold. New York: Norton, 1996.

The Trial. 1925. Translated by Breon Mitchell. New York: Schocken, 1998.

Keller, Gottfried. *Green Henry.* 1855. Translated by A. M. Holt. New York: Tusk Ivories, 2003.

Lawrence, D. H. *Sons and Lovers.* 1913. New York: Penguin, 1983.

Women in Love. 1920. Harmondsworth: Penguin, 1995.

Lewis, Wyndham. *Tarr.* 1918. Harmondsworth: Penguin, 1982.

Mann, Thomas. *Death in Venice.* 1912. Translated by Clayton Koelb. New York: Norton, 1994.

The Magic Mountain. 1924. Translated by John E. Woods. New York: Knopf, 2005.

Martin du Gard, Roger. *Jean Barois.* 1913. Translated by Stuart Gilbert. New York: Bobbs-Merrill, 1969.

Melville, Herman. *Moby Dick.* 1851. New York: Norton, 1967.

Musil, Robert. *The Man Without Qualities.* 1930, 1942. 2 vols. Translated by Sophie Wilkins. New York: Knopf, 1995.

Norris, Frank. *The Octopus: A Story of California.* 1901. New York: Signet, 1964.

Proust, Marcel. *Remembrance of Things Past.* 1913–27. 3 vols. Translated by C. K. Scott Moncrieff and Terence Kilmartin. New York: Random House, 1981.

Richardson, Dorothy. *Pilgrimage.* 1915–38. 4 vols. London: Virago, 1982.

Rilke, Rainer Maria. *The Notebooks of Malte Laurids Brigge.* 1910. Translated by Stephen Mitchell. New York: Vintage, 1985.

Sartre, Jean-Paul. *Nausea.* 1938. Translated by Lloyd Alexander. New York: New Directions, 2007.

Schnitzler, Arthur. "Fräulein Else." 1924. In *Desire and Delusion.* Translated by Margret Schaefer. Chicago: Ivan R. Dee, 2003.

   Lieutenant Gustl. 1901. Translated by Richard L. Simon. Los Angeles: Green Integer, 2003.

Stein, Gertrude. *The Making of Americans.* 1925. Normal, Ill.: Dalkey, 1999.

   Melanctha. 1909. In Carl Van Vechten, ed., *Selected Writings of Gertrude Stein.* New York: Vintage, 1962.

   Tender Buttons. 1914. In Carl Van Vechten, ed., *Selected Writings of Gertrude Stein.* New York: Vintage, 1962.

Steinbeck, John. *The Grapes of Wrath.* 1939. New York: Modern Library, 1952.

Stoker, Bram. *Dracula.* 1897. Harmondsworth: Penguin, 1993.

Tolstoy, Leo. *Anna Karenina.* 1851. Translated by Aylmer Maude. New York: Norton, 1970.

   "The Kreutzer Sonata." 1889. In *"The Kreutzer Sonata" and Other Stories.* Translated by David McDuff. Harmondsworth: Penguin, 1985.

Wilde, Oscar. *The Picture of Dorian Gray.* 1890. Harmondsworth: Penguin, 1985.

Woolf, Virginia. *A Room of One's Own.* 1929. New York: Harcourt, 1981.

   Jacob's Room. 1922. In *Jacob's Room & The Waves.* New York: Harcourt, 1959.

   Mrs. Dalloway. 1925. New York: Harcourt, 1981.

To the Lighthouse. 1927. New York: Harcourt, 1981.

The Waves. 1931. New York: Harcourt, 2006.

Zola, Émile. *La bête humaine.* 1890. Translated by Leonard Tancock. Harmondsworth: Penguin, 1977.

The Earth. 1887. Translated by Douglas Parmée. Harmondsworth: Penguin, 1980.

Germinal. 1885. Translated by L. W. Tancock. Harmondsworth: Penguin, 1971.

Nana. 1880. Translated by George Holden. Harmondsworth: Penguin, 1972.

The Debacle [1870–71]. 1892. Translated by Leonard Tancock. Harmondsworth: Penguin, 1972.

Notes

INTRODUCTION

1. Randall Stevenson, *Modernist Fiction: An Introduction* (Lexington: University of Kentucky Press, 1992), 8–9, 14–15; Jesse Matz, *The Modernist Novel: A Short Introduction* (Oxford: Blackwell, 2004), 8–9.
2. Pericles Lewis, *The Cambridge Introduction to Modernism* (Cambridge: Cambridge University Press, 2007), 1–10.
3. David Lodge, "Two Kinds of Modern Fiction," in *The Modes of Modern Writing: Metaphor, Metonymy, and the Typology of Modern Literature* (Ithaca: Cornell University Press, 1977), 45–46.
4. Erich Auerbach, *Mimesis* (Princeton: Princeton University Press, 1953); David Kadlec, *Mosaic Modernism: Anarchism, Pragmatism, Culture* (Baltimore: Johns Hopkins University Press, 2000); David Trotter, *The English Novel in History 1895–1920* (London: Routledge, 1993); Lewis, *Cambridge Introduction to Modernism*; Georg Lukács, "The Ideology of Modernism," in *Realism in Our Time: Literature and the Class Struggle* (New York: Harper, 1964), 17–46; José Ortega y Gasset, *The Dehumanization of Art* (Princeton: Princeton University Press, 1948); David Weir, *Decadence and the Making of Modernism* (Amherst: University of Massachusetts Press, 1995); Michael Valdez Moses, "Disorientalism: Conrad and the Imperial Origins of Modern Aesthetics," in *Modernism and Colonialism: British and Irish Literature, 1899–1939*, ed. Richard Begam and Michael Valdez Moses (Durham: Duke University Press, 2007), 43–69; Max Weber, "Science as a Vocation" [1918], in *From Max Weber: Essays in Sociology*, ed. H. H. Gerth and C. Wright Mills (New York: Oxford University Press, 1958), 129–56; Philip Weinstein, *Unknowing: The Work of Modernist Fiction* (Ithaca: Cornell University Press, 2005); Lionel Trilling, "On the Modern Element in Modern Literature," *Partisan Review* (January–February 1961): 3–30; John A. Lester Jr., *Journey Through Despair 1880–1914: Transformation in British Literary Culture* (Princeton: Princeton University Press, 1968); Paul B. Armstrong, *The Challenge of Bewilderment: Understanding and Representation in James, Conrad, and Ford* (Ithaca: Cornell University Press, 1987); Marjorie Perloff, *The Poetics of Indeterminacy: Rimbaud to Cage* (Princeton: Princeton University Press, 1981); Sara Haslam, *Fragmenting Modernism: Ford Madox Ford, the Novel and the Great War* (Manchester: Manchester University Press, 2002); James M. Mellard, *The Exploded Form: The Modernist Novel in*

America (Urbana: University of Illinois Press, 1980); Marshall Berman, *All that Is Solid Melts into Air: The Experience of Modernity* (New York: Penguin, 1982).

5. Lyotard does sketch what postmodernists believe positively in response to their incredulity, namely "many different language games" and "a heterogeneity of elements," but these fragmentary items replace any overall interpretation, and his definition of postmodernism is best known for the incredulity. Jean-François Lyotard, *The Postmodern Condition: A Report on Knowledge* [1979] (Minneapolis: University of Minnesota Press, 1984), xxiv.

6. Virginia Woolf, "Modern Fiction," in *The Common Reader: First Series* (New York: Harcourt Brace, 1925), 154.

7. Douglas Mao and Rebecca L. Walkowitz, "The New Modernist Studies," *PMLA* 123, 3 (May 2008): 737–48.

8. In an ambitious programmatic statement, Susan Stanford Friedman proposes re-conceiving modernism as a planetary phenomenon based on evidence from around the globe. She concedes that such an undertaking might "incorporate everything and lose all definitional cogency or analytical utility" (473) but then argues, for example, that the sort of imperialism captured in modernist novels had significant commonalities with the imperialism of the Tang Dynasty in China (AD 618–907). That and other examples of "modernity *before* the modernities of the post-1500 world system" and in non-Western countries, she contends, "combine periods of violent conquest with rapid technological change, world-systems of trade and cultural exchange, the bang/clash of different peoples and their world views, and new representational practices in the arts and other expressive domains" (481). Perhaps, but these basic structural features across space and time pale in comparison with their manifest differences, and to classify them all as modernist confounds sharp historical analysis and blurs discriminating cultural interpretation. Friedman, "Planetarity: Musing Modernist Studies," *Modernism/Modernity* 17, 3 (September 2010): 471–99.

9. *The Journals of André Gide* (New York: Knopf, 1948), vol. II, 271.

10. Woolf, "Modern Fiction," 151.

11. Virginia Woolf, "Mr. Bennett and Mrs. Brown" [1924], in *The Captain's Death Bed and Other Essays* (New York: Harcourt Brace, 1978), 110.

12. Monika Fludernik, "The Diachronization of Narratology," *Narrative* 11, 3 (October 2003): 331–48. Fludernik looks forward to more historical studies but reports that, as of 2003, "there has been comparatively little interest on a theoretical level in the history of narrative forms and functions" (331).

13. Allan Megill, "'Grand Narrative' and the Discipline of History," in *A New Philosophy of History*, ed. Frank Ankersmit and Hans Kellner (Chicago: University of Chicago Press, 1995), 152. See also Dorothy Ross, "Grand Narrative in American Historical Writing: From Romance to Uncertainty," *The American Historical Review* 100, 3 (June 1995): 651–77.

14. This scenario is derived from Weinstein, *Unknowing*, 21–76.

15. Stephen Kern, "Gender," in *The Culture of Love: Victorians to Moderns* (Cambridge: Harvard University Press, 1992), 191–217.

16. From Sir William Blackstone, *Commentaries on the Laws of England, 1765–69*, cited in Joan Perkin, *Women and Marriage in Nineteenth-Century England* (London: Routledge, 1989), 1–2. My survey of English law is from Perkin, *Women and Marriage*, 1–31, 292–310.

17. Rudolph Binion sees this change reflected in a "fictional assault on the family" around the turn of the century in "Fiction as Social Fantasy: Europe's Domestic Crisis of 1879–1914," *Journal of Social History* (Summer 1994): 679.

18. Mary Louise Roberts, *Civilization Without Sexes: Reconstructing Gender in Postwar France, 1917–1927* (Chicago: University of Chicago Press, 1994).

19. Chris Cook and John Paxton, *European Political Facts 1848–1918* (New York: Palgrave, 1978).

20. Lionel Trilling, "The Princess Casamassima," in *The Liberal Imagination* (New York: Harcourt Brace, 1950), 59.

21. Filippo Marinetti, "The Founding and Manifesto of Futurism," in *Marinetti: Selected Writings*, ed. R. W. Flint (New York: Farrar Straus, 1971), 42.

22. Jean-Michel Rabaté, *1913: The Cradle of Modernism* (Malden, Mass.: Wiley Blackwell, 2007).

23. Adam Hochschild, *King Leopold's Ghost: A Story of Greed, Terror, and Heroism in Colonial Africa* (New York: Mariner, 1998), 225–33.

24. The British Reform Acts of 1867 and 1884 quadrupled the electorate to 29 percent of men over the age of twenty. Belgium established universal male suffrage in 1893, Norway in 1898, Holland in 1917, Germany in 1918, Italy in 1919. Women won the right to vote in New Zealand in 1893, Finland in 1906, Germany, Poland, and England in 1918, Holland in 1919, the United States in 1920, and France in 1944. In the Western world by the 1880s the majority of men and women were literate. Mass education was promoted by increasing primary schooling, cheap mass circulation newspapers, and new lending libraries.

25. After 1877 the aristocracy ceased to dominate French ministries except for the military and diplomacy. Aristocratic presence in the British Cabinet dropped from forty-seven (1880–95) to thirteen (1905–14). Aristocratic officers in the Prussian army went from 65 percent in 1880 to 30 percent in 1913. Alan S. Kahan, "The Decline of Liberalism," in *Liberalism in Nineteenth-Century Europe: The Political Culture of Limited Suffrage* (New York: Palgrave, 2003), 173–201.

26. Harold Perkin, *The Rise of Professional Society* (London: Routledge, 1990).

27. Kahan, "The Decline of Liberalism," 190.

28. On the sacralization of politics in fascism, Nazism, and communism see Emilio Gentile, *Politics as Religion* (Princeton: Princeton University Press, 2006).

29. André Gide, "Journal of *The Counterfeiters*," in *C*, 425.

CHAPTER 1 CHARACTER

1. Joseph Conrad, *The Nigger of the "Narcissus"* [1897] (New York: Norton, 1979), 23, 85.

2. Djuna Barnes, *Nightwood* [1936] (New York: New Directions, 1961), 136.

3. Allyson Booth, *Postcards from the Trenches: Negotiating the Space Between Modernism and the First World War* (New York: Oxford University Press, 1996), 21.

4. Jean-Paul Sartre, *Nausea* [1938], translated by Lloyd Alexander (New York: New Directions, 2007), 100.

5. Ford Madox Ford, *The Good Soldier* [1915] (New York: Norton, 1995), 104.

6. Leo Bersani, *A Future for Astyanax: Character and Desire in Literature* (Boston: Little Brown, 1984), 56.

7. Ernst Mach, *The Analysis of Sensations* [1885] (New York: Dover, 1959), 22–29.

8. William James, *Principles of Psychology* (New York: Henry Holt, 1890), vol. 1, 239.

9. *The Standard Edition of the Complete Psychological Works of Sigmund Freud* (London: Hogarth, 1953), vol. XVI, 285.

10. Three paintings capture this same experience: Umberto Boccioni's *The Street Enters the House* (1911) with a woman penetrated by objects from the urban scene surrounding the balcony on which she stands, his *Materia* (1912) with his seated mother's head assaulted by waves of urban force lines and planes, and Ludwig Meidner's *The City and I* (1913), a self-portrait of him facing away from a city that seems to explode in his head.

11. Alfred Döblin, "*Ulysses* by Joyce," in *The Weimar Republic Sourcebook*, ed. Anton Kaes et al. (Berkeley: University of California Press, 1994), 514.

12. Wyndham Lewis, *Tarr* [1918] (Harmondsworth: Penguin, 1982), 70.

13. Virginia Woolf, *The Waves* [1931] (New York: Harcourt, 2006), 9.

14. Dennis Brown argues that "it was above all the recognition of 'shell-shock' which transformed the dissolving self of prewar literature into the chronically fragmented self of the twenties." *The Modernist Self in Twentieth-Century English Literature: A Study in Self-Fragmentation* (London: Macmillan, 1989), 20.

15. Hermann Broch, *The Sleepwalkers* [1931–32], translated by Willa and Edwin Muir (San Francisco: North Point Press, 1985), 407.

16. Hermann Hesse, *Steppenwolf* [1927], translated by Joseph Mileck and Horst Frenz (New York: Holt, 1963), 193, 57.

17. William Faulkner, *Light in August* [1932] (New York: Vintage, 1987), 543.

18. *Faulkner in the University: Class Conferences at the University of Virginia 1957–1958*, ed. Frederick L. Gwynn and Joseph L. Blotner (New York: Vintage, 1959), 72.

19. *Telegony* was coined by August Weismann in 1892 but was part of popular thinking back to antiquity. Some also argued that a woman could be permanently affected by a single coitus or even mental influences, so that a woman's baby might resemble a man she formerly loved, or something she saw during a pregnancy. On the broader historical significance of this concept see Stephen Kern, *A Cultural History of Causality: Science, Murder Novels, and Systems of Thought* (Princeton: Princeton University Press, 2004), 42–47.

20. George Chauncey, Jr., "From Sexual Inversion to Homosexuality: Medicine and the Changing Conceptualization of Female Deviance," *Salmagundi* (Fall 1982–Winter 1983): 122.

21. For evidence of this claim see Stephen Kern, *The Culture of Love: Victorians to Moderns* (Cambridge: Harvard University Press, 1992), 191–217.

22. Alfred Döblin, *Berlin Alexanderplatz: The Story of Franz Biberkopf* [1929], translated by Eugene Jolas (Harmondsworth: Penguin, 1978), 43.

23. "On the Teaching of Modern Literature" [1961], in Lionel Trilling, *Beyond Culture: Essays on Literature and Learning* (New York: Viking, 1965), 3–30.

24. Letter to Frank Budgen, August 16, 1921, in *Letters of James Joyce*, ed. Stuart Gilbert (London: Faber, 1957), vol. I, 170.

25. James Joyce, *Selected Letters of James Joyce*, ed. Richard Ellmann (New York: Viking, 1975), 181–82.

26. Ibid., 182.

27. Ibid., 187.

28. John Dos Passos, *U. S. A.* [1930, 1932, 1936] (New York: Library of America, 1996), 756–61.

29. In *The Odyssey* Homer describes Odysseus' handling of the bow as "like a harper," and after he strung it he "plucked it." In Joyce's "Aeolus" episode under the headline O, HARP EOLIAN!, Bloom "took a reel of dental floss from his waistcoat pocket and . . . twanged it smartly" (105).

30. Joyce's rendering of what Bloom remembers, imagines, thinks, feels, sees, hears, and reads while defecating is a major challenge to notions of the classical hero. For all the realists' commitment to rendering real life, they did not describe characters defecating. One exception is Tolstoy's "The Death of Ivan Ilych" (1886), which mentions that the terminal Ilych's defecations were a source of embarrassment, but Tolstoy does not attempt to render as if from within using stream-of-consciousness technique how Ilych experiences defecating or make it a humanizing moment as does Joyce with Bloom.

31. *Letters of James Joyce*, ed. Richard Ellmann (London: Faber, 1966), vol. II, 81. See also Keri Elizabeth Ames, "The Rebirth of Heroism from Homer's *Odyssey* to Joyce's *Ulysses*," in *Twenty-First Joyce*, ed. Ellen Carol Jones and Morris Beja (Gainesville: University of Florida Press, 2004), 157–78.

32. Thomas Vargish argues that "most major English novelists before George Eliot assumed the existence of a providential order to the cosmos and found evidence for a providential intention at work in it." *The Providential Aesthetic in Victorian Fiction* (Charlottesville: University Press of Virginia, 1985), 1. See also Carol Christ, "Aggression and Providential Death in George Eliot's Fiction," *Novel* 9 (Winter 1976): 130–40.

33. Jerome H. Buckley, *Season of Youth: The Bildungsroman from Dickens to Golding* (Cambridge: Harvard University Press, 1974), 17. See also Gregory Castle, *Reading the Modernist Bildungsroman* (Gainesville: University Press of Florida, 2006).

34. "At the start of the twentieth century, as though obeying some secret signal, Conrad and Mann, Musil and Rilke, Kafka and Joyce, all set about writing stories of 'formation' [*Bildung*] – in which the *Bildung* does not occur; in which objective culture, congealed in conventions and institutions, no longer helps to construct individual subjects, but wounds and disintegrates them." Franco

Moretti, *Modern Epic: The World System from Goethe to García Márquez* (London: Verso, 1996), 195.

35. Roberta Seret, *Voyage into Creativity: The Modern Künstlerroman* (New York: Lang, 1992).

36. Virginia Woolf, *The Diary of Virginia Woolf*, vol. II: *1920–24*, ed. Anne Olivier Bell, assisted by Andrew McNeillie (New York: Harcourt Brace, 1977), 13–14.

37. For Woolf's critique of the rationality that sustains "markets, tariffs, armaments, and war" see Edward L. Bishop, "The Subject in *Jacob's Room*," *Modern Language Studies* 38, 1 (Spring 1992): 169. On her critique of liberal rationalism, see Vincent Sherry, *The Great War and the Language of Modernism* (New York: Oxford University Press, 2003), 270–97.

38. On the autobiographical component of these novels see Seret, *Voyage into Creativity*, 9–10.

39. On this reading see Marian Eide, "The Woman of the Ballyhoura Hills: James Joyce and the Politics of Creativity," *Twentieth Century Literature* 44, 4 (Winter 1998): 377–93.

CHAPTER 2 EVENT

1. Henry James, "The Art of Fiction," in *The Future of the Novel*, ed. Leon Edel (New York: Vintage, 1956), 15–16.

2. Henry James, in *The Art of the Novel: Critical Prefaces by Henry James*, ed. Richard P. Blackmur (New York: Scribner's, 1962), 57.

3. Percy Lubbock notes this feature. "The view that [James] opens is as panoramic, often enough, as any of Thackeray's sweeping surveys, only the scale is different, with a word barely breathed in place of a dialogue, minutes for months, a turn of a head or an intercepted glance for a chronicle of crime or adulterous intrigue." *The Craft of Fiction* (New York: Viking, 1957), 149. Early James was indebted to melodramatic devices including highly moralized characters and momentous revelations of secret alliances. His later novels, however, moved away from melodrama and toward what Peter Brooks calls the "melodrama of consciousness" and of "ethical choice," as James devoted more attention to internal rather than external events. Peter Brooks, *The Melodramatic Imagination: Balzac, Henry James, Melodrama, and the Mode of Excess* (New Haven: Yale University Press, 1995), 153–57.

4. Maurice Maeterlinck, *The Treasure of the Humble* (New York: Dodd, Mead & Company, 1899), 105–06.

5. James Joyce, "Drama and Life" (1900), in *The Critical Writings of James Joyce*, ed. Ellsworth Mason and Richard Ellmann (New York: Viking, 1959), 45.

6. James Joyce, *Stephen Hero* (New York: New Directions, 1963), 211.

7. Morris Beja, *Epiphany in the Modern Novel* (Seattle: University of Washington Press, 1971), 83.

8. In Epiphany 1, Mr. Vance, holding a stick, visited James's home and told his mother that if James did not apologize an eagle would pull out his eyes. In Epiphany 15, two children tease a beggar, also gripping a stick, who threatens to

cut out "the livers and the lights [eyes]" of the children. Joyce combines these epiphanies into this pivotal moment in *Portrait*. See *The Workshop of Daedalus: James Joyce and the Raw Materials for "A Portrait of the Artist as a Young Man,"* ed. Robert Scholes and Richard M. Kain (Evanston: Northwestern University Press, 1965), 11, 25.

9. Virginia Woolf, "A Sketch of the Past," in *Moments of Being*, ed. Jeanne Schulkind (New York: Harcourt, 1985), 70.

10. Robert E. Spoo, "'Nestor' and the Nightmare: The Presence of the Great War in *Ulysses*," *Twentieth Century Literature* 32, 2 (Summer 1986): 137–54.

11. This argument is richly documented by Keith Gandal, who shows that his major modernist authors created Anglo characters (Tom Buchanan, Jake Barnes, Jason Compson) who were troubled by the Army's meritocratic procedures that gave rank and power to ethnic Americans or to soldiers who actually fought in the war (Jay Gatsby, Robert Cohn, Dalton Ames) and rivaled the Anglo men for sexually emancipated Anglo women (Daisy Buchanan, Brett Ashley, and Caddy Compson). Thus, they felt emasculated for not being in battle, not achieving important military positions, losing out to ethnic Americans and true war veterans, and being sexually inadequate. Gandal interprets these novels as responding to historical developments in the courtship narrative (the sexual emancipation of women) and the national and liberal narrative (the meritocratic practices in the American army mobilization that allowed ethnic Americans new power and status). *The Gun and the Pen: Hemingway, Fitzgerald, Faulkner, and the Fiction of Mobilization* (New York: Oxford University Press, 2008).

12. Quoted in Hermione Lee, *Virginia Woolf* (New York: Vintage, 1996), 338.

13. James M. Haule, "'Le Temps passé and the Original Typescript: An Early Version of the 'Time Passes' Section of *To the Lighthouse*," *Twentieth Century Literature* 29, 3 (Autumn 1983): 267–311; and James M. Haule, "*To the Lighthouse* and the Great War: The Evidence of Virginia Woolf's Revisions of 'Time Passes'," in *Virginia Woolf and War*, ed. Mark Hussey (Syracuse: Syracuse University Press, 1991), 164–79.

14. *Letters of Henry James*, ed. Percy Lubbock (New York: Scribner's, 1920), vol. 11, 384, 388.

15. Ford Madox Hueffer, "A Day of Battle," quoted in Samuel Hynes, *A War Imagined: The First World War and English Culture* (New York: Atheneum, 1960). Hynes's book is actually about the *in*ability of writers to imagine the war, as Ford wonders in that article "why [he] can write nothing . . . why [he] cannot even evoke pictures of the Somme or the flat lands round Ploegsteert" (105).

16. Ibid., 106.

17. Gertrude Stein, "How Writing is Written" [1934–35], in *The Gender of Modernism*, ed. Bonnie Kime Scott (Bloomington: Indiana University Press, 1990), 493.

18. That metaphor has a historical referent from this time, because a total eclipse on May 29, 1919 enabled Arthur Eddington to verify Einstein's General Theory of Relativity, specifically his hypothesis that space is curved, by observing the effect of the sun's gravitational force in curving light waves from stars

that appeared close to the sun, stars that cannot be seen when the sun is at full illumination.

19. Beja, *Epiphany in the Modern Novel*, 17.
20. E. M. Forster, *Aspects of the Novel* (New York: Harcourt Brace, 1927), 86.
21. Wayne C. Booth, *The Rhetoric of Fiction* (Chicago: University of Chicago Press, 1961), 126.
22. Brian Richardson, *Unlikely Stories: Causality and the Nature of Modern Narrative* (Newark: University of Delaware Press, 1997).
23. Gertrude Stein, *Tender Buttons* [1914], in *Selected Writings of Gertrude Stein*, ed. Carl Van Vechten (New York: Vintage, 1962), 508.
24. One internal narrator, Mr. Compson, explains these subversive concerns with overloaded Faulknerian prose: "Perhaps this is the pure and perfect incest: the brother realizing that the sister's virginity must be destroyed in order to have existed at all, taking that virginity in the person of the brother-in-law, the man whom he would be if he could become, metamorphosed into, the lover, the husband; by whom he would be despoiled, choose for despoiler, if he could become, metamorphose into the sister, the mistress, the bride" (77).
25. Albert Camus, *The Stranger* [1942], translated by Matthew Ward (New York: Vintage, 1988), 68.
26. In 1943 Jean-Paul Sartre argued that Camus's resistance to strong causality captures the absurdity of existence and recalibrates the scale of importance: "In this world [of *The Stranger*] that has been stripped of its causality and presented as absurd, the smallest incident has weight." "Camus' *The Outsider*," in *Jean-Paul Sartre: Literary and Philosophical Essays* (New York: Collier, 1955), 44.
27. T. S. Eliot, "Ulysses, Order, and Myth," *The Dial* 75 (1923): 480–83.
28. Modernist poets who integrated writings with myth include Ezra Pound and T. S. Eliot. Faulkner used biblical myth in *Absalom, Absalom!*, and Dos Passos used it in *Manhattan Transfer*. On Döblin's use of classical and biblical myth see Theodore Ziolkowski, *Dimensions of the Modern Novel* (Princeton: Princeton University Press, 1969), 99–137. On biblical and classical myth in several modernist novels see Kathleen Komar, *Pattern and Chaos: Multilinear Novels by Dos Passos, Döblin, Faulkner and Koeppen* (Columbia, S.C.: Camden House, 1983), 35–56.
29. Joseph Frank, "Spatial Form in Modern Literature" [1945], in *The Widening Gyre: Crisis and Mastery in Modern Literature* (Bloomington: Indiana University Press, 1968), 3–62, at 53–54. Subsequent references are to this edition. Ivo Vidan applies Frank's theory to novels by Conrad, Ford, Faulkner, Huxley, and Fitzgerald, in "Time Sequence in Spatial Fiction," in *Spatial Form in Narrative*, ed. Jeffrey R. Smitten and Ann Daghistany (Ithaca: Cornell University Press, 1981), 131–57.
30. *The Probabilistic Revolution*, ed. Lorenz Krüger, Lorraine J. Daston, and Michael Heidelberger, 2 vols. (Cambridge: MIT Press, 1987); Theodore M. Porter, *The Rise of Statistical Thinking 1820–1900* (Princeton: Princeton University Press, 1986), 315.
31. Fyodor Dostoevsky, *Crime and Punishment* [1866], translated by Jessie Coulson (New York: Norton, 1989), 57.

32. Thomas Vargish, *The Providential Aesthetic in Victorian Fiction* (Charlottesville: University Press of Virginia, 1985).

33. Leland Monk, *Standard Deviations: Chance and the Modern British Novel* (Stanford: Stanford University Press, 1993), 9.

34. André Gide, *Lafcadio's Adventures* [1914], translated by Dorothy Bussy (New York: Vintage, 1953), 195–96.

35. André Gide, "Faits-divers," *Nouvelle Revue Française* 30 (June 1, 1928): 841. See also "The Significance of the '*acte gratuit*,'" in *Modernist Conjectures: A Mainstream in European Literature 1910–1940*, by Douwe Fokkema and Elrud Ibsch (London: Hurst, 1987), 181–91.

36. Roy Jay Nelson, *Causality and Narrative in French Fiction from Zola to Robbe-Grillet* (Columbus: Ohio State University Press, 1990), 21–22.

37. Stephen Kern, *A Cultural History of Causality: Science, Murder Novels, and Systems of Thought* (Princeton: Princeton University Press, 2004), 13–14 and *passim*.

38. Letter to Louise Colet of January 16, 1852, in *The Selected Letters of Gustave Flaubert*, ed. Francis Steegmuller (New York: Vintage, 1953).

39. Henry James, "Preface" to *The Portrait of a Lady*, written for his collected works in 1908.

40. T. E. Hulme, "A Lecture on Modern Poetry" [1908], in *Further Speculations* (Lincoln: University of Nebraska Press, 1972), 72.

41. Wyndham Lewis, *Tarr* [1918] (Harmondsworth: Penguin, 1982), 311.

42. Forster, *Aspects of the Novel*, 26.

43. André Breton, *Nadja* [1928], translated by Richard Howard (New York: Grove, 1960), 18.

44. Gertrude Stein, "Portraits and Repetition" [1934], in *Look at Me Now and Here I Am: Writings and Lectures 1901–1945*, ed. Patricia Meyerowitz (Harmondsworth: Penguin, 1967), 110.

45. Lisa Ruddick explores Stein's rejection of the strong familial, bourgeois, and patriarchal plots of the nineteenth-century novel, which Stein claimed to have "killed." *Reading Gertrude Stein: Body, Text, Gnosis* (Ithaca: Cornell University Press, 1990), 124–28.

46. Virginia Woolf, "Modern Fiction" [1919], in *The Common Reader* (New York: Harcourt Brace, 1925), 154–55. A letter of August 28, 1930 explained that in *The Waves*, she was "writing to a rhythm and not to a plot."

47. For these earlier versions see E. L. Bishop, "The Shaping of *Jacob's Room*: Woolf's Manuscript Revisions," *Twentieth Century Literature* 32, 1 (Spring 1986): 115–35.

48. Brian McHale, "Telling Stories Again: On the Replenishment of Narrative in the Postmodernist Long Poem," *The Yearbook of English Studies* 30 (2000): 250.

49. T. S. Eliot, *The Waste Land: A Facsimile and Transcript of the Original Drafts Including the Annotations of Ezra Pound*, ed. Valerie Eliot (New York: Harcourt Brace, 1971), 5.

50. These first cuts are indicated in the facsimile edition with red ink for Pound's cuts and black ink for those that could have been made by Eliot or Pound. The original first page is crossed out in black ink. Ibid.

51. Ibid., 31.

52. *The Selected Letters of Ezra Pound, 1907–1941*, ed. D. D. Paige (New York: New Directions, 1971), 180.

53. John Hadfield, *Every Picture Tells a Story: Images of Victorian Life* (London: Herbert, 1985).

54. Leo Steinberg, "The Philosophical Brothel, Part 1," *Art News* 71, 5 (September 1972): 21, 40. See also William Rubin, "From Narrative to 'Iconic' in Picasso: The Buried Allegory in *Bread and Fruitdish on a Table* and the Role of *Les Demoiselles d'Avignon*," *Art Bulletin* 45, 4 (December 1983): 615–49.

55. Patricia Leighten, "Colonialism, *l'art nègre*, and *Les Demoiselles d'Avignon*," in *Picasso's "Les Demoiselles d'Avignon*," ed. Christopher Green (Cambridge: Cambridge University Press, 2001), 78–79.

56. "In Hardy, Conrad, and Ford, in Gertrude Stein, Joyce, and Lawrence, in Woolf and Faulkner, the parent is a mere alleged author, one who stupidly refused to admit that genealogical relations or family lines are factitious structures or 'creations,' that family is a misleading name for anarchy, and that generation and filiation are substitutes for significance." Robert Caserio, *Plot, Story, and the Novel: From Dickens and Poe to the Modern Period* (Princeton: Princeton University Press, 1979), 233.

57. On "the Great War's frustration of plot" see Allyson Booth, *Postcards from the Trenches: Negotiating the Space between Modernism and the First World War* (New York: Oxford University Press, 1996), 108–11.

58. Helen McAfee, "The Literature of Disillusion," *Atlantic Monthly* (August 1923): 225–26.

59. Philip Weinstein, *Unknowing: The Work of Modernist Fiction* (Ithaca: Cornell University Press, 2005), 99.

CHAPTER 3 SPACE

1. Henri Poincaré, *Science and Hypothesis* [1901] (New York: Dover, 1927), 52–56.

2. Jacob von Uexküll, *Umwelt und Innenwelt der Tiere* (Berlin, 1909).

3. Émile Durkheim and Marcel Mauss, *Primitive Classification* [1903] (Chicago: University of Chicago Press, 1970), 43–44, 82, 86.

4. José Ortega y Gasset, "Adám en el Paraiso" [1910], in *Obras Completas* (Madrid: Revista de Occidente, 1946), vol. 1, 471; "Verdad y perspectiva," *El Espectador* 1 (1916): 10ff.

5. Edgar Kaufmann and Ben Raeburn, *Frank Lloyd Wright: Writings and Buildings* (New York: New American Library, 1960), 314.

6. Dora Vallier, "Braque, la peinture et nous: propos de l'artiste recueillis," *Cahiers d'art* 29 (October 1954): 15–16.

7. Stéphane Mallarmé, "Sur Poë," *Oeuvres complètes* (Paris: Pléiade, 1954), 872.

8. Stéphane Mallarmé, "Mystery in Literature," in *Mallarmé: Selected Prose Poems, Essays, and Letters*, ed. Bradford Cook (Baltimore: Johns Hopkins University Press, 1956), 33.

9. On the democratization of spatial hierarchies see Stephen Kern, *The Culture of Time and Space 1880–1918* (Cambridge: Harvard University Press, 1983), 152–80.

10. Gertrude Stein, "A Transatlantic Interview" [1946], in *The Gender of Modernism*, ed. Bonnie Kime Scott (Bloomington: Indiana University Press, 1990), 502–03.

11. Michael Boccia, "The Novel as the Ambiguous Night: Djuna Barnes' *Nightwood*," in *Form as Content and Rhetoric in the Modern Novel* (New York: Lang, 1989).

12. Djuna Barnes, *Nightwood* [1936] (New York: New Directions, 1961), 126.

13. In "Djuna Barnes and Thelma Wood: The Vengeance of *Nightwood*," *Journal of Modern Literature* 18, 1 (Winter 1992): 5–18, Phillip Herring documents the influence of Thelma on the character of Robin but does not suggest her role in the novel's title.

14. E. M. Forster, *A Passage to India* [1924] (New York: Harcourt, 1984), 166.

15. Franz Kafka, *The Trial* [1925], translated by Breon Mitchell (New York: Schocken, 1998), 211.

16. Henri Bergson, *Essai sur les données immédiates de la conscience* (Paris: Felix Alcan, 1889), translated in 1910 as *Time and Free Will*.

17. Martin Heidegger, *Being and Time*, translated by John Macquarrie and Edward Robinson (New York: Harper, 1962), 149, 154–57.

18. Nicholas Dames, *Amnesiac Selves: Nostalgia, Forgetting, and British Fiction, 1810–1870* (Oxford: Oxford University Press, 2003), 3–4.

19. E. M. Forster, *Howards End* [1910] (New York: Norton, 1988), 22.

20. Ford Madox Ford, *Joseph Conrad: A Personal Remembrance* [1924] (New York: Ecco, 1989), 192–95.

21. Ian Watt, *Conrad and the Nineteenth Century* (Berkeley: University of California Press, 1979), 169–80.

22. Ford, *Joseph Conrad: A Personal Remembrance*, 204–05.

23. Ford Madox Ford, *Parade's End* [1924, 1925, 1926] (New York: Knopf, 1992), 330–33.

24. Other vividly impressionist scenes include Strether's discovery that Chad and Madame de Vionnet are lovers in *The Ambassadors* (459–68), the *Patna* running over the object that sank it in *Lord Jim* (26), and Biberkopf's learning of the death of Mieze from a newspaper article in *Berlin Alexanderplatz* (401–03).

25. Roy Pascal, *The Dual Voice: Free Indirect Speech and its Functioning in the Nineteenth-Century European Novel* (Manchester: Manchester University Press, 1977).

26. Trudi Tate, "*Mrs. Dalloway* and the Armenian Question," in *Modernism, History and the First World War* (Manchester: Manchester University Press, 1998), 147–70.

27. William James, *Principles of Psychology* [1890] (New York: Dover, 1950), vol. 1, 245.

28. William James, "Stream of Consciousness," in *Talks to Teachers* [1899] (New York: Holt, 1921), 15.

29. Edouard Dujardin, *"Les lauriers sont coupés," Revue indépendante* (May–August 1887).

30. On the evolution of the technique see Franco Moretti, *"Ulysses* and the Twentieth Century," in *Modern Epic: The World System from Goethe to Garcia Márquez* (London: Verso, 1996), 171.

31. May Sinclair, "The Novels of Dorothy Richardson," *Egoist* 5 (April 1918): 57–59. In fact, Edouard Dujardin was the first to use it throughout a novel in *Les lauriers sont coupés* (1887), translated as *We'll to the Woods No More* (New York: New Directions, 1938).

32. Ford Madox Ford, "A Haughty and Proud Generation," *Yale Review* 11 (July 1922): 717.

33. This argument about increasing authenticity is the thesis of my book *The Culture of Love: Victorians to Moderns* (Cambridge: Harvard University Press, 1992). I do not argue that modernist novels or their authors were more authentic, merely that the love experienced by the characters in their novels was more authentic, in the sense that Heidegger uses the term, that is, more aware of what it means to be in love.

34. Rainer Maria Rilke, *The Notebooks of Malte Laurids Brigge* [1910] (New York: Vintage, 1985), 22, 5.

35. Gertrude Stein, "Portraits and Repetition" [1934], in *Look at Me Now and Here I Am: Writings and Lectures 1901–1945*, ed. Patricia Meyerowitz (Harmondsworth: Penguin, 1967), 109.

36. For a reading of modernist interiority as a way of being in the world see David Herman, "1880–1945: Re-minding Modernism," in *The Emergence of Mind: Representations of Consciousness in Narrative Discourse in English*, ed. David Herman (Lincoln: University of Nebraska Press, 2011).

37. Elsewhere he argues against Gottfried Benn's argument that "there is no outer reality, there is only human consciousness." "The negation of outward reality," Lukács continues, "is present in almost all modernist literature." Georg Lukács, "The Ideology of Modernism" [1956], in *Realism in Our Time* (New York: Harper, 1964), 25.

38. For these figures see my introduction, p. 12.

39. John Dos Passos, *Manhattan Transfer* [1925] (Boston: Houghton Mifflin, 1953), 112.

40. Andrei Bely, *Petersburg* [1913–16], translated by Robert A. Maguire and John E. Malmstad (Bloomington: Indiana University Press, 1978), 12.

41. John Dos Passos, *Manhattan Transfer* [1925] (Boston: Houghton Mifflin, 1953), 365.

42. Franz Kafka, *The Castle* [1926], translated by Mark Harman (New York: Schocken, 1998), 99.

43. Samuel Smiles, *Thrift* [1875] (London: J. Murray, 1886), 70.

44. Frank Budgen, *James Joyce and the Making of Ulysses* (Bloomington: Indiana University Press, 1960), 122.

45. In 1920 Joyce gave Carlo Linati a schema of the novel that listed the symbol for "Wandering Rocks" as "sincronismi" (synchronizations), reproduced as an

appendix to Richard Ellmann, *Ulysses on the Liffey* (New York: Oxford University Press, 1972).

46. Gino Severini, "The Plastic Analogies of Dynamism – Futurist Manifesto 1913," in *Futurist Manifestos*, ed. Umbro Apollonio (New York: Viking, 1973), 121.

47. Pär Bergman, *"Modernolatria" et "Simultaneità": Recherches sur deux tendances dans l'avant-garde littéraire en Italie et en France à la veille de la première guerre mondiale* (Uppsala: Bonnier, 1962), x.

48. On simultaneity see Kern, *The Culture of Time and Space*, 67–81.

CHAPTER 4 TIME

1. This thematic division modifies the analysis of Gérard Genette, who divided time into order, duration, and frequency. *Narrative Discourse: An Essay in Method* (Ithaca: Cornell University Press, 1980). In *Narrative Discourse Revisited* (Ithaca: Cornell University Press, 1988), he replaced *duration* by *speed*, a confusing term because fast speed is redundant, and slow speed is oxymoronic. Pace is a more suitable focal theme for the distinction between slow and fast. Genette's frequency is mainly about Proust's use of iterative narratives. Frequency is a subtopic of repetition, itself a subtopic of order, as illustrated by the following order of narrative elements – abacada. That *order* includes *repetition* of the element *a*, which occurs at a *frequency* of every other element.

2. The goal of consensus at the heart of realism is the central argument of Elizabeth Deeds Ermarth, who interprets the realists' singular time frame as grounding the values and meanings in which characters reconcile conflicts and achieve closure. *Realism and Consensus in the English Novel: Time, Space and Narrative* (Princeton: Princeton University Press, 1983), 46.

3. Genette defines these terms and candidly apologizes for the "disgraces" of his terminology in *Narrative Discourse*, 40. *Analepsis*, from the Greek, meaning to take on something after the event, is a going back in a story any length of time, which can then proceed forward for a single moment up to many years. *Prolepsis* is literally to take on something in advance. Prolepses, like analepses, have different *reaches* (how far ahead or back they go) and *extents* (how long they last in terms of story time or text pages). I use these technical terms because the common substitutes are unacceptable. *Flashback* has cinematic and psychological associations that misleadingly suggest the speed of the move to the past and imply that the extent of the move will be brief. *Retrospection* suggests what characters do in memory, not a shift in the time frame of the narrative. Similar problems arise with *flashforward* and *anticipation*. Like retrospection, anticipation evokes human mental life and so is not suited to narrative reordering.

4. One possible technological explanation for the primacy of the present among modernists is the increasing influence of daily newspapers as suggested by Peter Fritzsche, who reports that in 1856 just 11 percent of German newspaper articles covered the past twenty-four hours, whereas by 1906 95 percent of the articles did. *Reading Berlin 1900* (Cambridge: Harvard University Press, 1996), 181.

5. Gertrude Stein, *Melanctha* [1909], in *Selected Writings of Gertrude Stein*, ed. Carl Van Vechten (New York: Vintage, 1962), 402.

6. Gertrude Stein, *Narration* (Chicago: University of Chicago Press, 1935), 25.

7. Gertrude Stein, "Sacred Emily," in *Geography and Plays* (Boston: Four Seas, 1922), 187.

8. Thornton Wilder, "Introduction" to Gertrude Stein, *Four in America* (New Haven: Yale University Press, 1947), v–vi.

9. William Faulkner, "Interview with Jean Stein Vanden Heuvel," in *Lion in the Garden: Interviews with William Faulkner, 1926–1962*, ed. James B. Merriweather and Michael Millgate (Lincoln: University of Nebraska Press, 1968), 255.

10. Philip Weinstein, *Becoming Faulkner: The Art and Life of William Faulkner* (Oxford: Oxford University Press, 2010), 52.

11. Wyndham Lewis, "Long Live the Vortex," *Blast* 1 (June 20, 1914): 7, 18, 147.

12. Ezra Pound, interview with Zinaida Vengerova, "Angliiskie futuristy," *Strelets* 1 (1915): 93–94, quoted by Jo-Anne Isaak in "The Revolution of a Poetics," in *Modernism: Challenges and Perspectives*, ed. Monique Chefdor et al. (Urbana: University of Illinois Press, 1986), 163–64.

13. Friedrich Nietzsche, *Thus Spoke Zarathustra*, translated by Walter Kaufmann (New York: Vintage, 1978), 139.

14. Friedrich Nietzsche, *Ecce Homo* (written in 1888, first published in 1908), translated by Walter Kaufmann (New York: Vintage, 1967), 258.

15. Nietzsche, *Zarathustra*, 228.

16. Filippo Marinetti, "Manifesto of Futurism," in *Marinetti: Selected Writings*, ed. R. W. Flint (New York: Noonday, 1971), 41.

17. Filippo Marinetti, "Destruction of Syntax – Imagination without Strings – Words-in-Freedom," in *Futurist Manifestos*, ed. Umbro Apollonio (New York: Viking, 1973), 98–99.

18. Genette, *Narrative Discourse Revisited*, 34.

19. Genette, *Narrative Discourse*, 95.

20. "He [Legrandin] brushed past us, and did not interrupt what he was saying to her, but gave us, out of the corner of his blue eye, a little sign which began and ended, so to speak, inside his eyelids and which, as it did not involve the least movement of his facial muscles, managed to pass quite unperceived by the lady; but, striving to compensate by the intensity of his feelings for the somewhat restricted field in which they had to find expression, he made that blue chink which was set apart for us sparkle with all the zest of an affability that went far beyond mere playfulness, almost touched the border-line of roguery; he subtilised the refinements of good-fellowship into a wink of connivance, a hint, a hidden meaning, a sacred understanding, all the mysteries of complicity, and finally elevated his assurances of friendship to the level of protestations of affection, even of a declaration of love, lighting up for us alone, with a secret and languid flame invisible to the chatelaine, an enamoured pupil in a countenance of ice." Marcel Proust, *Remembrance of Things Past* (1, 136–37).

21. Dermot Moran, *Introduction to Phenomenology* (London: Routledge, 2000), 124–63.

22. Eugen Bleuler, "Die Psychoanalyse Freuds," in *Jahrbuch für psychoanalytische und psychopathologische Forschungen* (Leipzig: Deuticke, 1910).

23. Anne Sealey, "The Strange Case of the Freudian Case History: The Role of Long Case Histories in the Development of Psychoanalysis," *History of the Human Sciences*, forthcoming.

24. Virginia Woolf, *The Waves* [1931] (New York: Harcourt, 2006), 92.

25. The clashing of public and private time nearly drove Kafka insane, as he explained in 1922. "It's impossible to sleep, impossible to wake, impossible to bear life or, more precisely, the successiveness of life. The clocks don't agree. The inner one rushes along in a devilish or demonic – in any case, inhuman – way while the outer one goes, falteringly, at its accustomed pace." *Tagebücher, 1910–1923* (Frankfurt: S. Fischer, 1951), 552.

26. William R. Everdell, *The First Moderns: Profiles in the Origins of Twentieth-Century Thought* (Chicago: University of Chicago Press, 1997), 351.

27. Paul Fussell, *The Great War and Modern Memory* (Oxford: Oxford University Press, 1975), 21.

28. Samuel Hynes, *A War Imagined: The First World War and English Culture* (New York: Atheneum, 1990), 431–33.

29. "Autobiography is the highest and most instructive form in which understanding of life confronts us." The language in which we think and the concepts we employ all originate in chronologically ordered time. Wilhelm Dilthey, *Pattern and Meaning in History* (New York: Harper, 1961), 85.

30. Sigmund Freud, "Beyond the Pleasure Principle," in *Standard Edition* (London: Hogarth, 1950), vol. XVIII, 28.

31. Peter Brooks, *Reading for the Plot: Design and Intention in Narrative* (New York: Knopf, 1984), 284–85.

32. Quoted in Merriweather and Millgate, eds., *Lion in the Garden*, 147–48. Aldous Huxley's *Eyeless in Gaza* [1936] (New York: Carroll & Graf, 1995), organized in six achronological chapters beginning in 1933, 1934, 1902, 1926, 1912, and 1931, is a homage to Faulkner. The narrator explains the method. "Somewhere in the mind a lunatic shuffled a pack of snapshots and dealt them out at random, shuffled once more and dealt them out in a different order, again and again, indefinitely. There was no chronology. The idiot remembered no distinction between before and after" (16–17).

33. Quoted in *Faulkner in the University: Class Conferences at the University of Virginia 1957–1958*, ed. Frederick L. Gwynn and Joseph L. Blotner (New York: Vintage, 1959), 94.

34. On the decline of those legacies see Daniel J. Singal, *William Faulkner: The Making of a Modernist* (Chapel Hill: University of North Carolina Press, 1977), 117–19.

35. Ford Madox Ford, *Joseph Conrad: A Personal Remembrance* [1924] (New York: Ecco, 1989), 136–37.

36. Ford Madox Ford, *The Good Soldier* [1915], ed. Martin Stannard (New York: Norton, 1995), 120.

37. Michael Valdez Moses, "Disorientalism: Conrad and the Imperial Origins of Modern Aesthetics," in *Modernism and Colonialism: British and Irish Literature,*

1899–1939, ed. Richard Begam and Michael Valdez Moses (Durham: Duke University Press, 2007), 43–69.

38. Ibid., 62.

39. Joseph Conrad, *Nostromo* [1904] (Oxford: Oxford University Press, 1984), 11.

40. Genette, *Narrative Discourse*, 117.

41. For these schemas see Richard Ellmann, *Ulysses on the Liffey* (New York: Oxford University Press, 1972), 186–87.

42. Shlomith Rimmon-Kenan, *Narrative Fiction* (London: Routledge, 1983), 58.

43. Gwynn and Blotner, eds., *Faulkner in the University*, 32.

44. Quoted in Jayne L. Walker, *The Making of a Modernist: Gertrude Stein* (Amherst: University of Massachusetts Press, 1984), 43.

45. Gertrude Stein, "How Writing is Written" [1934–35], in *The Gender of Modernism*, ed. Bonnie Kime Scott (Bloomington: Indiana University Press, 1990), 494.

46. Sigmund Freud, "The Aetiology of Hysteria," in *Standard Edition* (London: Hogarth, 1950), vol. III, 212.

47. Sigmund Freud, "From the History of an Infantile Neurosis," in *Standard Edition* (London: Hogarth, 1955), vol. XVII.

48. On the complex relation between the adult narrator Pip and the child Pip see Mary Galbraith, "Pip as 'Infant tongue' and as Adult Narrator in Chapter One of *Great Expectations*," in *Infant Tongues: The Voice of the Child in Literature*, ed. Mark A. Heberle et al. (Detroit: Wayne State University Press, 1994), 123–41.

49. "In response to a question how the novel began he replied. 'It began with a mental picture ... of the muddy seat of a little girl's drawers in a pear tree where she could see through a window where her grandmother's funeral was taking place and report what happened to her brothers on the ground below.'" Merriweather and Millgate, eds., *Lion in the Garden*, 244–45. In a prospective introduction to the novel for 1933, Faulkner wrote, "In *The Sound and the Fury* I had already put perhaps the only thing in literature which would ever move me very much: Caddy climbing the pear tree to look in the window at her grandmother's funeral while Quentin and Jason and Benjy and the negroes looked up at the muddy seat of her drawers." *The Sound and the Fury*, 2nd edition, ed. David Minter (New York: Norton, 1994), 227.

50. Morris Beja, *Epiphany in the Modern Novel* (Seattle: University of Washington Press, 1971), 18.

51. For these omissions see Roger Shattuck, *Marcel Proust* (New York: Viking, 1974), 120–21.

CHAPTER 5 FRAMEWORK

1. "Although self-problematizing beginnings may not be exclusive to modernist writing, the modernist period arguably intensified the ambiguity that the ragged edge implies." Melba Cuddy-Keane, "Virginia Woolf and Beginning's Ragged Edge," in *Narrative Beginnings: Theories and Practices*, ed. Brian Richardson (Lincoln: University of Nebraska Press, 2008), 98.

2. Hugh Kenner, "The Portrait in Perspective," in *James Joyce: Two Decades of Criticism*, ed. Seon Givens (New York: Vanguard, 1948), 137, 142.

3. Wayne C. Booth, *A Rhetoric of Irony* (Chicago: University of Chicago Press, 1974), 1–31.

4. Samuel Hynes argues that this novel "raises uncertainty about the nature of truth and reality to the level of a structural principle." "The Epistemology of *The Good Soldier*," in Ford Madox Ford, *The Good Soldier*, ed. Martin Stannard (New York: Norton, 1995), 310–17. In that volume Frank Kermode analyzes deception in the opening paragraphs of the novel (330–37), and Ian Watt analyzes abstraction and indirection in love in the first paragraph of James's *The Ambassadors* (465–84).

5. Ford Madox Ford, *The Good Soldier* [1915] (New York: Norton, 1995), 104, 156.

6. "The demise of genealogical thinking is roughly coterminous with the swerve away from linear narrative in twentieth-century novels." Patricia Drechsel Tobin, *Time and the Novel: The Genealogical Imperative* (Princeton: Princeton University Press, 1978), 5–8, 20.

7. André Gide, *Lafcadio's Adventures* [1914], translated by Dorothy Bussy (New York: Vintage, 1953), 14.

8. In "Das Vater-Sohn Motiv in der Dichtung 1880–1930," from *Stoff- und Motivgeschichte der deutschen Literatur* XI (1931), the German critic Kurt K. T. Wais surveys many of these works and concludes that the number of works dealing with father-son conflict between 1880 and 1930 is nearly equal to the number appearing in all of German literature before 1880. See also Stephen Kern, "Explosive Intimacy: Psychodynamics of the Victorian Family," *History of Childhood Quarterly* 1, 3 (Summer 1974): 437–62.

9. Alan Palmer, "Intermental Thought in the Novel: The Middlemarch Mind," *Style* 39, 4 (Winter 2005): 427–39.

10. Kermode locates such changes in the thirteenth century with "a new wave of Greek influence on Christian philosophy," but he subsequently speaks of the twentieth century as a unique age of crisis and is ready "to accept all manner of evidence that ours is a genuine end, a genuine beginning." *The Sense of an Ending: Studies in the Theory of Fiction* (Oxford: Oxford University Press, 1966), 67–68, 94. He draws on P. A. Sorokin, *The Crisis of our Age*, published in 1941, that attempts to quantify the religious crisis of the modernist period by counting the declining number of religious subjects in the arts.

11. Jacques Derrida interprets that grounding function as the goal of all metaphysical speculation in the Western world that seeks some "fundamental immobility and reassuring certitude" to life and thought. The ultimate originary moment is one of several ultimate grounding concepts such as essence and existence that are presented as the "fixed origin" that organizes the structure of everything else and makes it possible to master anxiety. "Structure, Sign and Play in the Discourse of the Human Sciences," in *Writing and Difference* (Chicago: University of Chicago Press, 1978), 278–81.

12. J. Hillis Miller, *The Disappearance of God: Five Nineteenth-Century Writers* (Cambridge: Harvard University Press, 1963), 6ff.

13. A number of novels about religious crises appeared later in the century: Jens Peter Jacobsen, *Niels Lyhne*, 1880; Mrs. Humphrey Ward, *Robert Elsmere*, 1888 and *Helbeck of Bannisdale*, 1898; Harold Frederic, *The Damnation of Theron Ware*, 1896; and Samuel Butler, *The Way of All Flesh*, 1903 (completed in 1884). They remain respectful of Christianity, however difficult Churches make the lives of its leaders.

14. Don Gifford with Robert Seidman, *Ulysses Annotated: Notes for James Joyce's "Ulysses"* (Berkeley: University of California Press, 1988), 13.

15. On these parodies of the Mass see Ruth M. Walsh, "In the Name of the Father and of the Son . . . Joyce's Use of the Mass in *Ulysses*," *James Joyce Quarterly* 6, 4 (Summer 1969): 321–47; Hugh Kenner, *Ulysses* (Baltimore: Johns Hopkins University Press, 1987), 34–35; Frederick K. Lang, *Ulysses and the Irish God* (Lewisburg: Bucknell University Press, 1993), 105–32.

16. The sense of an ending, Kermode argues, is a basic human need to order events as fundamentally as the paired concepts of *tick* and *tock*. *The Sense of an Ending*, 44–45. On endings in the novel see Alan Friedman, *The Turn of the Novel: The Transition to Modern Fiction* (Oxford: Oxford University Press, 1966); Marianna Torgovnick, *Closure in the Novel* (Princeton: Princeton University Press, 1981); D. A. Miller, *Narrative and its Discontents* (Princeton: Princeton University Press, 1981); William R. Thickstun, *Visionary Closure in the Modern Novel* (New York: St. Martin's Press, 1988).

17. Henry James, "The Art of Fiction" [1884], in *The Future of the Novel* (New York: Vintage, 1956), 8.

18. Joseph Conrad, "Henry James: An Appreciation" [1905], in *Notes on Life and Letters* (New York: Doubleday, 1923), 19.

19. Virginia Woolf, "The Russian Point of View," in *The Common Reader: First Series* (New York: Harcourt Brace, 1925), 180.

20. E. M. Forster, *Aspects of the Novel* (New York: Harcourt Brace, 1927), 95, 96.

21. Ford Madox Ford, "The Tradition of the Novel," in *Critical Writings of Ford Madox Ford*, ed. Frank MacShane (Lincoln: University of Nebraska Press, 1964), 17.

22. This thematic analysis is derived from Torgovnick, *Closure in the Novel*.

23. On essayism in Musil and others see Thomas Harrison, *Essayism: Conrad, Musil, and Pirandello* (Baltimore: Johns Hopkins University Press, 1992). For its role in "The Generation of 1905" see David S. Luft, *Robert Musil and the Crisis of European Culture 1880–1942* (Berkeley: University of California Press, 1980), 13–21.

24. Forster, *Aspects of the Novel*, 95.

25. For a discussion of the more open ending of the Gwendolen Harleth part of *Daniel Deronda*, the struggles of Eliot and Thackeray with poetic justice, and the decline of its role in Victorian endings see Margaret Mason Kenda, "Poetic Justice and the Ending Trick in the Victorian Novel," *Genre* 8 (1975): 336–51.

26. Michael Wheeler, *Death and the Future Life in Victorian Literature and Theology* (Cambridge: Cambridge University Press, 1990), 25.

27. Rainer Maria Rilke, *The Notebooks of Malte Laurids Brigge* [1910], translated by Stephen Mitchell (New York: Vintage, 1985), 9.

28. Ian P. Watt, "The Ending of *Lord Jim*," *Conradiana* 11 (1979): 4–21.

29. Djuna Barnes, *Nightwood* [1936] (New York: New Directions, 1961), 37. Barnes had considered titling her novel *Night Beast* before settling on *Nightwood*. For that fact and the ubiquity of the bestial in Barnes's writings and drawings see Bonnie Kime Scott, "Barnes Being 'Beast Familiar': Representation on the Margins of Modernism," *Review of Contemporary Fiction* 13, 3 (Fall 1993): 41–52.

30. James B. Scott, *Djuna Barnes* (Boston: Twayne, 1976), 103; Phillip Herring, "Djuna Barnes and Thelma Wood: The Vengeance of *Nightwood*," *Journal of Modern Literature* 18, 1 (Winter 1992): 16; Donna Gerstenberger, "The Radical Narrative of Djuna Barnes's *Nightwood*," in *Breaking the Sequence: Women's Experimental Fiction*, ed. Eileen G. Friedman and Miriam Fuchs (Princeton: Princeton University Press, 1989), 138.

31. For an elaboration of this claim and the larger argument about modernist authenticity in love see Stephen Kern, *The Culture of Love: Victorians to Moderns* (Cambridge: Harvard University Press, 1992), 350–51 and *passim*.

32. Henry James, *The Golden Bowl* [1904] (New York: Penguin, 1966), 421.

33. On this "scenic close-up ending" see "Gesture and the Ending of *The Golden Bowl*," in Torgovnick, *Closure in the Novel*, 143–56. In 1908 James formulated a strategy that does justice to the open-ended nature of life and the need to conclude a novel: "relations stop nowhere, and the exquisite problem of the artist is eternally but to draw, by a geometry of his own, the circle within which they shall happily *appear* to do so." Henry James, "Preface to *Roderick Hudson*" [1908], in *The Art of the Novel*, ed. Richard P. Blackmur (New York: Scribner's, 1934), 5.

34. In *James Joyce and the Burden of Disease* (Lexington: University of Kentucky Press, 1995), 58–61, Kathleen Ferris presents evidence that Bloom had syphilis. His possible infection from a prostitute might explain the death of Rudy, as a moment in *Ulysses* suggests: "Bridie Kelly! He [Bloom] will never forget the name, even remember the night: first night, the bridenight. They are entwined in nethermost darkness … She is the bride of darkness, a daughter of night. She dare not bear the sunnygolden babe of day. No, Leopold … That youthful illusion of thy strength was taken from thee – and in vain. No son of thy loins is by thee" (338). Ferris cites evidence that Bloom had symptoms of a form of neuro-syphilis, *tabes dorsalis*, that includes constipation, incontinence, and locomotor ataxia, known popularly as a syphilitic gait. See also David Kadlec, "Syphilis and James Joyce's *Ulysses*," in *Mosaic Modernism: Anarchism, Pragmatism, Culture* (Baltimore: Johns Hopkins University Press, 2000), 90–121, which interprets concern about syphilis in a broad cultural context of anarchism and feminism. Adding to Molly's fear may be the fact that there was no reliable test for syphilis in 1904; the first was developed by August von Wasserman only in 1906.

CHAPTER 6 TEXT

1. Gustave Flaubert, *Madame Bovary* [1857], translated by Francis Steegmuller (New York: Vintage, 1957), 216.

2. On Joyce's inventiveness with letters see Randy Malamud, "Letters: I AM A,'" in *The Language of Modernism* (Ann Arbor: University of Michigan Press, 1989), 159–64.

3. Gertrude Stein, *What Are Masterpieces* [1940] (New York: Pitman, 1970), 100.

4. John Dos Passos, *U. S. A.* [1930, 1932, 1936] (New York: Library of America, 1996), 756.

5. Eugene Jolas, "The Revolution of Language and James Joyce," in *Our Exagmination Round His Factification for Incamination of Work in Progress*, ed. Samuel Beckett et al. [1929] (New York: New Directions, 1962), 79, 83.

6. Ernest Hemingway, *A Farewell to Arms* (New York: Scribner's, 1929), 184.

7. Virginia Woolf, *A Room of One's Own* [1929] (New York: Harcourt, 1981), 12.

8. Faulkner's 1,287-word sentence in *Absalom, Absalom!* (116) is reputed to be the longest actual sentence in a modernist novel.

9. In *Tender Buttons* she wrote, "A sentence of a vagueness that is violence is authority and a mission and stumbling and also certainly also a prison." *Selected Writings of Gertrude Stein*, ed. Carl Van Vechten (New York: Vintage, 1962), 481.

10. See *The Linguistic Turn*, ed. Richard Rorty (Chicago: University of Chicago Press, 1967), who credits the first use of the term to Gustav Bergmann, *Logic and Reality* (Madison: University of Wisconsin Press, 1964), 177. The enormous significance of the linguistic turn was noted by George Steiner, who concluded that until the late nineteenth century, the most biting skeptics about knowledge such as David Hume remained confident in the ability of language to put their case with intelligible propositions. "This break of the covenant between word and world . . . constitutes one of the very few genuine revolutions of spirit in Western history and . . . defines modernity itself." George Steiner, *Real Presences* (Chicago: University of Chicago Press, 1989), 93.

11. Ludwig Wittgenstein, *Tractatus Logico-Philosophicus* [1922] (New York: Humanities Press, 1974), 19.

12. This historical shift was noted by John Fletcher and Malcolm Bradbury, who concluded that in the modernist novel there is "a progressive fading of that realism which has long been associated with the novel; language ceases to be what we see through, and becomes what we see." "The Introverted Novel," in *Modernism: A Guide to European Literature 1890–1930*, ed. Malcolm Bradbury and James McFarlane (Harmondsworth: Penguin, 1976), 401.

13. Hugo von Hofmannsthal, "The Letter of Lord Chandos," in *Selected Prose* (Princeton: Princeton University Press, 1952), 129–41.

14. For this interpretation see Jean-Joseph Goux, *The Coiners of Language* (Norman: University of Oklahoma Press, 1994).

15. Gertrude Stein, *Melanctha* [1909], in *Selected Writings of Gertrude Stein*, ed. Carl Van Vechten (New York: Vintage, 1962), 373.

16. On Moosbrugger's problems with language see Philip Payne, "Words that Bend Minds," in *Robert Musil's "The Man Without Qualities": A Critical Study* (Cambridge: Cambridge University Press, 1988), 123–29.

17. The French is also a single sentence, and the five participles are *évoquant, transportant, laissant, formant, jetant.* Marcel Proust, *À la recherche du temps perdu* (Paris: Gallimard, 1987), vol. 1, 387.

18. For advertising in *The Ambassadors* see Jennifer Wicke, *Advertising Fictions: Literature, Advertisement & Social Reading* (New York: Columbia University Press, 1988), 102–12.

19. Henry James, *The Ambassadors* [1903] (Harmondsworth: Penguin, 2003), 96–97.

20. Joyce "presents the overall dynamic of advertising in order to demonstrate the extent to which social relations, nationalist aspirations, power structures, class distinctions, gender constructions, and subjectivity itself, all intersect with and even depend upon the simulated universe of advertisements." Garry Leonard, "Joyce and Advertising: Advertising and Commodity Culture in Joyce's Fiction," *James Joyce Quarterly* 30.4/31.1 (1993): 574.

21. For Joyce's personal fascination with ads see Alfred Berger, "James Joyce, Adman," *James Joyce Quarterly* 3 (1965): 25–33.

22. For a reproduction and discussion of the likely basis for this image, a halftone photo in the April 2, 1909 issue of *Die Welt*, see M. David Bell, "The Search for Agendath Netaim: Some Progress, but No Solution," *James Joyce Quarterly* 12 (1974): 251–58.

23. Edwin W. Williams, "Agendath Netaim: Promised Land or Waste Land," *Modern Fiction Studies* 32, 2 (Summer 1986): 228–35.

24. "The city of things gave way to the city of signs, and the emphasis of the actual economies of major cities largely shifted from the production of goods to the production of signs, including advertising." Paula Geyh, *Cities, Citizens, and Technologies* (New York: Routledge, 2009), 17.

25. William Brevda, "How Do I Get to Broadway? Reading Dos Passos's 'Manhattan Transfer' Sign," *Texas Studies in Literature and Language* 38, 1 (Spring 1996): 32–51.

26. John Dos Passos, *Manhattan Transfer* [1925] (Boston: Houghton Mifflin, 1953), 195.

27. On these developments see my Introduction, pp. 1–20.

28. Dorothy Richardson, foreword to 1938 edition of *Pilgrimage* (1, 9).

29. Letter to Henry Savage, January 6, 1950, quoted in George H. Thomson, "Dorothy Richardson's Foreword to *Pilgrimage*," *Twentieth Century Literature* 42, 3 (Fall 1966): 344.

30. Dorothy Richardson, "Novels" [1948], in *The Gender of Modernism*, ed. Bonnie Kime Scott (Bloomington: Indiana University Press, 1990), 433.

31. Virginia Woolf, "Romance and the Heart," in *The Essays of Virginia Woolf*, vol. III: *1919–1924*, ed. Andrew McNeillie (New York: Harcourt Brace, 1988), 365–68, at 367.

32. As Elaine Showalter observes: "It is one thing to show that fiction before 1910 differed from fiction after 1910, and to label the differences metaphorically 'male' and 'female' ... It is another thing altogether to talk about female style when you mean female content. And it is the hardest of all to prove that there

are inherent sexual qualities to prose apart from its content, which was the crucial point Richardson wished to make." *A Literature of Their Own: British Women Novelists from Brontë to Lessing* (Princeton: Princeton University Press, 1977), 258.

33. Virginia Woolf, *A Room of One's Own* [1929] (New York: Harcourt, 1981), 76. In "Women and Fiction," also from 1929, Woolf added that the problem facing women writers is that "the very form of the sentence does not fit her. It is a sentence made by men; it is too loose, too heavy, too pompous for a woman's use." *Granite & Rainbow* (New York: Harcourt Brace, 1958), 81.

34. Yule F. Heibel argues that Kandinsky's paintings "ought to be seen in light of the renewed validity of anarchism as a form of political and cultural revivification in the immediate prewar period." "'They Danced on Volcanoes': Kandinsky's Breakthrough to Abstraction, the German Avant-Garde and the Eve of the First World War," *Art History* 12, 3 (September 1989): 355.

35. Rose-Carol Washton Long, "Occultism, Anarchism, and Abstraction: Kandinsky's Art of the Future," *Art Journal* 46, 1 (Spring 1987): 38–45.

36. Gustave Courbet, letter of December 25, 1861, in *Nineteenth-Century Theories of Art*, ed. Joshua C. Taylor (Berkeley: University of California Press, 1987), 347.

37. Wassily Kandinsky, "On the Spiritual in Art," in *Kandinsky: Complete Writings on Art*, ed. Kenneth C. Lindsay and Peter Vergo (New York: Da Capo Press, 1994).

38. Rose-Carol Washton Long, *Kandinsky: The Development of an Abstract Style* (Oxford: Oxford University Press, 1980), 26–41.

39. On the link between the Morocco Crisis and Kandinsky see Heibel, "'They Danced on Volcanoes,'" 342–61.

40. Wassily Kandinsky, *Composition IV* (1911), Tate Gallery, London.

41. Wassily Kandinsky, "Reminiscences/Three Pictures," in *Kandinsky: Complete Writings on Art*, ed. Kenneth C. Lindsay and Peter Vergo (New York: Da Capo Press, 1994), 384–85.

42. Giacomo Balla, *Speeding Car + Light + Noise* (1913), Zurich Kunsthaus, and *Abstract Speed* (1913), private collection, reproduced in *Futurism & Futurisms*, ed. Pontus Hultén (New York: Abbeville Press, 1986), 79, 77.

43. Kasimir Malevich, "From Cubism and Futurism to Suprematism: The New Realism in Painting," in *K. S. Malevich: Essays on Art, 1915–1933*, ed. Troels Andersen (Copenhagen: Borgen, 1968), vol. 1, 19–41.

44. Kasimir Malevich to Alexander Benois, May, 1916, quoted in Jo-Anne Isaak, "The Revolution of a Poetics," in *Modernism: Challenges and Perspectives*, ed. Monique Chefdor et al. (Urbana: University of Illinois Press, 1986), 168.

45. For a picture of that installation see *Primitivism, Cubism, Abstraction: The Early Twentieth Century*, ed. Charles Harrison et al. (New Haven: Yale University Press, 1993), 236.

46. Kasimir Malevich, "Suprematism" [1927], in *Modern Artists on Art: Ten Unabridged Essays*, by Robert L. Herbert (Englewood Cliffs, N.J.: Prentice Hall, 1964), 95.

47. Wyndham Lewis, "Enemy of the Stars," *Blast I* [1914] (Santa Rosa: Black Sparrow Press, 1962), 64.

48. "War . . . presented me with a subject-matter so consonant with the austerity of that 'abstract' vision I had developed, that it was an easy transition . . . When Mars with his mailed finger showed me a shell-crater and a skeleton with a couple of shivered tree-stumps behind it, I was still in my 'abstract' element." Wyndham Lewis, *Rude Assignment: A Narrative of My Career Up-to-Date* (London: Hutchinson, 1950), 128.

49. Ibid., 129.

50. Gertrude Stein, "A Transatlantic Interview 1946," in *The Gender of Modernism*, ed. Bonnie Kime Scott (Bloomington: Indiana University Press, 1990), 504.

51. While Stein despaired of producing a fully abstract text, one without sense, critics have seen her work as moving in that direction. Richard Kostelanetz views many of Stein's post-World War I writings as "nonrepresentational, lacking even a suggestion of anything outside themselves." She produced "abstract writing [that] is based exclusively upon materials indigenous to the medium of language: words that are unified by elements other than syntax and semantics." He also relates her "acoherent" style to the contemporary "atonal music" of the time. *The Yale Gertrude Stein* (New Haven: Yale University Press, 1980), xxii–xxiv.

52. Ball's poetry and the selection from his diary are in *Dada Art and Anti-Art*, ed. Hans Richter (New York: M. H. Abrams, 1970), 41–43.

53. *The Diary of Virginia Woolf*, vol. III: *1925–1930*, ed. Anne Olivier Bell assisted by Andrew McNeillie (New York: Harcourt Brace, 1980), 76.

54. On this passage and abstraction in Woolf see Christine Froula, "Picturing the World: The Quest for the Thing Itself in *To the Lighthouse*," in *Virginia Woolf and the Bloomsbury Avant-Garde: War, Civilization, Modernity* (New York: Columbia University Press, 2005), 129–73.

55. In a similar spirit, Willa Cather urged that novelists "break away from mere verisimilitude" and follow modern abstract painting "to present their scene by suggestion rather than by enumeration." To that end she called for a new kind of "defurnished novel" stripped of the realistic excess that clutters the realist novels of Balzac. "How wonderful it would be," she proposed, "if we could throw all the furniture out of the window; and along with it, all the meaningless reiterations concerning physical sensations, all the tiresome old patterns, and leave the room as bare as the stage of a Greek theatre . . . for the play of emotions." Willa Cather, "The Novel Démeublé," *New Republic* 30 (April 12, 1922): 5–6.

56. Hermann Broch, *The Sleepwalkers* [1931–32], translated by Willa and Edwin Muir (San Francisco: North Point Press, 1985), 398.

57. Quoted in Anna Balakian, *André Breton: Magus of Surrealism* (New York: Oxford University Press, 1971), 20, 27.

58. André Breton, *Manifestoes of Surrealism* (Ann Arbor: University of Michigan Press, 1972), 26.

59. Ibid., 14.

60. Ibid., 6, 7.

61. Breton's other surrealist novels are *Communicating Vessels* (1932) and *Mad Love* (1937).

62. André Breton, *Nadja* [1928], translated by Richard Howard (New York: Grove, 1960), 79.
63. The sexualized face is in Magritte's *The Rape* (1934). The literary reference is from Breton's report of the first surreal phrase that occurred to him as he was falling asleep – "something like: 'there is a man cut in two by the window.'" Breton, *Manifestoes of Surrealism*, 21.
64. Françoise Gilot and Carlton Lake, *Life with Picasso* (New York: McGraw-Hill, 1964), 70.
65. Gregory L. Ulmer, "The Object of Post-Criticism," in *The Anti-Aesthetic: Essays on Postmodern Culture*, ed. Hal Foster (Port Townsend, Wash.: Bay Press, 1983), 84, a judgment underscored by Marjorie Perloff, *The Futurist Moment: Avant-Garde, Avant-Guerre, and the Language of Rupture* (Chicago: University of Chicago Press, 1986), 46.
66. Jürgen Stenzel, "Mit Kleister und Schere: Zur Handschrift von *Berlin Alexanderplatz*," *Text + Kritik* 13/14 (1972): 39–44. In "Der Bau des epischen Werkes" (1929) Döblin wrote, "In the course of writing one historical book or another, it has happened that I could hardly restrain myself from simply copying entire documents." Alfred Döblin, *Aufsätze zur Literatur* (Freiburg: Olten, 1963), 114.
67. David B. Dollenmayer, *The Berlin Novels of Alfred Döblin* (Berkeley: University of California Press, 1988), 74. For Döblin's adding sections 1 and 2 after reading Joyce see Breon Mitchell, *James Joyce and the German Novel 1922–1933* (Athens: Ohio University Press, 1976), 138–39.

CHAPTER 7 NARRATOR

1. D. A. Miller, *The Novel and the Police* (Berkeley: University of California Press, 1988), 52–54.
2. Henry James, "Preface to *The American*," in *The Art of the Novel: Critical Prefaces by Henry James*, ed. Richard P. Blackmur (New York: Scribner's, 1934), 37.
3. These critics include Percy Lubbock in 1921, Cleanth Brooks and Robert Penn Warren in 1943, F. K. Stanzel and Norman Friedman in 1955, and Wayne Booth in 1961. Gérard Genette, *Narrative Discourse: An Essay in Method* [1972] (Ithaca: Cornell University Press, 1980), 187–88.
4. Wayne Booth, "Distance and Point of View," *Essays in Criticism* 11 (1961): 60–79.
5. Genette, *Narrative Discourse*, 186.
6. Ibid., 189.
7. Henry James, *What Maisie Knew* [1897] (Harmondsworth: Penguin, 1985), 24.
8. Rudolph Binion interprets this novel as one of dozens of works by Gide, Ibsen, Strindberg, Synge, Zola, Hauptmann, Tolstoy, Butler, and others in the years 1879–1914, which assailed the institutions of family and marriage out of a shared sense of guilt over the widespread adoption of birth control within marriage. *Past Impersonal: Group Process in Human History* (Dekalb: Northern Illinois University Press, 2005), 29. Thus, Maisie's father declares, "There *are* no family women – hanged if there are! None of them want any children – hanged if they do!" (73).

9. Henry James, *The Ambassadors* [1903] (Harmondsworth: Penguin, 2003), 34.

10. Henry James, *The Golden Bowl* [1904] (New York: Penguin, 1966), 454.

11. For the proliferation of spaces in modernist culture see Stephen Kern, *The Culture of Time and Space 1880–1918* (Cambridge: Harvard University Press, 1983), 131–52.

12. Friedrich Nietzsche, *On the Genealogy of Morals* (New York: Vintage, 1967), 119.

13. Gide first used *en abyme* to refer to such a literary function in 1893. On *mis en abyme* see Lucien Dällenbach, *The Mirror in the Text* (Chicago: University of Chicago Press, 1989), 8, 30–35.

14. André Gide, "Journal of *The Counterfeiters*," in *C*, 425.

15. Virginia Woolf, "Modern Fiction," in *The Common Reader* (New York: Harcourt Brace, 1925), 155.

16. E. M. Forster, *A Passage to India* [1924] (New York: Harcourt, 1984), 165–66.

17. Hermann Broch, *The Sleepwalkers* [1931–32], translated by Willa and Edwin Muir (San Francisco: North Point Press, 1985), 575.

18. On Broch's interpretation of relativity theory and application in the novel see Ernestine Schlant, "Hermann Broch and Modern Physics," *Germanic Review* 78, 53 (Spring 1978): 69–75.

19. Wylie Sypher, "The Cubist Novel," in *Rococo to Cubism in Art and Literature* (New York: Vintage, 1960), 295–311.

20. A notable exception is Mark Twain's poorly educated, albeit shrewd, narrator of *The Adventures of Huckleberry Finn* (1884) who begins, "You don't know about me, without you have read a book by the name of 'The Adventures of Tom Sawyer,' but that ain't no matter."

21. In *Light in August* Faulkner layers multiple voices increasingly removed from conscious thought with punctuation and typography. Double quotation marks set off direct speech, single quotation marks indicate a character's thought, and at the deepest layer italics indicate thoughts of which a character is almost, or even entirely, unaware.

22. Hermann Broch, *Gesammelte Werke* (Zürich: Rhein-Verlag, 1957), vol. VIII, 33. On Broch's indebtedness to Joyce see *James Joyce und die Gegenwart*, published in 1936, based on a lecture in 1932. Breon Mitchell, *James Joyce and the German Novel 1922–1933* (Athens: Ohio University Press, 1976), 161.

23. These parodies are identified in Don Gifford with Robert J. Seidman, *Ulysses Annotated: Notes for James Joyce's "Ulysses"* (Berkeley: University of California Press, 1988), 314–81.

24. Letter of March 20, 1920 in *Selected Letters of James Joyce*, ed. Richard Ellmann (New York: Viking, 1975), 251–52. A number of these anthologies are cited in Andrew Gibson, *Joyce's Revenge: History, Politics, and Aesthetics in "Ulysses"* (Oxford: Oxford University Press, 2002), 172–73.

25. M. M. Bakhtin, "Discourse in the Novel," in *The Dialogic Imagination: Four Essays*, ed. Michael Holquist (Austin: University of Texas Press, 1981), 262–63.

26. Bakhtin, "Discourse in the Novel," 306–07.

27. Nancy Glazener contrasts Bakhtin's interpretation of heteroglossia in Dickens with a distinctly modernist heteroglossia in Gertrude Stein's "The Gentle

Lena" that includes the roles of the unconscious and ideology that are not present in realist heteroglossia. See "Dialogic Subversion: Bakhtin, the Novel and Gertrude Stein," in *Bakhtin and Cultural Theory*, ed. Ken Kirschkop and David Shepherd (Manchester: Manchester University Press, 1989), 165–72.

28. For a definition of "absolute heteroglossia" see Tony Crowley, "Bakhtin and the History of the Language," in *Bakhtin and Cultural Theory*, ed. Kirschkop and Shepherd, 197.

29. The name comes from *A Portrait of the Artist as a Young Man*, where the idiom of a character pervades the narrator's idiom. In Joyce's line "Every morning, therefore, Uncle Charles repaired to his outhouse," the word *repaired* is more typical of Uncle Charles than of the narrator. Hugh Kenner, *Joyce's Voices* (Berkeley: University of California Press, 1978), 17–21.

30. Letter of January 3, 1920 in *Selected Letters of James Joyce*, 246.

31. Bakhtin, "Discourse in the Novel," 316. Bakhtin locates these zones in Turgenev, but they abound more in Joyce.

32. Brian McHale refers to the impact of these voices as a "contamination." While in the "normal" episodes of *Ulysses* there is a "parallax between adjacent sentences of a character's interior discourse and authorial discourse, there is [in "Nausicaa"] an even finer-grained parallax *within* a character's discourse, a kind of micro-parallax." *Constructing Postmodernism* (London: Routledge, 1992), 51–52. On voices in this episode see Suzette Henke, "Gerty MacDowell: Joyce's Sentimental Heroine," in *Women in Joyce*, ed. Suzette Henke and Elaine Unkeless (Urbana: University of Illinois Press, 1982), 132–49.

33. On problems with *omniscience* in narrative see Jonathan Culler, "Omniscience," *Narrative* 12, 1 (January 2004): 22–34.

34. "The 'omniscient narrator,' so often compared to God, in fact embodies not God's perspective but that of society in general. He reports general social knowledge in tones approximating those of a tour guide, a gossip columnist, or a university professor, depending on the exact object of social knowledge at hand." Pericles Lewis, *Modernism, Nationalism, and the Novel* (Cambridge: Cambridge University Press, 2000), 17.

35. Andrei Bely, *Petersburg* [1913–16], translated by Robert A. Maguire and John E. Malmstad (Bloomington: Indiana University Press, 1978), 48.

36. *The Critical Writings of Ford Madox Ford*, ed. Frank MacShane (Lincoln: University of Nebraska Press, 1964), 68.

37. James Phelan identifies six types of unreliable narration: misreporting, mis-reading, misevaluating, underreporting, underreading, and underregarding. "The Implied Author, Unreliability, and Ethical Positioning," in *Living To Tell About It: A Rhetoric and Ethics of Character Narration* (Ithaca: Cornell University Press, 2005), 31–65.

38. Ford Madox Ford, *The Good Soldier* [1915] (New York: Norton, 1995), 12.

39. E. M. Forster acknowledged a similar intentional ignorance of crucial things about his own character, specifically what actually happened to Adela in the Marabar Caves. "In the cave it is either a man, or the supernatural, or an illusion. And even if I know! My writing mind therefore is a blur here – i.e. I will it to remain a blur,

and to be uncertain, as I am of many facts of daily life." Quoted in P. N. Furbank, *E. M. Forster: A Life*, 2 vols. (London: Secker and Warburg, 1977), vol. II, 125.

40. Brian McHale, *Postmodernist Fiction* (London: Routledge, 1987), 9, 10.

41. Philip Weinstein, *Unknowing: The Work of Modernist Fiction* (Ithaca: Cornell University Press, 2005), 257.

CONCLUSION

1. Virginia Woolf, "Mr. Bennett and Mrs. Brown," in *The Captain's Death Bed and Other Essays* (New York: Harcourt Brace, 1978), 117.

2. David Daiches, *The Novel and the Modern World* (Chicago: University of Chicago Press, 1970), 26–27.

3. David S. Thatcher, *Nietzsche in England 1890–1914: The Growth of a Reputation* (Toronto: University of Toronto Press, 1970); John Burt Foster, Jr., *Heirs to Dionysus: A Nietzschean Current in Literary Modernism* (Princeton: Princeton University Press, 1981); Steven E. Aschheim, *The Nietzsche Legacy in Germany 1890–1990* (Berkeley: University of California Press, 1992); Douglas Smith, *Transvaluations: Nietzsche in France 1872–1972* (Oxford: Oxford University Press, 1996).

4. Rustom Barucha, "Forster's Friends," *Raritan* 4 (Spring 1986): 105–22.

5. Christopher Lasch, *Haven in a Heartless World: The Family Besieged* (New York: Basic, 1977).

6. On this crisis see Pericles Lewis, *Modernism, Nationalism, and the Novel* (Cambridge: Cambridge University Press, 2000), 10, 52–96.

7. Ford Madox Ford, *Parade's End* [1924, 1925, 1926] (New York: Knopf, 1992), 330.

8. G. O. Trevelyan, *Cawnpore* (London, 1865), quoted in Patrick Brantlinger, *Rule of Darkness: British Literature and Imperialism, 1830–1914* (Ithaca: Cornell University Press, 1988), 203.

9. Dickens also published a story about the Mutiny, "The Perils of Certain English Prisoners," shortly after the event. In it Captain Carton seeks revenge against "villains" who destroyed British property, murdered men, "murdered their little children, and worse than murdered their wives and daughters." He believes that he holds his commission "by the allowance of God," and will use it "to exterminate these people from the face of the earth." Quoted in ibid., 199–200, 208.

10. Jean-Joseph Goux, *The Coiners of Language* (Norman: University of Oklahoma Press, 1994).

11. Seth Moglin argues that American literary modernism generally is a mourning of injuries inflicted by capitalism. *Mourning Modernity: Literary Modernism and the Injuries of American Capitalism* (Stanford: Stanford University Press, 2007).

12. Victor Hugo, *Les Misérables* [1862], translated by Norman Denny (Harmondsworth: Penguin, 1976), Pt. V, Bk. I, Ch. 20.

13. André Gide, *Dostoevsky* [1923] (New York: New Directions, 1961), 90.

14. On the pervasiveness of Lawrence's reworking of especially Genesis, Exodus, John, and Revelation, see T. R. Wright, *D. H. Lawrence and the Bible* (Cambridge: Cambridge University Press, 2000).

15. J. Mitchell Morse, *Sympathetic Alien: James Joyce and Catholicism* (New York: New York University Press, 1959); Frederick K. Lang, *"Ulysses" and the Irish God* (Lewisburg, Pa.: Bucknell University Press, 1993); Roy Gottfried, *Joyce's Misbelief* (Gainesville: University Press of Florida, 2007); Cóilín Owens, *James Joyce's Painful Case* (Gainesville: University Press of Florida, 2008).

16. Roger Martin du Gard, *Jean Barois* [1913], translated by Stuart Gilbert (New York: Bobbs-Merrill, 1969), 112, 344.

17. Rudolph Binion identifies "post-Christian survivals" of the afterlife, original sin, and absolute reality in *After Christianity: Christian Survivals in Post-Christian Culture* (Durango, Colo.: Logbridge-Rhodes, 1986). Vincent Pecora identifies a "secularized religion" in the modernist novel, "the overcoming but also the distortion and reemergence of received religious concepts and patterns of thought" in *Secularization and Cultural Criticism: Religion, Nation, & Modernity* (Chicago: University of Chicago Press, 2006), 23–24. Pericles Lewis analyzes how James, Proust, Kafka, Woolf, and Joyce sought "to understand religious experience anew" and craft characters who retain a "residuum of the sacred" after conventional belief is gone. *Religious Experience and the Modernist Novel* (Cambridge: Cambridge University Press, 2010), 19, 6.

18. The autobiographical characters are Pontellier (Chopin), Roquentin (Sartre), Morel (Lawrence), Henderson (Richardson), Dedalus (Joyce), Tarr (Lewis), Breton (Breton), Haller (Hesse), Müller (Broch), Jack (Dos Passos), Brigge (Rilke), Marcel (Proust), Baraglioul and Edouard (Gide), and Briscoe (Woolf).

19. Virginia Woolf, "A Sketch of the Past," in *Moments of Being: Unpublished Autobiographical Writings*, ed. Jeanne Schulkind (New York: Harcourt Brace, 1985), 72.

20. Frank Budgen, *James Joyce and the Making of "Ulysses"* (Bloomington: Indiana University Press, 1960), 21.

21. The house of fiction and the associated imagery are from James's Preface to *The Portrait of a Lady*.

Index